THE
WATCHMAKER'S
DAUGHTER

ALSO BY LARRY LOFTIS

The Princess Spy
Code Name: Lise
Into the Lion's Mouth

THE WATCHMAKER'S DAUGHTER

THE TRUE STORY OF WORLD WAR II HEROINE CORRIE TEN BOOM

LARRY LOFTIS

WM

WILLIAM MORROW
An Imprint of HarperCollinsPublishers

HarperCollins books may be purchased for educational, business, or sales promotional use. For information, please email the Special Markets Department at SPsales@harpercollins.com.

FIRST EDITION

Designed by Bonni Leon-Berman

Library of Congress Cataloging-in-Publication Data has been applied for.

ISBN 978-0-06-323458-1 (hardcover)
ISBN 978-0-06-331966-0 (international edition)

23 24 25 26 27 LBC 5 4 3 2 1

For Steve Price—a true Casper ten Boom

Daring to do what is right,
not what fancy may tell you,
valiantly grasping occasions,
not cravenly doubting—
freedom comes only through deeds,
not through thoughts taking wing.
Faint not nor fear,
but go out to the storm and the action,
trusting in God whose commandment
you faithfully follow;
freedom, exultant, will welcome
your spirit with joy.

—*Dietrich Bonhoeffer*

CONTENTS

DRAMATIS PERSONAE

Ten Boom Family	Nickname	Relationship
Arnolda Johanna	Nollie	Corrie's older sister
Cocky van Woerden		Corrie's niece, Nollie's daughter
Peter van Woerden		Corrie's nephew, Nollie's son
Casper	Opa	Corrie's father
Cornelia Arnolda Johanna	Corrie (Tante Kees)	
Elisabeth	Betsie (Tante Bep)	Corrie's oldest sister
Willem		Corrie's brother
Christiaan Johanes	Kik	Corrie's nephew, Willem's son
Beje Permanent Refugees	**Nickname**	
Hansje Frankfort-Israels	Thea	
Ronnie Gazan		
Mary van Itallie		
Mirjam de Jong		
Leendert Kip		
Meta Monsanto	Tante Martha	
Paula Monsanto		
Meijer Mossel	Eusi	
Nel		
Hans Poley		
Mr. de Vries		
Henk Wessels		
Henk Wiedijk		
Dutch Resistance	**Nickname**	
Hans van Messel		
Reynout Siertsema	Arnold (code name)	
Herman Sluring	Pickwick, Uncle Herman	
Others	**Role**	
Lieutenant Hans Rahms	German military judge	

PROLOGUE

HE CUT AN IMPOSING FIGURE.

Handsome and broad-shouldered, Lieutenant Hans Rahms looked chiseled in his German uniform, and his erect posture and placid expression suggested a model Nazi soldier. But he was more than an SS officer supervising a prison; he was the military judge who would decide Corrie's fate. In essence, Rahms was judge, jury, and executioner. With a wave of his hand he could send someone to the gallows or a concentration camp.

As Corrie stood before his desk she saw a number of papers—*her* papers. These were her notes for various underground activities—including ration cards—which contained the names and addresses of friends, Jews, and Resistance workers. The Gestapo had found them during a search of the Beje and apparently had just given them to the prison.

"Can you explain these pages?" Rahms asked.

Corrie's heart pounded. Aside from incriminating her for several capital crimes, every name on that list was in danger. If the Gestapo found them, underground workers would be arrested and sent to concentration camps or shot. Jews named in the papers would be rounded up for shipment to a death camp. But what could she tell the lieutenant—that those were not her notes? No, this was the end. For her, for everyone.

"No, I can't."

Chapter 1

THE WATCHMAKERS

TICK. TICK. TICK.

It was a soothing sound, methodical and predictable. Willem ten Boom's shop at Barteljorisstraat 19 in Haarlem, Holland, was small, and his ticking watches seemed to invite conversation and friendship. He had rented the house in 1837 to launch his watchmaking venture, a dramatic break from his father's gardening trade. Like most buildings in town, the first floor housed the business, while the second and third floors provided residential quarters.

In 1841 Willem married Geertruida van Gogh, and three years later something unusual happened at the Beje—as the ten Boom residence came to be known. The local Dutch Reformed minister, Dominee Witteveen, called on Willem one day with a peculiar plea: "You know the Scriptures tell us to pray for the peace of Jerusalem, and the blessing of the Jews." It was an odd request at the time—few Dutch Christians had heard of praying for Israel—but Willem agreed. "I have always loved God's ancient people," he told Witteveen; "they gave us our Bible and our Savior."

With this simple encouragement, Willem began inviting friends over to pray for Jerusalem and the Jews. It was a legacy he would pass on to his children and grandchildren.

In 1856 Geertruida died of tuberculosis, and two years later Willem married Elisabeth Bell. Their first child, Casper, was born a year later. Casper apprenticed under his father in the family business for several years, and when he turned eighteen he opened a watch shop in Rapenburg, the Jewish quarter of Amsterdam.

He settled into the community, admiring his neighbors. "As long as I can remember," he shared later, "the portrait of Isaac da Costa* has been hanging in our living room. This man of God, with his burning heart for Israel, his own people, has had a strong influence on our family."

Casper often joined the Amsterdam Jews in their Sabbaths and holy days, studied the Talmud with them, and was pleasantly surprised when they asked him to explain the fulfillment of Old Testament prophecies in the New Testament.

When he was twenty-five, Casper married a young Dutchwoman named Cornelia ("Cor") Luitingh. They had their first child in 1885, Elisabeth ("Betsie"), followed by sibling Willem the next year. In 1890 they had another daughter, Arnolda ("Nollie") Johanna, and a third daughter—a premature, sickly child—on April 15, 1892.

They named her Cornelia ("Corrie") Arnolda Johanna.

Cor recorded in her diary both anguish and hope: "The Lord gave us a very little, weak baby—Corrie. Oh, what a poor little thing she was. Nearly dead, she looked bluish white, and I never saw anything so pitiful. Nobody thought she would live."

Live she did, although she was only six months old when grandfather Willem died. But Willem had planned all along that Casper would continue the family trade, so upon his death Casper and Cor returned to Haarlem to take over the shop. A

---

* Isaac da Costa, a lawyer and poet, was a Portuguese Jew who had converted to Christianity. Throughout his life he worked to have Dutch Christians pray for Jerusalem and the Jews.

few years later, in 1897, Elisabeth moved out of the Beje so that Casper, Cor, and the children could move in.

Casper picked up where his father left off, honing his watchmaking skills by apprenticing under Hoü, widely considered the best in the world. In his shop at the Beje, Casper hung an engraving by a Dutch artist of a watchmaker at his desk.

The watchmaker engraving.

The English translation reads:

PEOPLE'S TRADES/THE WATCHMAKER

One has to be prepared for when the time is over.
O man, arrange your state of soul
as long as the clock is still going;

For when the weight has come to the end
of this short time that we live,
You can't pay anybody anywhere to pull the weight up again,
Not through art, or money, or respect of man.

Casper at work in the Beje shop.

It was an apt summary of Casper ten Boom's life.

He hoped to pass the trade on to his son, but shortly before he turned eighteen Willem told his father he didn't want to continue in the business, saying he felt called to be a minister. Though disappointed, Casper understood and gave his blessing for his son to go to the University of Leiden to study theology. Twelve-year-old Corrie, however, announced to her father that *she* wanted to become a watchmaker. Thankful that someone in the family would carry on the business, he began to apprentice her.

Willem completed his theological studies in 1916, and would eventually accept a position with a church in Zuylen, a picturesque town on the outskirts of Utrecht. To his surprise, the church allowed him one day a week to continue his studies at the

The ten Boom family in 1902. Left to right: *Betsie, Nollie, Casper, Willem, Cor, and Corrie.*

famous university there. Immediately, Willem immersed himself in a subject that fascinated and worried him: anti-Semitism. This cancer had taken root in Germany and France, and he couldn't study it enough. "I was captivated by the study of anti-Semitism from the start," he told his fiancée Tine van Veen one day, "but now that I am really getting into it, it is taking possession of me. I can no longer get away from it. The Jewish question is haunting me. It is so dangerous. Anti-Semitism has repercussions which will affect the whole world."

Little did Willem know how prophetic his words would be.

Corrie, meanwhile, worked diligently to become a competent assistant to her father. She had her own workbench in the shop, and Casper expected her to be punctual, diligent, and persistent. Without fail, however, he was also encouraging. Though he was now recognized as the best watchmaker in Holland, one day he told her: "Girl, I trust that you will become a more able watch repairer than your father."

As the years went by, Corrie longed to improve her skills and she pressed her father: "Papa, too often when a broken watch is brought in, I have to ask you or the watchmaker what the

The ten Boom children in 1910. Left to right: *Nollie, Corrie, Willem, and Betsie.*

problem is. I would like to know more about the insides of a watch."

At the time, though, watchmaking schools existed only in Switzerland, and Casper couldn't afford to send his daughter there. Still, he and Corrie kept that goal in the forefront of their minds; somehow they would find a way.

Not long after, Corrie was proofreading one of her father's articles for his weekly watchmaker's magazine. The story focused on an extraordinary watch—easily the most expensive in the world—that had been ordered and made for the emperor of Austria. He had since abdicated, however, and could no longer afford it. Made of heavy gold, it was the first pocket watch that played a tune—the "Ranz des Vaches"—a Swiss folk song. Casper closed the article by congratulating the lucky watchmaker who would eventually sell it.

Some days later one of the shop's regular customers came in with a special request. "I would like to have a watch that nobody else has," the man announced. "Do you know if that is possible? I do not mind what the price is."

Casper mentioned the Ranz des Vaches watch and the price, noting that it was located in Switzerland. The man paid for it on the spot, saying that he was going to Switzerland that week and would collect it himself. Casper's commission on the sale was so great that it covered Corrie's school and apprenticeship in two Swiss watchmaking factories.

The watchmaker's daughter would become a watchmaker herself.

When Corrie finished her Swiss apprenticeship she returned home to again assist her father in the shop. On October 17, 1921, Corrie's mother, Cor, died. Casper was heartbroken, and Corrie recorded his words as he looked one last time at the woman he loved.

"This is the saddest day of my life. Thank you, Lord, for giving her to me."

That very year Corrie became the first licensed female watchmaker in Holland. In due time she handled the bulk of business that came into the ten Boom shop.

Willem, meanwhile, continued to preach and write about anti-Semitism, and in 1925 the Dutch Society for Israel asked if he would consider a special job as missionary to the Jews in Amsterdam. In preparation for this work, the society suggested that Willem take off a year for study at the Institutum Judaicum in Leipzig, Germany. Willem couldn't accept fast enough, and once in Germany he began research for a PhD. Over the next three years he worked on his doctoral

Casper and the ten Boom watch shop, about 1905.

dissertation: "Entstehung des Modernen Rassenantisemitismus in Frankreich und Deutschland" (The birth of modern racial anti-Semitism in France and Germany).

While Willem was writing his dissertation in Leipzig, Adolf Hitler was preparing to publish his own work: the anti-Semitic *Mein Kampf.** Although Willem was unaware of Hitler's book, he had seen enough to discern that trouble was just around the corner. In a letter to Tine, he wrote: "I expect that in a few years' time, there will be worse pogroms than ever before. Countless Jews from the east will come across the border to seek refuge in our country. We must prepare for that situation."

Willem received his PhD in 1928, his anti-Semitism dissertation being published two years after Hitler's second volume of *Mein Kampf,* and just five years before Hitler's rise to power. This young Dutch scholar—educated and published in Germany—had thrown down the gauntlet, as it were, within the belly of the beast. It would prove to be the beginning of a long, frightful clash between the ten Booms and the Nazis.

WHEN WILLEM FINISHED his studies he began his ministry to the Jews. A few days every week he would visit the Jewish quarter of Amsterdam, engaging some in discussion, offering Bibles to others. And in typical ten Boom fashion, he opened his home to everyone in need. It was called *Theodotion*—gift of God. Within a few short years, that very home would be called upon to save Jewish lives.

On January 30, 1933, German president Paul von Hindenburg—under pressure from his cabinet advisors and

---

* *Mein Kampf* was published in two volumes, the first appearing in 1925, the second in 1926.

Dr. Willem ten Boom

against his better judgment*—appointed Adolf Hitler as chancellor of Germany. Queen Wilhelmina, observing the German situation on behalf of her Netherlands, knew the appointment spelled trouble. "Old President Hindenburg was still at the helm," she recalled, "but Mussolini had shown us how quickly fascist forces can remove lawful authority. I did not doubt that Hitler would soon establish a dictatorship."

Once installed, Hitler wasted no time in persecuting Jews. On April 1 he instituted a one-day boycott of Jewish businesses. Throughout the country, prospective patrons were barred by Nazi SA† men from entering Jewish shops. Many Germans, however, were outraged and refused to comply. In Berlin, for example, Julie Bonhoeffer—Lutheran pastor Dietrich Bonhoeffer's ninety-year-old grandmother—pushed past a Nazi cordon to make her purchase in a Jewish business.

But the boycott was just a warm-up. Six days later the Nazi government barred Jews from all civil service jobs, including schools and universities, which resulted in the dismissal of all Jewish pro-

---

*   Hindenburg disliked Hitler and had previously told General Kurt von Hammerstein that he had "no intention whatsoever of making that Austrian corporal either Minister of Defense or Chancellor of the Reich." For the origin of "Bohemian" corporal, which Hindenburg used initially and later preferred, see the endnotes.

†   The SA (Sturmabteilung, or "Storm Detachment"), one of Hitler's two Nazi paramilitary organizations (the SS being the other), was formed in 1920. Known as "Brownshirts" or storm troopers, these men were used by Hitler as an instrument of street terror.

fessors. In addition, Jews were prohibited from practicing law or medicine. In all, some forty-two laws were enacted to discriminate against Jews. The following year nineteen more laws were passed, and in 1935, another twenty-nine. The Nuremberg Laws, as the 1935 enactments were known, stripped German Jews of their citizenship, forbade them from marrying Aryans, and even outlawed extramarital affairs between Jews and non-Jews.

The following March, Hitler ordered his troops to reoccupy the Rhineland, an area bordering the Rhine River that Germany had lost during World War I. It was an act of aggression, but the international community—perhaps reluctant to oppose a country reclaiming former lands—remained largely silent. On the diplomatic side, Hitler worked to keep everyone calm; the German Foreign Office repeatedly assured the Netherlands government that the Reich would respect Dutch neutrality.

That summer Berlin hosted the 1936 Olympics and Hitler, desirous of putting Germany's best foot forward, relaxed his persecution of Jews. After the games, however, when most of the international press was gone, the Nazi attacks accelerated. Jews were now prohibited from staying in hotels, patronizing restaurants or shops owned by non-Jews, or even sitting in parks reserved for Aryans.

The Nazis didn't limit themselves to persecution of Jews; they went after Christians as well. In 1937 they arrested Martin Niemöller, influential Berlin pastor and head of the anti-Nazi Confessing Church. His crime, they charged, was "malicious attacks against the state." He was fined, given a short prison sentence, and then freed. Upon hearing the news of Niemöller's release, however, Hitler ordered his re-arrest, and Niemöller was sent to the Sachsenhausen concentration camp.*

---

* Niemöller would spend the next seven years—mostly in solitary confinement—at the Sachsenhausen and Dachau concentration camps. He is famous for his confession: "First they came for the Jews. I was silent. I was not a Jew.

In Holland, though, things were fairly normal. In 1937 Crown Princess Juliana married Bernhard of Lippe-Biesterfeld, a prince from—of all places—Germany. That same year the ten Booms celebrated the hundred-year anniversary of their watch business. Corrie was proud that her lineage as a watchmaker dated back to grandfather Willem, who had first opened the watchmaking shop at the Beje. Life in Haarlem was peaceful, but things would change before a year had passed.

In March 1938 Germany annexed Austria, and some 183,000 Austrian Jews suffered the same persecution as Jews in Germany. By the summer, most Jewish businesses in the Reich had been taken over by Germans. The fall, however, brought a glimmer of hope. On September 29, British prime minister Neville Chamberlain and French prime minister Edouard Daladier met with Hitler in Munich and signed an accord recognizing Germany's annexation of the Sudetenland region of Czechoslovakia. Upon arriving in London, Chamberlain announced that the Munich Agreement had secured "peace in our time."

In the Netherlands, however, Queen Wilhelmina believed otherwise. "The main question was what national-socialism would mean for the rest of Europe," she later wrote. "By the spring of 1938, when Hitler invaded Austria, the answer was plain to me. German policy would result in a European catastrophe.

"No sooner had Hitler got hold of Austria than he began to stir up trouble in Czechoslovakia. . . . Hitler's land-hunger had not been appeased. It had already become obvious to me that Hitler would go further, that for him the attainment of one object only meant that he could start working on the realization of his next territorial wish, and that he would involve the whole of Europe in his game as soon as he considered the time ripe for it.

Then they came for the Communists. I was silent. I was not a Communist. Then they came for the trade unionists. I was silent. I was not a trade unionist. Then they came for me. There was no one left to speak for me."

The prelude to the treacherous attack on our own country had begun."

Notwithstanding the Munich Agreement, Hitler continued his rage against Jews. Less than a month after the accord, on October 27, eighteen thousand German Jews were arrested, packed into cattle cars, and entrained to the Polish border. The Grynszpan family—who had just been expelled from Hanover—was among the deported. When the train arrived at the Polish border, Berta Grynszpan mailed a letter to her seventeen-year-old brother, Herschel, who was living in Paris. Hearing about his family's treatment—especially the transfer to Poland without food or water—the boy became enraged.

On the morning of November 6 Herschel purchased a gun and proceeded to the German embassy. He asked to see the ambassador, Johannes von Welczeck, but the diplomat slipped out without meeting him. Herschel insisted on seeing someone to whom he could deliver an important document, and he was ushered into the office of Third Secretary Ernst vom Rath. When vom Rath asked to see the document, Herschel shouted: "You are a *sale boche* [filthy kraut] and here, in the name of twelve thousand persecuted Jews, is your document!"

Herschel fired five times, three shots missing, but two hitting vom Rath in the abdomen. Herschel was arrested and vom Rath was rushed to the hospital, triggering a backlash reminiscent of that following the assassination of Archduke Franz Ferdinand in 1914.*

When news of the shooting reached Berlin, Hitler's propaganda minister, Joseph Goebbels, seized the opportunity to further persecution of Jews. He ordered all newspapers not only to

---

* Austrian Archduke Franz Ferdinand was assassinated in Sarajevo on June 28, 1914, by Gavrilo Princip, a nineteen-year-old Bosnian Serb. The event is considered the most immediate cause of World War I.

cover the story, but to make it the dominant news. "All German newspapers must carry large-scale reportage on the assassination attempt against the life of the third secretary in the German Embassy in Paris," he instructed. "The news must completely dominate page 1. . . . It should be pointed out in several editorials that this assassination attempt perpetrated by a Jew must have the most serious consequences for Jews in Germany."

Editors complied with Goebbels's directive, and the crisis expanded when news of vom Rath's death reached Hitler in Munich at nine p.m., November 9. Demonstrations against Jewish homes and businesses were to be allowed, Hitler decided, and police withdrawn. Some three hours later Gestapo chief Heinrich Müller dispatched an order to police throughout the country: "Actions against Jews, especially against their synagogues, will take place throughout the Reich shortly. They are not to be interfered with. . . . Preparations are to be made for the arrest of about 20,000 to 30,000 Jews in the Reich."

Individual branches of the SA received their own instructions within the hour. In Cologne, for example, SA members were directed to set fire to all synagogues at four a.m., followed by attacks on Jewish shops and homes two hours later.

The destruction unleashed by Hitler's Nazis that night was breathtaking. The event became known as Kristallnacht—Night of the Broken Glass. By the time the mayhem subsided on the evening of November 10, some two thousand synagogues had been burned, almost seventy-five hundred Jewish businesses had been ravaged, at least ninety-six Jews had been killed, and another thirty thousand arrested and sent to concentration camps.

When Hollanders heard the news, some protested and others issued warnings, but the reaction was mixed. Many were unaware of the Kristallnacht horrors, while those who knew assumed such atrocities would never occur in the Netherlands.

Nevertheless, Dutch hearts, filled with compassion, donated 400,000 guilders in a nationwide collection to assist Jews who had fled to Holland.

BUSINESS IN THE Beje carried on as usual, meanwhile, and the watch shop continued to grow. To help meet demand, Casper hired a man named Mr. Ineke to assist with watch repair, and a woman named Henny van Dantzig to help with sales. In addition, the ten Booms had a number of suppliers in Germany, and Casper and Corrie would regularly exchange correspondence and materials with them. As the last weeks of 1938 ticked by, however, Corrie noticed something unusual.

Where those suppliers were Jewish-owned companies, her mail to them was being returned, "Address Unknown."

Chapter 2

HITLER YOUTH

IT SEEMED ODD THAT IN the spring of 1939 a German would come to Haarlem to apprentice for Casper ten Boom, Holland's best watchmaker. Germany, after all, had annexed Austria and the Czech Sudetenland a year earlier,* and Adolf Hitler appeared hell-bent on acquiring more territory. Yet for the ten Booms, it was business as usual. Casper's reputation was known now in much of Europe, and the ten Boom shop had employed numerous German apprentices over the years.

This hire, though, was different. Otto Altschuler was tall and handsome, and had come to the Beje—as the ten Boom watch shop was known—with a recommendation from a well-respected firm in Berlin. He was a good employee and quite courteous to Casper—whom everyone called Opa (grandfather)—but there was an edge about Otto that Corrie couldn't place. As a competent watchmaker herself, she became her father's chief assistant and heir apparent, and worked closely with apprentices.

The first tip-off occurred one day when Otto proudly announced that he was a member of the Hitler Youth. This meant

---

* Germany annexed the Czech Sudetenland in March 1938, and began to occupy it on October 5, 1938. By March 15, 1939, the occupation was complete, and Hitler added Bohemia and Moravia to his conquests.

nothing to the ten Booms, but it would have been alarming to anyone in Germany. Founded in 1922, the Hitler Youth was a Nazi organization for boys aged fourteen to eighteen. Per Hitler's guidelines, members were required to be "slim and slender, swift as greyhounds, tough as leather, and hard as Krupp steel."

On December 1, 1936, the Führer had enacted a law outlawing all non-Nazi youth organizations, declaring: "All of the German youth in the Reich is organized within the Hitler Youth. The German youth, besides being reared within the family and schools, shall be educated physically, intellectually and morally in the spirit of National Socialism."

First and foremost, the Hitler Youth was a propaganda tool for indoctrinating young minds in Nazi ideology. And the re-education started long before the teenage years. From the age of six until ten, boys served in a pre–Hitler Youth apprenticeship where they were given performance books to record their progress through Nazi ideals. At ten, each boy was subjected to tests in athletics, camping, and Nazi history. If he passed, he graduated into the Jungvolk ("Young Folk"), where he took an oath:

> In the presence of this blood banner, which represents our Führer, I swear to devote all of my energies and strength to the savior of our country, Adolf Hitler. I am willing and ready to give up my life for him, so help me God.

Girls were not excluded from the indoctrination. From ages ten to fourteen, they were enrolled in an organization called the Jungmaedel ("Young Maidens"). Like their male counterparts, they would go on long marches and attend classes on National Socialist ideology, but they also were encouraged to become healthy mothers of strong Nazi children. At fourteen, girls would progress to the Bund Deutscher Maedel ("League of German Maidens"), where the indoctrination continued.

When boys turned fourteen, they were inducted into the Hitler Youth proper, remaining there until they turned eighteen and passed directly into the German army. From the outset the organization's purpose was to groom boys as paramilitary street thugs like the SA. They were trained in the use of rifles and machine guns, and would attend a monthlong military camp. Not surprisingly, Hitler Youth worked alongside the SA in orchestrating the terrors of Kristallnacht.

Parents who instructed their children not to join the Hitler Youth were threatened with prison and told that their boys would be sent to orphanages. And the threats were effective: by the end of 1938, Hitler Youth numbered almost eight million. Yet there were some four million young men who had not joined, so in March 1939 the Reich enacted a law conscripting all boys into Hitler Youth in the same fashion as eighteen-year-olds were drafted into the army.

AS DAYS PASSED the ten Booms noticed that Otto was unlike their previous German apprentices. At first it was subtle criticisms of Dutch people and products, followed by his proclamation, "The world will see what Germans can do." Not long after that Otto told Corrie that the Old Testament was the Jews' "Book of Lies."

Opa, however, wasn't worried. "He has been taught wrong," he told Corrie. "By watching us, seeing that we love this Book and are truthful people, he will realize his error."

Some weeks later, though, Otto's sinister side revealed itself. Otto's landlord came by the Beje one day to inform the ten Booms about their young German employee. She had been changing the sheets on Otto's bed that morning and found something under his pillow. She removed from her purse a knife with a curving ten-inch blade.

Again Opa gave Otto the benefit of the doubt. "The boy is probably only frightened," he said, "alone in a strange country. He probably bought it to protect himself."

Corrie mused the assessment. Otto was indeed alone, and he spoke no Dutch. Aside from Opa, Betsie, and Corrie—who all spoke German—he had no one to talk to. Perhaps Father was right.

As time went on, though, Corrie noticed something else. Otto seemed to be cold and disrespectful toward Mr. Christoffels— an elderly gentleman Opa had hired to assist with repairs— but maybe it was just thoughtlessness. She mentioned it to her brother Willem when he was visiting one day, and he brushed aside Corrie's wishful thinking. "It's very deliberate," he said. "It's because Christoffels is old. The old have no value to the State. They're also harder to train in the new ways of thinking. Germany is systematically teaching disrespect for old age."

Hearing the discussion, Opa countered that Otto was always courteous to him, and that he was a good bit older than Christoffels.

"You're different," Willem said. "You're the boss. That's another part of the system: respect for authority. It is the old and the weak who are to be eliminated."

Corrie and Opa could only shake their heads. Was such a nefarious ideology even possible?

Some days later they received their answer. One morning Mr. Christoffels stumbled into the shop, his cheek bleeding and his jacket torn. He was missing his hat so Corrie rushed into the street to retrieve it. Retracing the path the old man took to work, she noticed a group of people who seemed to be having words with someone: Otto. She asked one of the bystanders what had happened and he said that when Christoffels turned a corner into the alley, Otto was waiting. He slammed the old man into the side of a building and ground his face against the bricks. Corrie was aghast; her worst fears about Otto were true.

For the first time in more than sixty years of business, Opa had to fire an employee. He tried to reason with Otto, explaining why his behavior was improper, but Otto remained stone-faced. Opa let him know that his employment was over and Otto calmly collected his tools without a word.

At the door Otto turned back and Corrie shivered. It was the most ominous look of contempt she had ever seen.

Chapter 3

PERSECUTION

IN BERLIN, TIME WAS OF the essence. From the day Hitler came to power in 1933, German military leaders had plotted to do away with him—either by assassination or by arrest and trial. In 1938 the so-called Generals' Plot* to oust or kill Hitler involved the highest leaders of the German army, the Wehrmacht. Due to a number of logistical problems, however, the plot failed to materialize. Beginning in the fall of 1939, General Franz Halder, chief of the Army General Staff, had been carrying a loaded pistol in his pocket when he met with Hitler, determined to shoot the Führer himself. Unfortunately, he could never do it. He realized eventually that he was an army officer, not an assassin, and someone else would have to do the dirty work.

Without a coup, Wehrmacht leaders were hamstrung; Hitler

---

* The Generals' Plot, as it came to be known, was supported by virtually every senior German officer of the Wehrmacht and Abwehr (military intelligence), including: General Walther von Brauchitsch, commander in chief of the army; General Franz Halder, chief of the Army General Staff; General Ludwig Beck, Halder's predecessor; General Gerd von Rundstedt, commander in chief of Army Group No. 1; General Erwin von Witzleben, commander of III Army Corps; and Abwehr chief Admiral Wilhelm Canaris. Three notable exceptions to this list were Hitler's principal Wehrmacht supporters: General Alfred Jodl and Field Marshal Wilhelm Keitel, war criminals who were executed at the Nuremberg Trials, and Field Marshal Walter Model, who committed suicide on April 21, 1945.

demanded that they invade Poland so on September 1, 1939, they did. France and England immediately declared war against Germany, thus commencing World War II.

Now, in the early months of 1940, Hitler demanded more, asking his generals to prepare for invasions of Norway, Denmark, Belgium, and the Netherlands.

Staunch anti-Nazi officers knew this was their last chance; they would either have to assassinate the Führer or sabotage his plans. Colonel Hans Oster,* assistant to Abwehr chief Admiral Wilhelm Canaris, believed that if the Western nations could put up a stout defense, then Hitler's leadership would be crippled, making a coup easier. The idea had originated with Halder in late 1939,[†] but Oster's contact with the Dutch military attaché in Berlin, Major Gijsbertus Jacobus Sas, now provided an efficient leak channel.

For Oster this was Plan B to stop Hitler. Plan A was the coup attempt, but at every turn the Wehrmacht generals seemed to lose their opportunity.

And so the clock continued to tick.

On April 3, 1940, Oster advised Sas that Germany would invade Denmark and Norway six days later, on April 9. He asked Sans not only to warn the Danes and Norwegians, but also to notify the British. In addition, he had his friend Josef Müller pass this information along to the Vatican. The warning was not enough, though, as the Wehrmacht successfully invaded both countries.

Now more than ever Oster was intent on thwarting the invasion of Holland. On May 9 he had dinner with Sas and afterward they drove to the armed forces headquarters so Oster could see if there were any new developments. The Dutchman waited

---

* Oster so loathed Hitler that among Abwehr colleagues, he referred to him as "the pig."
† The plan was dubbed "set-back theory."

in the car while Oster snooped inside for details. After twenty minutes he returned, dispirited.

"My dear friend," he told Sas, "now it is really all over. . . . The pig [Hitler] has gone off to the Western front, now it is definitely over. I hope that we shall meet again after this war."

At once Sas notified The Hague with a specific message for the Defense Ministry: "Tomorrow at dawn. Hold tight." He then alerted his friend Georges Goethals, the Belgian military attaché.

But Sas's previous cries of "wolf"—all of which had been inaccurate—had worn out the Dutch and Belgian generals. The Holland invasion alone had been scheduled and then canceled *twenty-nine* times. So tired of these warnings was General H. G. Winkelman, the Dutch commander in chief, that he told Sas that his source (Oster) was "pitiful." And so the Netherlands and Belgium largely ignored the latest Oster-Sas warning, assuming it was yet another false alarm.

At three a.m. on May 10 the German Eighteenth Army crossed the IJssel, Holland's defensive line. At dawn the Luftwaffe dispatched eleven hundred aircraft to bomb airfields and drop two airborne divisions into South Holland. To counter the Eighteenth Army's 141 Panzers, General Winkelman had a mere twenty-six armored cars, and not a single tank. The Dutch air force was equally outgunned: it had just one hundred thirty-two serviceable fighters, only seventy-two of which were modern.[*]

Hitler's plan was to drop airborne troops on the three airfields surrounding The Hague, seize the capital, and capture Queen Wilhelmina and her cabinet.

To his surprise, Dutch resistance was stout.

※ ※ ※

---

[*]   Before the day was out, it lost sixty-two of them.

Corrie jerked up in her bed at the pounding concussions. *Bombs!*

Explosion after explosion, all sounding like they were falling next door. The Germans were bombing the Schiphol airport, she knew, scarcely five miles away. She raced into Betsie's room and found her sister sitting up, pale and shaking. They held each other tightly, trembling as a flickering red glow flashed through the window after each blast.

"Lord, make us strong," they prayed. "Give us strength to help others. . . . Take away our fear. Give us trust."

ENRAGED THAT HITLER had broken his promise to respect Netherlands' neutrality, Dutch queen Wilhelmina went to the radio to encourage her people to remain vigilant.

From her bomb shelter in The Hague she called the king of England to ask for assistance. The British had already provided some troops, but the number was wholly inadequate to counter the invasion.

As the early hours of the invasion dragged on, German airborne units captured a number of key bridges, but not the airfields at The Hague. Dutch infantry, with effective use of artillery, drove two Wehrmacht regiments from the area. At Rotterdam, German units—one landing on the Nieuwe Maas river by seaplane—also faced stiff opposition.

The tide began to turn the morning of May 12, however, when an armored division of the Eighteenth Army smashed through the Grebbe Line—a forward defense line in central Holland. That afternoon the Ninth Panzer Division crossed bridges at Moerdijk and Dordrecht and reached the Nieuwe Maas. The Dutch blocked entrance into Rotterdam, though, by sealing bridges on the northern ends.

At daybreak on the thirteenth, Winkelman advised Queen Wilhelmina that The Hague was no longer safe, and that she needed to leave. Together with her principal advisors she proceeded to the Hook of Holland, where her party boarded a British destroyer bound for England. As it turned out, they left just in time.

The next morning, May 14, an annoyed and impatient Hitler issued a directive to his generals: "The power of resistance of the Dutch Army has proved to be stronger than was anticipated. Politically as well as military considerations require that this resistance be broken *speedily*."

The tactic Hitler decided to employ was the terror bombing of Rotterdam. Surely the Dutch would recall, he surmised, the fate of Warsaw the prior fall.*

Later that morning a lone German officer crossed the bridge at Rotterdam displaying a white flag. The message he carried was that Rotterdam had to surrender or else it would be bombed.

Immediately the Dutch began negotiations, sending an officer to the German headquarters near the bridge to discuss terms. As the Dutchman made his way back across the bridge to deliver the German demands, however, the Luftwaffe was already on its way.

A few hours later central Rotterdam lay in ruins. It surrendered, and at dusk that evening General Winkelman ordered his troops to lay down their arms. The next morning, May 15, he signed the official capitulation. The city's death toll was twenty-one hundred, another twenty-seven hundred wounded, and more than seventy-eight thousand made homeless.

In Haarlem, the ten Booms grew discouraged.

"The darkest time during those five days," Corrie remembered, "was when our royal family left, our Queen Wilhelmina for England and Crown Princess Juliana for Canada. We knew

---

* From September 1 to 25, 1939, the Luftwaffe pounded Warsaw. On the twenty-fifth alone it dropped 560 tons of high explosive and 72 tons of incendiary bombs.

German invasion of Netherlands and Belgium, courtesy of
Life *magazine, May 27, 1940. Haarlem is ten miles west of*
Amsterdam.

then that our case was hopeless. There were not many times that I cried, but when I heard about the royal family leaving the country, I was heartbroken and wept.

"For the Dutch people, the Queen was our security—we loved her."

With control of the country, Hitler installed an ardent Nazi, Dr. Arthur Seyss-Inquart, as Reich commissioner of the Netherlands. Seyss-Inquart, a pleasant-mannered Viennese lawyer, had longed for a unification of Austria and Germany. After the Anschluss in March 1938, Hitler installed him as Austrian chancellor, and then the following month as Reich governor. In October 1939, with Germany's successful invasion of Poland, Seyss-Inquart became its deputy governor-general.

Now, with the occupation of the Netherlands, Hitler moved the seasoned Seyss-Inquart to his new position. And to assist

Seyss-Inquart, Hitler appointed another Austrian, Hanns Albin Rauter, as the Higher SS and Police Leader, and head of all SS troops. While junior to Seyss-Inquart in the civil administration, Rauter held a higher SS rank and reported directly to the *Reichsführer*, SS chief Heinrich Himmler.

An imposing figure, Rauter was tall and tough-looking, with a stern discipline and blunt personality to match. A fanatical and radical Nazi, he was also ruthless.

Seemingly to lull their subjects into complacency, Seyss-Inquart and Rauter implemented their reign of terror slowly. At first they gave the impression that the occupation would be friendly. Hitler saw the Dutch as fellow Aryans,* after all, and respected their prosperity and cultural heritage. In a show of good faith, Seyss-Inquart freed all Dutch military prisoners taken during the four-day war.

The following month Hermann Goering promised the Dutch that their standard of living would not fall below that of their German neighbors, and for a while local shops experienced a tremendous boon; German soldiers spent freely, and the occupation didn't seem so bad after all. Corrie recalled the dramatic increase in business in the early months after the invasion: "Soldiers frequently visited our store, for they were getting good wages and watches were among the first things they bought. . . . I listened to them excitedly discussing their purchases, they seemed like young men anywhere off on a holiday. Most of them selected women's watches for mothers and sweethearts back home. Indeed, the shop never made so much money as during that first year of the war."

An eleven-year-old girl in Arhem, Adriaantje Hepburn-Ruston—later known to millions as Audrey Hepburn—also re-

* Hitler told Anton Mussert, leader of the National Socialist Movement of the Netherlands (NSB), that the best representatives of the Germanic race could be found in the Netherlands and Norway.

membered the time: "The Germans tried to be civil and to win our hearts. The first few months we didn't know quite what had happened. . . . A child is a child; I just went to school."

Yet the occupation honeymoon was over within six months.

ON SEPTEMBER 12 Queen Wilhelmina broadcast on the BBC another message to her countrymen, saying, "A nation which has vitality and determination cannot be conquered simply by force of arms. . . . Magnificent manifestations of unity and independence . . . help us to feel confidence in a future which will render to us all a free and independent country under God's blessing."

Like Prime Minister Winston Churchill for the British, the queen provided a glimmer of hope for the Dutch, who desperately needed inspiration and courage to face what was to come.

The following month Seyss-Inquart announced that Jewish civil servants and professors were to be expelled from their posts. At once student protests began, first at Delft Technological University, then at the University of Leiden and other schools. Students began boycotting their classes, and Delft and Leiden temporarily closed.

To counter the rebellion, the Nazis cracked down with nationwide university raids, arresting students and professors alike. It was a foretaste of things to come, and many other Jewish professionals—doctors, lawyers, and architects—resigned from their posts.

Yet there was more in store for Jews. In 1941 Seyss-Inquart instituted a new policy: all Jewish citizens of the Netherlands were to have their personal identity cards marked with a large *J*. Soon thereafter they were required to wear a yellow Star of David on their coats. So appalled at the persecution was Casper ten Boom that he reported in line to receive a Star of David. In his mind, it was the only way for him to protest the injustice; he would suffer alongside his Jewish brothers.*

What hit everyone in Holland, however, was the rationing of food and other goods. For decades the Dutch had a large export surplus of butter, cheese, fruit, and vegetables. Seyss-Inquart now redirected all of those exports—and much of the domestic produce—to Germany. Corrie remembered receiving ration cards that, during the first year of occupation, could be used to purchase food and commodities actually found in stores. Each week, though, the newspapers would announce what the ration coupons could be exchanged for.

The other adjustment was the lack of available news. Seyss-Inquart controlled the newspapers, which meant that only German propaganda would be included. "Long glowing reports of the successes of the German army on its various fronts," Corrie recalled, and "eulogies of German leaders, denunciation of traitors and saboteurs, appeals for the unity of the 'Nordic peoples.'"

Without legitimate newspapers, the Dutch had only one source for outside news: radio. Each week they would turn to the BBC to hear a message from their exiled queen. The German occupiers were well aware of the encouragement that would come through the BBC, of course, so they outlawed radios; every Hollander now had to turn them in to Nazi authorities. Like many others, the ten Booms had no intention of being cut off from news and the queen's broadcasts.

Peter, Nollie's son, had an idea. Since the ten Booms had two radios, they could appear compliant by turning in one, and secretly hiding the other. In the stairwell, in a curve just above Casper's room, Peter inserted the smaller radio and replaced the boards. The other radio Corrie would turn in at the Vroom & Dreesmann department store where the collection occurred.

---

* Corrie and Betsie later persuaded their father not to wear the star in public.

"Is this the only radio you own?" the army clerk asked her.

"Yes."

The German glanced at the paper in front of him. "Ten Boom, Casper, ten Boom, Elisabeth, at the same address. Do either of them own a radio?"

Corrie held his gaze. "No."

As she exited the building she began to tremble. It was the first time in her life she had lied.

BACK HOME SHE and Betsie took turns every night listening to the Free Dutch broadcasts; while one crouched over the radio, the other would play the piano as loudly as possible. The news, though, was dreadful: German offensives everywhere were successful. And that, more than anything, troubled the British. The Germans had repaired the bomb damage to Holland's airfields and now used them as forward bases for Luftwaffe attacks on England.

Night after night Corrie lay in bed, trembling at the sound of Luftwaffe bombers heading west. Soon, though, the British retaliated with attacks on Germany. Often German fighters would intercept Royal Air Force (RAF) aircraft over Haarlem, and one night a dogfight raged above the Beje. Through her window she couldn't see the planes, but the fiery streak of tracer bullets left no doubt about the action.

As the summer of 1941 rolled on the Dutch government in exile worked to establish their own network to broadcast into the Netherlands. On July 28 Radio Oranje transmitted its first message, and Queen Wilhelmina minced no words. Rather than referring to the occupiers as Germans, she called them *moffen*, an old Dutch ethnic slur meaning an unwashed and backward people.

Recognizing the effectiveness of the BBC and Radio Oranje,

Seyss-Inquart issued a "Measure for the Protection of the Dutch Population Against Untrue Information." It stated that the Dutch should be protected from "false news," and that only Nazi stations would be officially sanctioned. As expected, the law declared that anyone caught listening to the BBC or Radio Oranje would be severely punished.

Corrie and the ten Booms had no intention of obeying the law, but kept the sound low when tuning in. Food, however, remained a problem. Germany had invaded Russia on July 22 and the hundreds of thousands of German troops marching east needed daily rations, which meant that more produce from the Netherlands would be siphoned off and sent to the Wehrmacht.

On afternoons when weather permitted, Corrie would walk with her father through the neighborhood, and each passing day she saw more evidence of persecution. Shop windows, restaurants, theaters, and even concert halls had placards that read: JEWS WILL NOT BE SERVED. At parks, signs simply warned: NO JEWS.

As summer turned to fall, Corrie noticed a disturbing sequence of events. First it was watches that had been repaired, but whose owners had not returned to collect them. Then a house on Nollie's block suddenly became deserted. Not long after that another watch shop—owned by a Jewish man Corrie knew as Mr. Kan—didn't open for business. Opa knocked on the door one day, wondering if his colleague was ill, but no one answered. As they passed the shop on succeeding days they noticed that it had become dark and shuttered.

A few weeks later, as Corrie and her father walked through the Grote Markt in downtown Haarlem, they came upon a cordon of police and soldiers. As they approached, Corrie was repelled at what she saw. Countless men, women, and children, all wearing the Star of David, were being herded into the back of a truck.

"Father," Corrie cried. "Those poor people."

The police cordon then opened and the truck pulled through. Opa nodded. "Those poor people."

Corrie glanced at her father and saw that he was not looking at the departing truck, but at the soldiers.

"I pity the poor Germans, Corrie. They have touched the apple of God's eye."*

OVER THE NEXT few days Corrie spoke with her father and Betsie about what they could do to help their Jewish neighbors. Hiding them in the Beje was an obvious answer, but they had limited space and no hiding places. And the risk was immediate and severe: anyone caught sheltering Jews would be sent to a prison or concentration camp.

Yet that was precisely what Willem was already doing. Soon after the occupation he had created a hiding area beneath the floor in his study. When the Gestapo came for random searches, any Jews he harbored would slip into the secret place.

Behind the scenes, the British were doing everything they could to assist their Dutch allies. The RAF's periodic dog-fights over Holland weren't making a significant impact on the war, but the British had a secret weapon: the Special Operations Executive. Founded in 1940, the SOE was created to fill a void. Unlike MI6, the professional organization that conducted foreign espionage, the SOE was tasked to do the dirty work: arming Resistance fighters, sabotage (especially against bridges, trains, and German ammo dumps), counterintelligence, and

---

* In the Old Testament, Israel is twice referred to as the apple of God's eye. Deuteronomy 32:10 provides: "In a desert land he [God] found him [Jacob, representing Israel], in a barren and howling waste. He shielded him and cared for him; he guarded him as the apple of his eye." Similarly, in Psalms 17:8 David prays: "Keep me as the apple of your eye; hide me in the shadow of your wings."

even assassinations. In short, Winston Churchill's directive for the SOE was to "set Europe ablaze." All agents were trained to kill using any weapon, including knives, or even with their bare hands. For this reason they were dubbed spies, commandos, or simply "Baker Street Irregulars."

The Germans called them "terrorists."

In almost all cases where the SOE sought operatives for occupied territories, they recruited nationals who spoke the language without an accent, and who knew the particular area where they were being sent. The SOE had made significant progress in France, and London wanted to do the same in the Netherlands. In September they dropped two agents by parachute into Holland, followed by Thys Taconis, a sabotage expert, and H. M. G. Lauwers, his radio operator, on November 6.

Radio operators—who received arduous training in codes and wireless sets—were London's best source for eyewitness reports, and for establishing drops of arms for distribution to Resistance fighters.

The two agents dropped in September had mixed success: while one made it back to England with useful information in February 1942, the other was lost at sea. Taconis and Lauwers, meanwhile, had set up operations in Arnhem and The Hague, respectively.

On March 18, after a little more than four months of secret wireless communication, London received from Lauwers a request to drop in another agent, which the Dutch section of SOE said they would do immediately.

Only it wasn't Lauwers.

Chapter 4

RAZZIAS

ALSO OPERATING IN THE HAGUE in 1942 was a crafty Abwehr counterespionage officer, Major Hermann Giskes. One of his agents—a man named Ridderhof—ran a haulage service that could provide trucks for drops London might be ordering. In a stroke of luck Ridderhof had met Taconis, and through him learned of Lauwers and his radio, along with their general plans. All of this information went directly to Giskes, who began an operation he dubbed "North Pole."

On March 6, Lauwers had just begun a transmission to London when his landlord informed him that there were four black cars outside. Lauwers immediately fled, but in his pocket were three of the ciphered messages he was about to send. Giskes's men arrested him as he made his way down the street, and the incriminating evidence in his pocket left no alibi. The Germans also arrested the landlord and his wife, and confiscated the radio.

As a general rule, captured spies during World War II were given the option of working with the enemy or execution.* If the agent chose the former, the captors would "play back" or "turn" his radio, as it is called. This meant that the agent would agree

---

* The British made it easy for German spies captured in England: either work with MI5 (which supervised double agents) or be sent to the Tower of London.

to send messages to London (or Berlin in the case of captured German spies) dictated by his captors without revealing that he had been captured by the enemy. The SOE had contingencies for this risk, however, and each radio operator had a set of pre-planned security checks to ensure that he had not been compromised; if the checks were missing from the transmission, the home office would know that the agent had been arrested and the radio turned.

To his credit, Lauwers followed the SOE protocol, omitting all security checks in his transmissions for Giskes. London, unfortunately, disregarded the warning, assuming that Lauwers had been negligent or in a hurry. From this point on, Giskes would have SOE's Dutch section sending him a steady supply of agents, all of whom would parachute into the arms of awaiting German soldiers.*

In Haarlem, the Nazi vise grip began to close in around the ten Booms as well. On Sunday, Corrie, Betsie, and Opa went to a service at the Dutch Reformed Church in Velsen, where Nollie's eighteen-year-old son, Peter, played the organ. The Velsen organ was one of the finest in Holland, and Peter had won the post in a competition against forty more experienced musicians.

The church was filled to capacity, and the ten Booms squeezed into one of the last available pews. As Peter listened to the sermon from his organ loft, his mind began to wander. This very day, May 10, marked the two-year anniversary of the occupation. "My patriotic spirit awakened," he remembered, "I decided that something should be done on this Sunday morning to demonstrate that we still were real Dutchmen at heart, something to express our faith and hope in a day of victory when we would again be a free people."

---

* By war's end, the SOE had dispatched fifty-six agents into Holland. Of those, forty-three parachuted into German reception parties, thirty-six of whom were executed.

Eighteen-year-old Peter van Woerden at the organ. On the wall to his right is an image of Johann Sebastian Bach, a devout Christian who often signed his sheet music "S.D.G."—Soli Deo Gloria ("To God Alone Be the Glory").

When the service ended, instead of playing a traditional hymn, he pulled out every stop to full volume and began playing the "Wilhelmus," the national anthem of the Netherlands.

Below him the congregation rustled. Everyone in the church knew a recent Seyss-Inquart edict made playing or singing the "Wilhelmus" a crime. Opa, though eighty-two now, was the first on his feet. Others followed. Suddenly, from somewhere behind them, Corrie heard a voice begin to sing the words. Then another. And another. Within seconds the entire congregation was on its feet, all proudly and defiantly singing the outlawed anthem.

Many wept.

Corrie remembered the moment vividly: "We sang at the top of our lungs, sang our oneness, our hope, our love for Queen and country. On this anniversary of defeat it seemed almost for a moment that we were victors."

The ten Booms waited for Peter awhile after the service at the side door of the church; half the congregation, it seemed, wanted to hug him, shake his hand, or pat him on the back. As Corrie reflected on the situation, she grew discouraged. The Gestapo would hear about this soon, and then what? Peter most certainly would be arrested, and perhaps others who sang.

Little did Corrie know, the recently appointed Nazi mayor of Velsen attended the service, determined to see if the church complied with the new law.

THE NEXT MORNING Peter felt someone shaking him.

"Peter! Wake up," cried Cocky, his little sister. "Please, Peter, wake up!"

Peter opened his eyes. "Uh? What's the matter? . . . Oh, it's you. Come on now, let me go back to sleep, will you?"

Cocky shook him again. "Listen to me. You must get up— this instant. The police have come! They're downstairs. Peter! Are you listening to me? The police are downstairs, and they say you are to go to prison."

Peter went with her downstairs and the Dutch officers calmly announced that he was under arrest.

"It's because of the 'Wilhelmus,'" Cocky whispered.

The policemen allowed Peter to return to his room to collect a change of clothes, and as he packed, his mother appeared in the doorway.

"Peter," Nollie said softly, "this is going to be a dangerous ex- perience for you. We don't know what is going to happen, where they are going to take you. But I know, son, that if the Lord is with you, we don't have to fear anything at all. Let's get down on our knees for a moment."

Nollie began to pray, but Peter's heart was far away. While he had grown up in a Christian home and played the organ for his church, he felt that religion was for older people, especially women. Religion was not for him. Not at eighteen, in any case.

When they returned downstairs the officers flanked Peter and led him away without further discussion.

At the police station he was taken to a cold, gray interrogation room. One by one various Germans—most presumably Gestapo—asked him the same questions again and again. Evidently they thought he was an important Resistance operative, perhaps even a leader. As he pondered his situation between questions, he heard something incredible: outside a street musician was playing a famous Dutch hymn. As Peter sat there, the words to the melody came to him:

> O surround us with Thy grace, Lord Jesus, forever
> That the attacks of the enemy will harm us never.

Another officer came in, breaking Peter's momentary respite, and took him to a second room for more questions. Then another. Finally, a guard let him out into a small yard that seemed to be an outside holding cell. Bunched in the corner, a number of Jews were surrounded by German guards. After a while a truck came and everyone was ordered into the back. As Peter took his seat, a young officer entered and announced that if anyone said a word, he would be shot.

They arrived without incident at their destination— Amsterdam prison—and Peter received his personal allotment: blanket, cup, fork, and spoon. He was then taken to a small cell that had two other occupants: a contractor accused of espionage, and a gangster who had been arrested for burglary. "Smart Mels," as he was called, regularly displayed his underworld talent by stealing bread around the prison when they were let outside. Peter later learned that Mels had lived a hard life, more than a third of it behind bars.

..

ON WEDNESDAY MORNING, as Corrie and her father set up their workbenches in the shop, Cocky burst into the room.

"Opa! Tante Corrie! They came for Peter! They took him away!"

Cocky didn't know where Peter had been taken, though, and it wasn't until Saturday that Corrie found out that he had been imprisoned in Amsterdam.

For two weeks Corrie waited and worried. No news came about Peter, but another danger emerged. One night, just shy of the eight p.m. curfew, she heard a knock on the Beje's alley door. She opened to find a woman in a fur coat—odd for the summer—clutching a suitcase.

"My name is Kleermaker," the woman said. "I'm a Jew."

Corrie invited her in and introduced her to her father and Betsie. Mrs. Kleermaker's story sounded all too familiar. Her husband had been arrested several months before, and her son had gone into hiding. The family owned a clothing store but the SD had ordered her to close it and she was afraid to return to her apartment, which was just above the business. She had heard, she said, that the ten Boom family had befriended a Jewish man recently.

"In this household," Opa chimed in, "God's people are always welcome."

"We have four empty beds upstairs," Betsie added. "Your problem will be choosing which one to sleep in!"

TWO NIGHTS LATER Corrie heard another knock on the alley door just before eight o'clock. She opened to find an elderly Jewish couple—frightened to death—holding their last possessions. They expressed the same story, and Corrie took them in. The danger and risk, she knew, posed a problem. The ten Booms now harbored three Jews, and the Beje was located only a half block from the Haarlem police headquarters. The next day she visited Willem for advice and help. She told him about the Jews and asked if he could find a place for them in the country.

"It's getting harder," he said. "They're feeling the food shortage now even on the farms. I still have addresses, yes, a few. But they won't take anyone without a ration card."

"Without a ration card! But Jews aren't issued ration cards!"

Willem mused a moment. "I know. And ration cards can't be counterfeited. They're changed too often and they're too easy to spot."

So how in the world were they going to get ration cards? Corrie asked.

"You steal them."

The word "steal" caught in Corrie's conscience. "Then, Willem, could you steal . . . I mean . . . could you get three stolen cards?"

Willem shook his head. The Gestapo watched him night and day, he said. "It will be far better for you to develop your own sources. The less connection with me—the less connection with anyone else—the better."

On the train ride home Corrie racked her brain to think of a source. One name came to mind: Fred Koornstra, who used to work for the utility company and read the Beje's electric meter each month. From what she recalled, he now worked in the Food Office, the very place where they distributed ration cards.

That evening after dinner she paid Fred a visit, a bit uneasy about whether he would help or turn her in. After some small talk, she explained that she had been housing three Jews, and that another two had arrived that afternoon—all needing ration cards.

"Is there any way you can give out extra cards? More than you report?"

Fred shook his head. Every card was accounted for, he said, and then the numbers were double-checked. He thought for a moment and then had an idea.

"Unless . . . Unless there should be a holdup. The Food Office in Utrecht was robbed last month. . . . If it happened at noon, when just the record clerk and I are there . . . and they found us tied and gagged . . ."

Corrie waited as Fred processed how the fake crime could be committed.

"How many do you need?" he finally asked.

"One hundred."

OVER AT AMSTERDAM prison, Peter languished. Nights were long and as he lay on his thin straw mattress, his mind returned again and again to his family. He thought about his parents and siblings, remembering how they looked sitting around the dinner table. Without fail, though, each night his thoughts would be broken by another prisoner's weeping. At dawn, Peter knew, that man would be executed.

"Prison under a Nazi regime for a political offense suddenly turns one's thoughts to serious matters," he remembered of the time. "As night after night I experienced agonizing thoughts, hearing the cry of the doomed, as every day we heard on the pipes* the news of young men taken from their cells and shot down somewhere in the streets as a reprisal measure of the occupying forces, the danger of my situation made me lay my religion in the balance."

As if on cue, the next day or so he received a parcel from home. It contained clean clothes, a handkerchief, and a small

---

* The prisoners learned how to communicate with others in the cell block by tapping on the heating pipes.

piece of soap. Hidden in a sock, too, he found a small New Testament. Peter couldn't understand how it wasn't discovered during inspection, but he was grateful to have something to read, something meaningful. He read and reread the pages, and to his surprise the Scriptures came alive.

"It seemed suddenly to be a personal letter to me," he wrote later, "with words of cheer and help for the many trying situations that arose daily. The Christ it spoke about no longer seemed like the subject of a hagiography, but real, like a friend of mine. I began to realize that Jesus Christ had not only died for the world in a general way, but that He had given His life for me, that I, by faith and trusting Him, could have eternal life."

He prayed and at once his spirits lifted. "Inside I felt free, almost light, with a sort of joy. Circumstances no longer infuriated me. I had come to prison to find Christ, an unfailing Friend."

A WEEK AFTER Corrie's visit with Fred Koornstra, he stopped by the Beje. Corrie was shaken by what she saw: Fred's eyes were a greenish purple, and his lower lip was cut and swollen.

Before she could comment, Fred said, "My friend took very naturally to the part."

He set on the table a manila folder with exactly one hundred ration cards, adding that he could provide another one hundred cards every month. Corrie was ecstatic—hundreds of Jewish lives would be saved—but it was too risky for her to pick them up at his house every month. She had another idea. Could he come to the Beje dressed in his old meterman uniform? The meter was on the inside of the house, after all, so he could give her the cards out of sight of prying eyes. Fred said he was game, and Corrie found a place in the stairs where he could hide the cards when he "checked the meter."

A few nights later Corrie took in another four Jews: a woman and her three children. Later that evening, well past curfew, the alley doorbell rang again. Assuming that another Jew had been told about the Beje, Corrie dashed downstairs. To her amazement, the visitor was her nephew Kik, Willem's son.

"Get your bicycle," he said. "I have some people I want you to meet."

"Now? After curfew?"

Kik didn't answer and Corrie fetched her tireless bike. Down the dark streets they pedaled, then over a canal, and Corrie realized that they were in the Aerdenhout suburb. Kik led her to a house shrouded with trees, and a young maid was waiting for them at the door. Kik carried both bikes inside and placed them in the foyer alongside countless others.

As they made their way to the drawing room, none other than Corrie's old friend Pickwick greeted them with coffee. His real name was Herman Sluring, and he was one of the ten Booms' best customers. Fabulously wealthy, he bought the Beje's most expensive watches and often joined the family upstairs for conversation. On the one-hundred-year anniversary of the shop he had sent an enormous bouquet of flowers, and later came to the party. Everyone loved him and he was affectionately referred to as either "Uncle Herman" (Peter's favorite name for him) or "Pickwick," a name Corrie and Betsie had given him after realizing he looked like an illustrator's sketch of Charles Dickens's famous character.

Short, fat, bald, and cross-eyed, Pickwick was not much to look at, but he was a fine Christian gentleman who loved children and was kind and generous.

He began introducing Corrie and Kik to the other guests and Corrie immediately understood that these were underground Resistance workers; everyone was called "Mrs. Smit" or "Mr. Smit." The leadership of the Resistance, she learned, worked in liaison with the British and the Free Dutch forces fighting in other cities, and Pickwick seemed to be in charge of the Haarlem cell.

Moments later he introduced Corrie to the group as "the head of an operation here in this city"; until that moment, Corrie simply saw herself as helping her Jewish neighbors.

One by one Pickwick identified the others, each with a particular skill or contribution: one could prepare false identity papers; another could produce a car with government plates; still another could forge signatures.

Corrie understood that she had crossed the Rubicon: she was now part of the Dutch Resistance.

MEANWHILE IN AMSTERDAM, a thirteen-year-old Jewish girl named Anne Frank started a diary on her birthday, June 12. Amsterdam had the country's largest Jewish population, and the Nazis targeted it first. In her initial diary entry, Anne recalled the avalanche of persecution initiated by the Nazis:

"Our freedom was severely restricted by a series of anti-Jewish decrees: Jews were required to wear a yellow star; Jews were required to turn in bicycles; Jews were forbidden to use streetcars; Jews were forbidden to ride in cars, even their own; Jews were required to do their shopping between 3 and 5 p.m.; Jews were required to frequent only Jewish-owned barbershops and beauty parlors; Jews were forbidden to be out on the streets between 8 p.m. and 6 a.m.; Jews were forbidden to attend theaters, movies or any other forms of entertainment; Jews were forbidden to use swimming pools, tennis courts, hockey fields or any other athletic fields; Jews were forbidden to go rowing; Jews were forbidden to take part in any athletic activity in public; Jews were forbidden to sit in their gardens or those of friends after 8 p.m.; Jews were forbidden to visit Christians in their homes; Jews were required to attend Jewish schools."

More horrors awaited Holland's Jews, though, as Anne would soon discover.

✳ ✳ ✳

On June 15 Peter was released from prison. No fanfare—a few short formalities and he returned to the streets of Amsterdam. Back at his church, though, things had changed. The sermons from the pulpit had become vague and meek. Then his job: due to the need for electricity to run the trains, his position as organist had been eliminated. The other change he noticed was that food had become scarcer by the day; the notion of a normal meal was out of the question. Staples like bread and potatoes were now impossible to find, and Hollanders were forced to eat what *was* available.

Flowers. Tulip bulbs, for example, were boiled or fried and used as a replacement for potatoes.

Peter also noticed that the persecution of Jews had worsened: now every Jew captured by the Nazis was transported to a concentration camp and executed. He wasn't Jewish, but he was in the crosshairs of a new Nazi program: *razzias*. Because of a manpower shortage in Germany—military service being compulsory for adult males—the country lacked sufficient workers to operate factories. As such, they began raiding areas of occupied territories and sending the captured young men to Germany for forced labor. Peter had a certificate showing that he worked for an ecclesiastical organization, however, which exempted him from being "drafted" for such work. Or so he thought.

A week later he attended a conference for Christian workers in the neighboring town of Hilversum. As he left the building two policemen seized him, each holding an arm. They told him he was under arrest and Peter suspected he was caught up in a *razzia*. He tried to protest, saying he was exempt from transport to Germany, but one of the officers cut him off.

"Save it. You can explain it to the authorities."

Peter spent the night in a dirty, dank cell with several drunks.

In the morning he was taken to the German commander's office. Asked why he had not already gone to Germany to work in a factory, Peter said he was a preacher and therefore exempt.

"Can you prove that?"

Peter removed the ecclesiastical certificate from his wallet and showed him.

The officer glanced at it and laughed. "We don't believe those certificates anymore. Here in Holland, every boy seems to think that he's a minister. Furthermore, sonny, you don't look like a preacher to me. You're too young. I'm going to send you to Germany to work along with the rest."

Chapter 5

DIVING UNDER

PETER KNEW HE HAD ONE shot, and that the jig would be up in thirty seconds. Amsterdam prison was bad enough; if he went to Germany he knew he'd never come back.

"Sir, just a moment," he said. "I have other proof that I'm a preacher."

"Well, what is it?"

"Let me have just five minutes of your time to preach for you a Gospel message. Then you can judge whether I'm telling you the truth or not."

The commander sat back and stared at him for what seemed like days. He motioned to another officer and they had a short conversation that Peter couldn't hear. Suddenly the German looked up, exasperated, and pointed to the door.

"RRRRRAUS!"

Peter bolted before his luck changed.

The *razzias* continued, though, and with more severity than ever. At every important place in the city, he noticed, soldiers did not ask questions; they simply arrested boys and sent them to Germany. From this point on, if he went out in public he'd need a disguise, church certificate notwithstanding. With a little help from his sisters, he began dressing as a girl whenever he left the house. Surprisingly, the scarfs and skirts worked; on several occasions soldiers even whistled at him.

As days passed, however, even disguises were insufficient as Gestapo "recruiting agents" raided homes without notice, nabbing any boys they found. There was no alternative at this point: Peter would have to "dive under."

*Onderduikers,** they were called—Dutch boys who had to disappear and hide from house to house just as the Jews were doing. Jews were "divers," too, but the consequences of being caught were radically different. For the non-Jewish Dutchmen, it meant forced labor; for the Jew, it meant death.

Beginning with a special census in January 1941, the Nazis had begun targeting Jews for deportation to Germany. The Jewish census gave them the records needed for later roundups, which commenced the following summer. In June 1942 the *Zentralstelle,* the German office orchestrating deportations, announced that commencing July 14, all Jews would be sent to work in Germany under the supervision of the police. Few complied with the order, however, so the Germans raided homes in Amsterdam, arresting and holding as hostages some seven hundred fifty Jews that very day. The reprisal had the desired effect: over the next two weeks some six thousand Jews reported for transport to Westerbork, a transit station in northeastern Netherlands that the Nazis used as a staging point for deportations to concentration camps.

One such family caught in the maelstrom was the Frank family. On July 9 Anne recorded what it was like for Jewish divers: "Mother called me at five-thirty. . . . The four of us were wrapped in so many layers of clothes it looked as if we were going off to spend the night in a refrigerator. . . . No Jew in our situa-

---

* Literally, the term means "people who go underwater."

tion would dare leave the house with a suitcase full of clothes. I was wearing two undershirts, three pairs of underpants, a dress, and over that a skirt, a jacket, a raincoat, two pairs of stockings, heavy shoes, a cap, a scarf, and lots more.

"The stripped beds, the breakfast things on the table, the pound of meat for the cat in the kitchen—all of these created the impression that we'd left in a hurry. But we weren't interested in impressions. We just wanted to get out of there, to get away and reach our destination in safety. Nothing else mattered."

Anne Frank's family found a place to hide at her father's office building at 263 Prinsengracht. With a highly irregular layout, the structure allowed them to disappear in the upper floors. The ground floor housed a warehouse with various spaces for stockrooms, workrooms, and milling. In the corner the building had an office, through which one could access the second, third, and fourth floors. The second level contained three offices, and a stairwell led up to the third floor, where there were more small rooms and a bathroom. The fourth floor contained two tiny rooms and the attic. It was in these third- and fourth-floor rooms that the Frank family took refuge.

The Franks were happy to have a place to stay, but the cramped quarters and confinement were stifling. "Not being able to go outside upsets me more than I can say," Anne wrote in her diary on September 28, "and I'm terrified our hiding place will be discovered and that we'll be shot."

Indeed, the rooms were easy to find once you were on the third floor. To add a measure of security, a carpenter built in a bookcase at the entrance; if pushed or pulled in the right place, it would swing open. They dubbed their new home the "Secret Annex."

AT THE SAME time, Audrey Hepburn recorded what it was like in Arnhem: "I'd go to the station* with my mother to take a train and I'd see cattle trucks filled with Jews . . . the worst kind of horror. . . . I saw families with little children, with babies, herded into meat wagons—trains of big wooden vans with just a little slat open at the top. . . . And on the platform were soldiers herding more Jewish families with their poor little bundles and small children. There would be families together and they would separate them, saying, 'The men go there and the women go there.' Then they would take the babies and put them in another van."

These babies—and their destination—would soon come to the attention of Corrie ten Boom.

MEANWHILE IN DELFT, a small town some thirty miles south of Haarlem, a tall eighteen-year-old boy arrived on the campus of Delft Technological University. His name was Hans Poley. Up until September 1942 the Nazis had largely ignored the colleges after the initial raids in 1941. If you weren't Jewish, it was perhaps the last safe haven. That was about to change. Hans noticed that while everything appeared normal on the surface, the students and faculty were on edge.

Nazi commissioner Seyss-Inquart was in fact planning to address Dutch universities, but his first priority was rounding up Jews. So the raids on Jewish neighborhoods in Amsterdam continued, with thousands arrested in September.

Anne Frank recorded in her diary the shocking news pouring in to the Secret Annex: "Our many Jewish friends and acquain-

---

* The Arnhem Centraal Station was just two blocks from Hepburn's apartment on Jansbinnensingel.

tances are being taken away in droves," she wrote on October 9. "The Gestapo is treating them very roughly and transporting them in cattle cars to Westerbork. . . . The people get almost nothing to eat, much less drink, as water is available only one hour a day, and there's only one toilet and sink for several thousand people. Men and women sleep in the same room, and women and children often have their heads shaved. . . . We assume that most of them are being murdered. The English radio says they're being gassed."

Yet there was more. To quell recent acts of sabotage against German authorities, the Gestapo began unspeakable reprisals. "Leading citizens," Anne wrote, "are taken prisoner to await their execution. If the Gestapo can't find the saboteur, they simply grab five hostages and line them up against the wall."

In London, Queen Wilhelmina—heartbroken over reports of the barbarism—gave a radio address on October 17: "With great attention and profound anxiety I follow your increasing difficulties and sufferings . . . the bitter distress of thousands in prisons and concentration camps. . . . I share whole-heartedly in your indignation and sorrow at the fate of our Jewish countrymen; and with my whole people I feel this inhuman treatment, this systematic extermination of those countrymen who have lived for centuries with us in our beloved homeland, as something done to us personally."

OVER ENSUING WEEKS the persecution intensified. On November 19 Anne Frank added to her diary: "Night after night, green and gray military vehicles cruise the streets. They knock on every door, asking whether any Jews live there. If so, the whole family is immediately taken away. . . . It's impossible to escape their clutches unless you go into hiding. They often go around with lists. . . . They frequently offer a bounty, so much per head. . . . In the evenings when it's dark, I often see long lines of good, innocent people, accompanied by crying children, walking on and on, ordered about by a handful of men who bully and beat them until they nearly drop dead. No one is spared. The sick, the elderly, children, babies and pregnant women—all are marched to their death."

IN EARLY DECEMBER rumors spread that the Nazis would soon resume raids and mass arrests at all Dutch universities. Sensing the impending danger, Delft University announced that the Christmas holidays would start early—"due to a shortage of coal for heating."

Over the break Hans decided to leave Delft and find a hiding place with relatives in Zeeland, located in the southwest corner of Holland. As the least populated province in the Netherlands, it was the last place the Germans would conduct raids. Not long after he arrived he fell in love with a beautiful seventeen-year-old girl named Mies. She was from nearby Goes, and she, too, was smitten. Each afternoon Hans would meet her at the train station to walk her home after her studies at the local teachers' college. They decided they wanted to get married, but the practicality of that was nil.

After the New Year the evil occurring in Amsterdam worsened by the day. Seyss-Inquart not only resumed raids in Amsterdam, he made a special effort to round up and deport orphans, the elderly, and the ill.

* * *

From glimpses through her window each day, Anne Frank witnessed exactly what she had feared. On January 13, 1943, she wrote: "Terrible things are happening outside. At any time of night and day, poor helpless people are being dragged out of their homes. . . . Families are torn apart; men, women and children are separated. Children come home from school to find that their parents have disappeared. Women return from shopping to find their houses sealed, their families gone. The Christians in Holland are also living in fear because their sons are being sent to Germany. Everyone is scared."

And the Nazis weren't the only adversary the Dutch faced; as winter set in, food disappeared—save sugar beets, tulip bulbs, and maybe a slice of bread or two a day. Families didn't have enough to feed themselves, much less divers they didn't know. Dutch homes also had no electricity, and no heat.

Life in the Netherlands was cold, miserable, and dangerous.

One morning at the beginning of February, Corrie noticed that Mr. Christoffels had failed to join their morning Bible study, and then did not appear for work. She checked with his landlady and her heart broke with the news.

The old man had frozen to death in his bed.

AFTER THE SUCCESSFUL roundup of Jews, Seyss-Inquart turned his attention to the non-Jewish Dutch. When students returned to campuses for the winter semester, the Nazis pounced. On February 6 the Gestapo launched nationwide raids on universities, arresting tens of thousands of students. The choice given to boys was to either sign a Nazi pledge of loyalty or be sent to Germany for forced labor.

To avoid signing the oath, Hans decided not to return to Delft. "The battle against national socialism was not just a battle with arms," he explained, "it was ideological, a religious battle."

✳ ✳ ✳

On April 24 Corrie, Betsie, and Opa gathered around their small radio to hear Queen Wilhelmina's broadcast from London. Knowing that what she said would make its way back to Hitler, Her Royal Highness minced no words: "I want to raise a fiery protest against the cunningly organized and constantly extended manhunt which the German hordes, assisted by national traitors, are carrying out all over the country. Our language lacks the words to describe these infamous practices."

NEAR THE END of the month—the deadline for submitting university loyalty oaths—the Nazis announced that students who had not signed one were to report for deportation to Germany. To ensure compliance Hanns Rauter, the Gestapo high commander, warned that those who did not report would subject their parents to arrest.

Hans knew that the Nazis would check not only the houses of parents, but the houses of relatives. He would have to find another place to hide. That place would be the Beje. Hans's mother knew Corrie through a church ministry for handicapped children, and talk one day led to Hans's predicament.

"He can stay with us until we find a more suitable place for him," Corrie told Mrs. Poley.

The description of the hideout—a house with two women in their fifties and a father in his eighties—didn't seem too exciting to Hans, but his options were scant. Corrie and the Poleys agreed that Hans would arrive at the Beje the second week of May.

TO ASSIST DIVERS and Jews in finding hideouts, a most unusual collaboration had been formed in late 1942. Mrs. Helena T. Kuipers-Rietberg, a housewife and mother of five, teamed up with Reverend F. Slomp, a Calvinist pastor who had been expelled from his pulpit due to anti-Nazi preaching and activities. Together they formed an underground organization called the Landelijke Organisatie voor Hulp aan Onderduikers,* or LO, which expanded rapidly across Holland. Due to Reverend Slomp's connections in the Reformed Church, most of the members of the LO were devout Calvinists whose religious convictions and sense of sacrifice compelled them to join.

In Haarlem, the Dutchman who headed and supervised the LO was none other than Uncle Herman—the jolly and rotund "Pickwick."

The LO's work was delicate, though, since they had to pair divers with host families, most of whom did not have enough room to house an entire Jewish family. When a home was large enough to bring in a second family, it usually meant that the Jews had to live in basements or upstairs rooms. When infants and children were involved, the LO tried to place them with rural hosts in the northeastern provinces. Often, the LO would pay the foster parents for the child's board.

Hosts in rural areas were ideal for adults, too, since divers could assist the family as farm laborers, a "job" that would appear perfectly normal to Gestapo agents. But regardless of the location of the host family, divers were encouraged not to tell their families of the new hideout, and certainly not to visit home. The hosts had an additional risk because if a diver was caught, he could be tortured into confessing the identity of his host family, as well as his contacts within the LO. Eventually the Gestapo would work their way up the chain of command and capture a leader.

Like Mrs. Kuipers-Rietberg. She was arrested in the spring and sent to a German concentration camp, where she died.

---

* National Organization for Help to Hiders.

Chapter 6

THE ANGELS' DEN

ON MAY 13, 1943, JUST AFTER SUNDOWN but before curfew, Hans Poley made his way along back streets to the Beje. Arriving at the ten Booms' alley entrance, he pressed the buzzer and a middle-aged woman answered the door.

"Welcome! Come in, quickly. I'm Tante Kees,* and I do hope that you'll be very happy here."

Corrie led him up the stairs and into the main living area, where Betsie was sewing and Opa was sitting by the coal stove.

"Father, this is Hans. He will stay with us for some time."

Hans looked over at the elderly gentleman. His hair and beard were snow-white, and he was peering up over his gold-rimmed glasses.

"Well, my boy, we are glad that you trust us to offer you shelter, but we have to expect our ultimate protection from our Father in heaven. We do hope that our Lord will bless your stay. Sit down here."

Before taking his seat, Hans introduced himself to the woman who had been sewing.

"I will be your Tante Bep from now on," Betsie said.

---

* Kees was a boy's name, but as a youth Corrie was a tomboy and acquired it as a nickname.

It was clear, Hans figured, that everyone who stayed in the Beje was considered extended family, and that Corrie and Betsie were aunts.

"We cannot offer you much in the way of companionship of your own age," Betsie added, "but we shall certainly get on well."

Hans sat down and Opa began a soft interrogation. He asked Hans about himself, his background, his convictions, and why he needed to hide. Hans explained the situation at the universities and said that he had become a diver. Opa nodded, saying that he had several grandsons in the same predicament. He also said that he was the chairman of the board of the Dreefschool (elementary and high school), and that last year they had received an affidavit requiring the board to declare that they had no Jewish students. He persuaded the board to refuse to answer it.

When he concluded his questions, Opa glanced at his watch and saw that it was a quarter past nine. "Children, it's time for an old man to go to bed. We shall say our evening prayers. Please, Bep, hand me the Bible."

He began reading from Psalm 121: "Where does my help come from? My help comes from the Lord, the Maker of heaven and earth. . . ." When he finished he began praying, asking God to protect friends who had disappeared, his grandsons, and then the queen herself. "We ask Your special blessing for our beloved Queen Wilhelmina," he prayed, "on whose shoulders You have laid such a heavy burden. Be her strength so she can guide us according to Your will."

After Opa retired, Corrie led Hans up a short flight of curving steps as she explained that the building was complicated because originally there were two houses. As they passed down a corridor, Hans noticed a few doors opening to tiny rooms, and then a door at the end of the hall. Corrie opened that door and Hans was amazed to see a furnished room that spanned the width of the house. Beneath the steeply inclined roof it had two beds and some creatively crafted closets.

"Stay away from the windows," Corrie said. "We have lace curtains, but the neighbors shouldn't notice anything out of the ordinary. Also, the shop and the workshop behind it are out of bounds for you. But make yourself at home as much as you like in this room. Oh, Hans, I hope you will be happy here."

Corrie motioned to the beds. "We may get more guests like you, so you probably won't be alone in this room for long." She then led him back down the corridor and opened a door to a small space containing a water tap on a white enamel basin. "You can wash here. It's somewhat primitive, but it will have to do for the time being."

Hans replied that he had been camping many times, and that the accommodations were fine. "I'm just very grateful that you're willing to put up with me and take the risks that you do."

That evening as Hans lay in bed, the Damiate bells of the old St. Bavo Church chimed. From his position in the top side of the house, it seemed as if the bells rang directly over him. The tune playing was a familiar one to every Haarlemer, and somehow it comforted Hans, mitigating the fact that his free life was over.

He thought of Mies, wondering what he would tell her about his new home, and then he fell fast asleep.

In the morning Corrie gave him a full tour of the Beje. Given the age of the building, it had no central heating or even baths and showers. There were two coal stoves—one in the living room and another in the parlor—and two toilets—one on the second floor and one in the basement. There was the cold-water tap that Corrie had showed him the night before, but that was it; a "bath" meant the wash bowl and water jug.

Still, there was a warmth and happiness here that few Dutch homes enjoyed. Later that day Hans met the rest of the "family": Mr. Ineke, who assisted Opa and Corrie in the shop; Henny van Dantzig, a cheerful woman in her thirties who helped with sales;

and then Snoetje, the ten Boom cat. Pitch-black, Snoetje would roam the house. During meals, she would find her way to the dinner table for handouts. Stepping gingerly from one shoulder to the next, she would make her way around the table until she had enough scraps for her own meal.

That evening the ten Booms added another guest: Hansje Frankfort-Israels. She went by Thea, and for several minutes she told her story. She and her husband were Jewish and they worked at the Het Apeldoornsche Bosch, a home for mentally handicapped Jews. In January, she said, the Germans raided the place and began to kick and beat the patients. "The Germans took those poor people outside and herded them through the gate with shouts and sticks toward the railway cars designed for cattle transport. Then they stacked them one on top of the other and carried them off to Germany. Many of them were dead before they crossed the border."

As Thea spoke, Hans glanced over at Betsie and noticed tears in her eyes. Corrie, though, listened with clenched fists.

Thea explained that she and her husband fled and had been on the run ever since. So that they could find places to stay though, they had to separate. She had not heard from him in weeks.

With Hans and Thea, the Beje had its first two permanent refugees: a Dutch diver and a Jewish woman. Corrie intended to bring in many more, especially Jews.

On Sunday, May 18, everyone in the Beje celebrated Opa's eighty-fourth birthday. Nollie and her husband Flip came by for the day, as did Willem. When everyone settled in the living room, Corrie asked Willem if he couldn't find a farm where Hans could hide and help a rural family. Willem thought the question was premature without inquiring of Hans's wishes, but Corrie quickly rebutted.

"There is more to it," she said. "I've been thinking about what Thea told us. There will be much need for shelter for our Jewish people. There will always be more Dutchmen who will provide a home to non-Jews than to Jews. We are willing to help Jews, so let us shelter as many as we can."

No one could argue with Corrie's logic, and Willem said he'd look into it.

THAT SAME DAY Anne Frank recorded in her diary how she had witnessed a dogfight high in the sky a few nights earlier, and Allied airmen had to parachute from their burning plane. They were Canadians, she found out later, and five crewmen had safely bailed out. The pilot, however, burned to death, and the Gestapo quickly captured the four remaining men.

Early that morning the danger hit frighteningly close, and Anne wrote: "Last night the guns were making so much noise that Mother shut the window. This was followed by a loud boom, which sounded as if a firebomb had landed beside my bed. 'Lights! Lights!' I screamed. . . . I expected the room to burst into flames at any moment."

These scenes would repeat again and again for Anne, and for everyone in Amsterdam and Haarlem.

HANS, MEANWHILE, GREW accustomed to the ten Boom routine. He and Corrie would rise first and have breakfast together around seven-thirty. Opa and Betsie would come down around eight-thirty, eat, and then Opa would take his place by the stove or in the workshop. Corrie had long since taken over the bulk of work on watches, and Hans admired her craftsmanship.

"Now look at this," she said one morning as she turned on the BBC and fiddled with an old chain watch. "At the first boom of Big Ben, it will be 8:00 a.m. to the second. At that moment I time the difference with this mother watch." Corrie checked the second hand of the watch and when the boom sounded she said the chain watch was only three seconds off. "During the day," she added, "this will be the standard for all other clocks and watches in the shop and in repair. It's the first thing I do every morning."

Hans understood that Corrie was fifty-one now and had been at the trade for more than thirty years. Like her father, she enjoyed the intricate challenge of watchmaking and repair, and she took great pride in her work. Her new passion, though, was hiding Jews.

In late May, Hans discovered how he could help without leaving the house. Every week his mother had been stopping by the Beje to bring clean clothes, recent news, and—most importantly—letters from Mies. On one occasion he found in his package a copy of the "Wilhelmus," the Dutch national anthem. To print it was illegal, as was selling or buying it.

Hans beamed and showed it to Corrie. Opa glanced over and said, "I think, my boy, it is fitting to read it aloud to all of us." Hans was well aware that Opa and everyone else knew the words by heart, but it was a mini-celebration that they had a copy of the contraband. "The hymn dates back more than four hundred years," Hans recalled, "to William of Orange's flight for religious freedom for the Low Countries under Spanish rule. Now its old words took on a new and very personal meaning for each of us. William had a deep trust that the Almighty would vindicate the struggle and the sacrifices, and the words echoed our own situation."

> But unto God, the greatest
> of Majesties, I owe
> obedience, first and latest
> For justice wills it so.

Hans tacked the paper to the sloping roof over his bed, and the document gave him an idea. He couldn't be seen outside, of course, but he could help in another way. His mother had dropped off a typewriter one day and he figured this would be his contribution: underground pamphlets. The Resistance had an active network to disseminate news and encouragement through fliers, and the plea was always the same: "Multiply and pass on!"

He mentioned the idea to Corrie, and a day or so later she came in with a first job. A customer who worked in the town hall had come in for a repair, she said, and he explained how the Nazis required the town staff to provide addresses for the young men they wished to send off to German factories. She handed Hans a paper.

"A farewell address," she said, "from a Dutch government official who resigned because he couldn't accept the German treatment of Jews. I thought you'd like to copy it, so he let me borrow it for a day."

Hans read it quickly:

I feel the need to explain briefly to you, as my staff, what has been the motive for handing in my resignation on September 12, 1940. That day it became clear to me that in our country the so-called Aryan declaration will become mandatory. This means that, when considering applications or planning staff moves, we shall be obliged to investigate whether the person involved is of Jewish descent. However dear my vocation may be to me, because of this measure I felt obliged to hand in my resignation, as my conscience as a Christian and as a Dutchman will never allow me to put this question to anyone ever. . . .

THE MAN WAS right, Hans knew, that his future was precarious. Nazi reprisals against letters like this were severe, as were punishments for anyone copying or disseminating them. He assured Corrie that he would type out a number of copies so the man could distribute them to his colleagues.

On June 8 the Gestapo carried out more *razzia* raids all over Holland; hundreds of Dutch boys would be sent to Germany the next day. The increased danger also brought the ten Booms their third resident, and second Jew: Mary van Itallie. She was a petite forty-two-year-old daughter of a University of Amsterdam professor, and her story was worse than Thea's. When the Germans began persecuting Dutch Jews, she told the ten Booms, her parents committed suicide rather than face a death camp like Auschwitz. To her credit, despite the trauma Mary remained positive and upbeat. She believed that goodness and truth would eventually prevail, and she fit in well with everyone at the Beje.

Shortly after Mary arrived, Corrie took in two more Dutch divers: Henk Wessels and Leendert Kip. No one asked their ages, but Henk looked eighteen, and Leendert twenty-five. Henk had a choirboy face and his quiet and cheerful disposition matched. Leendert was the opposite—mature-looking, with a mischievous grin—he was talkative and opinionated. Their occupations, though, seemed mismatched: the choirboy was actually a young lawyer, and the opinionated one a schoolteacher.

The ten Boom refugees now counted five—Hans, Thea, Mary, Henk, and Leendert—and as a group they discussed how to better hide themselves in the old house. Hans thought the attic might be a good spot and he investigated the dust-covered space. The attic door was too obvious, he concluded, so he nailed the original hatch shut and sawed a new one in a less obvious place. When they tested it during an emergency drill, however, it was clear that the attic wouldn't work; it took too long to get everyone up and the hatch closed.

Corrie, though, had an idea. "I'll ask Pickwick. I'm sure he'll know someone who can help us."

A few days later an architect showed up at the Beje. Like most Resistance workers, he went by the name "Mr. Smit." It appeared that he inspected all Haarlem Resistance hideouts as he wanted to review the Beje's entire security system. Corrie showed him the cubbyhole in the stairwell for hiding ration cards, and Mr. Smit approved. Then she explained to him her safe/not safe system: if a wooden "Alpina Watches" sign hung in the dining room window, it was safe to enter; otherwise not. Then there was the mirror outside the window that revealed who was approaching; if the Gestapo or police appeared, the door between the shop and house could be shut and locked, thus providing valuable extra time for refugees to scramble for hiding places.

Smit made his way upstairs and marveled at the eccentric layout of the house, the crooked walls, and the irregular floor levels. "Miss ten Boom, if all houses were constructed like this one, you would see before you a less worried man."

Corrie followed him as he made his way to her bedroom on the top floor.

"This is it!" Smit cried. "You want your hiding place as high as possible. Gives you the best chance to reach it while the search is on below."

"But . . . this is my bedroom."

Smit ignored her and began moving furniture and measuring. After a few minutes he motioned to the back of her bedroom. "This is where the false wall will go!"

With a pencil he sketched a line about thirty inches from the wall. "One layer of bricks will be enough. A fake closet at the left in front of it and a sliding panel in the back of the closet should do it. My lady, this will be great. I'll be just as proud of this as of the beautiful houses I've built."

Over the next two days workmen came by with tools hidden inside newspapers and bricks tucked away in briefcases. In no time Corrie had a brick wall in her bedroom, which was promptly covered by plaster. At one end the false wall ended with a wooden linen closet, which provided entrance into the hiding space. On the bottom shelf it contained a sliding secret panel—a

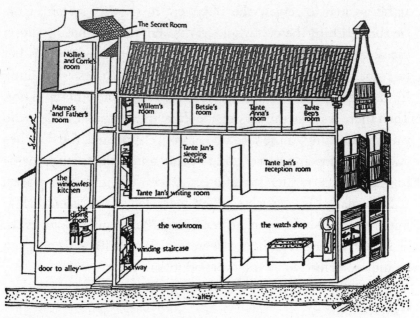

Beje layout showing the secret hiding place.

masterpiece of craftsmanship—that was three feet wide by two feet high. It was set in tight-fitting grooves so that when closed, no cracks or seams appeared. A counterweight and wheel allowed the piece to move easily, and a thin layer of rubber was placed at the bottom to mask the noise of closing it.

A fresh coat of paint was applied to the wall and closet, and when it dried Corrie placed linens and towels on the shelving. On the bottom, in front of the sliding panel, she placed two large sewing boxes. The work was so professional that the paint and caulking looked original, complete with marks of grime, water stains, and chipped and peeling molding. Looking at the false wall in a room where she had lived for fifty years, she couldn't imagine that it had not been part of the original construction some one hundred fifty years ago.

Mr. Smit came by for a final inspection a few days later and he gave Corrie survival and security advice. "Keep a water jug in there," he said. "Change the water once a week. Hardtack and vitamins keep indefinitely. Anytime there is anyone in the house whose presence is unofficial, all possessions except the clothes on his back must be stored in here."

He pounded the wall above the closet and admired the construction. "The Gestapo could search for a year. They'll never find this one."

When the hiding place was finished, Corrie and the refugees gave it a name: *engelen den*—the "Angels' Den." Leendert—who was an amateur electrician—wired the house with an alarm system to give the refugees time to scamper upstairs before the Gestapo arrived. A buzzer was placed at the top of the stairs so that everyone in the house could hear it. Then he placed buttons to activate the buzzer in various spots around the house: beneath

Left: *Linen closet with the bottom sliding panel closed.*
Right: *Closet with sliding panel open.*

the dining room windowsill, in the downstairs hallway, beside the Beje's front door, beneath the windows of one bedroom, behind the shop counter, and one at each workbench.

On Saturday, June 26, Corrie decided it was time for a test. Without warning, she activated the buzzer that night and the refugees scrambled out of bed, down the hall, and into the hiding place. When the panel closed she set sewing boxes in front of it and then checked her watch.

Three minutes, twenty-eight seconds.

That wasn't going to cut it. Mr. Smit had advised a time of one minute to have all refugees in, but that seemed impossible. Corrie called everyone out, gave the time, and told them that they needed to get it down to a minute and a half.

"Let's run through all the actions," Leendert said, "and see where we can save time."

The two biggest consumers of valuable seconds were turning the mattresses—in case the Gestapo felt to see if they were still warm—and getting everyone into the space.

To eliminate one bed turn and one through the hatch, Hans offered to sleep each night in the Angels' Den. "That would mean one less person to evacuate," he said. "I could also store the stuff you carry. Everyone could then crawl in much easier."

Corrie liked the idea, adding that she would be inspecting everyone's room. A piece of clothing left behind, a letter, even cigar ashes might tip off the Gestapo. She made the rounds and found the first violation in Hans's room. "You'll have to take down that picture of your fiancée," she said. Hans hated to take Mies out of his daily view, but Tante Kees was right and he removed it.

Corrie let everyone know that she'd run another test soon, and that ninety seconds was their goal.

The Nazis, meanwhile, continued *razzias* to snatch more boys. At Flip and Nollie's house, they knew that Peter and his brothers were at risk, but they didn't have the fortune of a house where they could build a false wall. Instead they rearranged their kitchen to utilize a small potato cellar beneath the floor. They enlarged the trapdoor and kept a rug over it, over which they placed the kitchen table. Not ideal, but better than nothing.

On Flip's birthday Corrie, Betsie, and Opa stopped by to celebrate. Pickwick had been generous enough to give them a perfect gift to bring along: a quarter pound of English tea. When they arrived, Nollie and Flip were out and Cocky was

A practice run, June 1943. Thea helping Mary out of the Angels' Den secret entrance.

upstairs cleaning a bedroom. As she opened a window to shake out her dust rag, she noticed a group of soldiers surrounding the block and running from house to house. A *razzia*! She raced downstairs and found her brother.

"Peter, hurry! Hide! The Germans are coming. Quick, go to the kitchen!"

Cocky lifted the trapdoor and Peter jumped in. Corrie and Betsie helped with the rug and the table, and then all three hustled to throw on a tablecloth and set out five place settings. Moments later the Nazis kicked in the front door. From his huddled position in the cellar, Peter heard the strident tromping of leather boots above him.

"Are there any boys here?" a German asked Cocky.

Corrie glanced at her niece and cringed; notwithstanding the circumstances, Cocky had been taught to never, ever lie.

"Yes, sir," she replied. "There's one under the table."

Chapter 7

THE BABIES

PETER GASPED. HUDDLED IN THE dark, his heart pounded so loudly he thought the Germans might hear.

Before Corrie could intercede, the soldier seized a corner of the tablecloth and flung it back. Cocky burst into laughter and the soldiers glared at her.

"Don't take us for fools," one of them snapped.

With that, the Germans turned and stormed out. Peter had dodged another bullet.

THE NEXT NIGHT at the Beje the alarm sounded, waking up Hans in the Angels' Den. Jumping up, he tossed his blankets aside and lifted the panel door. Thea arrived first, crawling into the dark space with her night bag. Hans helped her and whispered, "Keep moving to the end." Mary arrived next, scrambling in with her bag.

"Move on until you feel Thea," he whispered.

Moments later Leendert clambered in with his briefcase, followed by Henk. When Henk's feet cleared the entrance, Hans eased the panel down. Behind it he could hear Corrie sliding the sewing boxes in. Everyone remained silent for several moments, listening. Without a light, the Angels' Den was pitch dark, and

with five standing shoulder to shoulder, it was already claustrophobic.

Like a coffin.

"Come this way a bit," Hans said to Henk. "If they shoot
through the panel, then at least they won't hurt you."

Mary stood behind Hans, shivering against his shoulder.

"Hans, stop it. Don't say those things. I know you're right, but
I hate it."

Everyone listened for a while but they heard nothing until a
car stopped in front of the Beje. A minute or so later it drove off.

"We don't have any food in here," Leendert uttered. "Another
thing we overlooked!"

Everyone froze as footsteps sounded in Corrie's room. A
cough, a sneeze, a sniffle would reveal their presence. They
waited several moments, each slowly inhaling and exhaling the
trapped and spoiled air.

"All right, you can come out now," Corrie announced. "Two
minutes, four seconds this time."

Hans and the others breathed a sigh of relief, but every face
revealed anguish and fright. This wasn't a game, they knew, and
not only had they missed the ninety-second mark, they had forgotten to put food in the place.

Everyone went downstairs for hot chocolate, nerves still on
edge. For the first time in his life Hans experienced real fear, and
Thea and Mary looked pale and traumatized.

NOT LONG AFTER Corrie's test, she discovered a frightening
problem. At a Jewish nursery in Amsterdam the Nazis planned
to kill one hundred babies, their parents likely en route to concentration camps. Sickened by the scenario, Corrie longed for a
way to help.

The Creche, as the nursery was called, was located across the street from the Hollandsche Schouwburg, a former theater the Germans used as a deportation center for sending Jews to West- erbork. The Hollandsche Schouwburg and Creche were closely linked, as the former held Jewish adults, while the latter kept babies and small children.

Secreting the infants out under the nose of the Nazis, however, was easier said than done. The obsessively organized Germans kept detailed lists containing the name of every child coming into or leaving the center.

Those running the buildings, however, devised a plan. Walter Süskind, the thirty-five-year-old Jewish manager of the Hol- landsche Schouwburg, started by recruiting Felix Halverstad, an associate at the theater who kept the books for both venues. Next Süskind brought in Henriëtte Henriques Pimentel, the sixty- six-year-old Jewish director of the Creche.

The escape would be enacted in two stages. First, Felix would alter the books of the Creche to eliminate names of babies taken out. If the Germans reviewed the records, there must be no trace that these children had ever been at the Creche. Second, Walter would coordinate with Henriëtte on transporting the infants. The scheme was tricky, though, as the German guards across the street at the Hollandsche Schouwburg monitored the Creche.

They needed a distraction, as well as couriers who could carry the babies. Corrie mentioned the matter to Hans and the others at the Beje, and everyone wanted to assist.

"We will save them," one of the boys said. Corrie asked how, and he said, "We will steal them."

The young man's boldness and bravery impressed Corrie, but she knew that none of her boys could even safely leave the house.

Serendipitously, some days later a group of young German soldiers showed up at the Beje seeking help. How they heard about the ten Booms and their work, Corrie didn't know.

"We don't like to work any longer for Adolf Hitler," one of

them confided. "We will not kill the Jewish people. Can you help us?"

The soldiers' approach in broad daylight heightened danger, but Corrie accepted the risk and invited them in. Like her Jews and Dutch divers, these Germans needed a way to disappear. Corrie couldn't believe her good fortune.

She could help, she told them, but in exchange they would have to give up their uniforms.

The soldiers readily agreed; if they were to blend in, they'd need civilian clothes anyway. After Corrie gathered a shirt and pants for each, she passed along their uniforms to her Dutch boys so that they could appear at the Creche with Wehrmacht authority.

Still, the rescue was complicated. Walter, Felix, and Henriëtte—coordinating with Betty Goudsmit-Oudkerk, a seventeen-year-old nurse—planned to smuggle the children out in backpacks, boxes, shopping bags, or laundry baskets. From there they would need to be escorted to a close hideout where they could be housed for a few hours. Henriëtte enlisted the aid of Johan van Hulst, headmaster of the Reformed Teacher Training College next door, who agreed to hide the children in his building. He would then work with the underground, the plan went, to transport the children by train or tram to Limburg or Friesland, where they would be relocated to accepting families.

Corrie's "soldiers" apparently provided the escort.

All one hundred babies were saved.*

***

On Monday, June 28, Corrie burst into the boys' room at seven a.m. with "Rise and shine." It was Hans's birthday and

---

* The Pimentel–Süskind–van Hulst escape line worked well, eventually saving between six hundred to one thousand Jewish infants.

Corrie had planned a small party. They all traipsed downstairs for breakfast and everyone sang the traditional Dutch birthday song, "Lan zal hij leven" (Long shall he live). The ten Booms presented Hans with a book, and that afternoon he received a heartwarming gift when his parents handed him a letter from Mies. Exchanging letters often risked Gestapo attention, so they had agreed on a once-per-month schedule. Still, each letter brought a blessing. "The strengthening words in those pages brought new confidence and hope for me," he remembered.

Not long after the party the shop phone rang and Corrie answered.

"We have a man's watch here that's giving us trouble," the caller said. "We can't find anyone to repair it. For one thing, the face is very old-fashioned."

Corrie recognized it immediately as code: they were trying to find a hiding place for a Jew whose features gave him away. "Send the watch over," she said, "and I'll see what we can do in our own shop."

At seven that evening the alley doorbell rang. Corrie invited her "watch repair" in and observed his "old-fashioned" features: early thirties, thin, balding, and with protruding ears and small glasses. She closed the door and he gave a polite bow and then removed a pipe from his coat.

"The very first thing I must ask is whether or not I should leave behind my good friend the pipe? Meijer Mossel and his pipe are not easily separated. But for you, kind lady, should the smell get into your drapes, I would gladly say goodbye to my friend nicotine."

Corrie laughed. "Of course you must keep your pipe! My father smokes a cigar—when he can find one these days."

"Ah, these days! What do you expect when barbarians have overrun the camp?"

Corrie led him upstairs into the dining room and before she

could introduce him, Mossel blurted: "Is that your father? Why, if he were Jewish, he might be a patriarch."

"Sir," Opa returned, "we may be God's children by grace, but you are a son of His chosen people by birthright."

After introductions Mossel gave the group a little of his background, telling them that he had been the cantor* of the Jewish Community in Amsterdam. "But now," he went on, "where is my Torah? . . . Where is my congregation?" Most of his family had been arrested, he said, and his wife and children had relocated to a farm in northern Holland. The farm owners had rejected him "for obvious reasons," he added, referencing his features.

A few minutes later Mossel became more emotional, venting his distress. "You ask why I did not go to the Joodse Schouwburg† when the summons came? Why my wife and family did not go? I'll tell you why. My only purpose in life is to sing praises to Adonai, the Lord. I am a *Yehude*, a *Yid*. That means one who praises Adonai. Can I praise Adonai when they have killed me? Then I would be a martyr, yes, but can a martyr sing the praise of Adonai? So, *hinneh*,‡ here I am, at your mercy."

Mossel then turned to Opa. "You will allow me to say my prayers and sing my praises in this house?"

Before Opa could respond, Corrie said, "Of course you can say your prayers here." She then told him he could sleep in the boys' room with Hans, Leendert, and Henk, but asked if the Beje's nonkosher food would be a problem.

"Should I rather starve and die," Mossel replied, "or eat nonkosher and live to praise my Master? Your food will be my pleasure, Madam!"

---

*   The synagogue official who conducts liturgical parts of a service, and sings or chants the prayers.
†   Since the Hollandsche Schouwburg was now being used exclusively for processing Jews, it was often referred to as the Joodse Schouwburg.
‡   A Hebrew word of transition that could be rendered in English as, "now," "yes," or "look."

Corrie nodded. "But please stop calling me 'Madam.' Everybody here calls me Tante Kees." She asked what everyone should call him and Mossel shrugged. His name was Meijer, he said, but perhaps he should go by something else? "Why not Winston or Wolfgang?"

After a few suggestions, Mossel turned to Hans. "It is your birthday, I understand. Would you do me the favor of naming me?"

Hans didn't hesitate. "Sir, we shall call you Eusi."

"Eusi, Eusi," Mossel repeated. "Where do you get that?"

"Oh, it's just a kind of pet name for the youngest member of the family. In my home—and in my friends' homes—everyone calls the youngest brother Eusi."

Mossel nodded. "All right, Eusi it will be." He turned to Betsie: "My lady, allow me to introduce myself. I am Eusi. And you have earned my lasting gratitude by accepting me into your home."

Betsie smiled. "Welcome here, Eusi. May your stay be a happy one for all of us. And please, call me Tante Bep."

While food was extremely scarce in Haarlem, one day Corrie and Betsie noticed in the newspaper a coupon for pork sausage. The ten Booms had not seen meat in weeks, so they were delighted to get it. Corrie wondered, though—notwithstanding his earlier comment—if Eusi would eat such nonkosher food.

When mealtime came, Betsie produced from the oven a pork and potatoes casserole. "Eusi, the day has come." She dished out a sizable serving onto his plate and Eusi couldn't resist the aroma of a delicious hot meal.

Savoring the first bite of pork, he nodded. "Of course, there's a provision for this in the Talmud. And I'm going to start hunting for it . . . just as soon as dinner's over."

On one point, however, Eusi would not budge. A few nights later while Corrie made hot chocolate, Leendert casually mentioned he overheard Nollie say that if she were asked whether she was sheltering a Jew, she would answer "yes." In her opinion, the Ninth Commandment not to give false testimony against one's neighbor left her no alternative. God was fully able, she reckoned, to take care of the situation arising from her obedience.

Hearing Leendert's remarks, Eusi stormed up to him. "Tell me I did not hear you correctly," he said in a rising voice. "Tell me I misunderstood. Do I hear that she would rather sacrifice lives than lie?"

Before Leendert could answer, Corrie was there. "Sh, be quiet, be quiet. Eusi, please sit down, and let's talk about this."

"What is there to talk about? Lives are at stake, and you want to talk?"

"You know God's commandment," Corrie said. "'You shall not give false testimony,' as well as we do—"

"Yes, yes, I expected that." Exasperated, Eusi began an Old Testament history lesson, reminding Corrie about Rahab and the Hebrew midwives—all of whom had lied to honor God's cause. Corrie listened without response, and Eusi concluded his lecture.

"But, here we are, under your roof. We have trusted our lives to you, Tante Kees. I demand that you tell us that you will not betray us, if you can help it. If I can't trust you, I must find another place to stay."

Corrie and Eusi sat down at the dining table and Corrie took his hands. "Eusi, I promise, we will not betray any of you, if we can possibly help it."

Both parties understood that what constituted "if we can help it" was vague at best, but Eusi was mollified. "Thank you, Tante Kees. I believe you and trust you."

Reflecting later on the incident, Hans wrote: "Many Dutch Christians faced radical changes in those summer months in 1943. Until then, lying, stealing, killing, and blackmailing were crimes before God and before Dutch society. But a demonic re-gime had taken hold of our country and our civilization, and we had to choose: follow their evil directives or suffer the conse-quences; help those in need or stand disinterestedly on the side-lines. However long one tried to avoid a choice . . . the moment of truth would finally come."

Every member of the ten Boom family would be tested in this way time and again.

Nollie's son Peter, for one, invited and embraced the danger. Since Corrie's stolen ration cards could not feed all the Jews in the area, he sought another way to help. For Jews without cards, food had to be purchased on the black market, but with what money?

One day while playing the piano at home, he thought: *What about a concert for family and acquaintances to raise money for Jews?* He ran the idea by his parents and they approved. Flip and Nollie warned, though, that such an undertaking would be dangerous because no public concerts—or even a large gathering—could be held without obtaining a special permit from Nazi authorities. Peter had the answer: a private concert in a secret location.

He had a friend who owned a small auditorium and, sure enough, the man agreed to let him use it. With the help of his parents, Peter sent out a number of secret invitations to extended family and friends. When the afternoon of the concert arrived, he donned his sister's clothes over his own and headed to the auditorium. Slipping in through a back door, he removed his feminine accouterments and made his way onstage and smiled.

Before him sat an audience of some one hundred guests, al-most the exact number of invitations he had sent. He took his place on the piano bench and began the concert. Minutes later the sound of pounding arose from the auditorium's main en-trance, and then the doors smashed open.

A dozen German soldiers rushed in, rifles leveled, and someone behind Peter tapped his arm. He turned to see a German officer holding one of the invitations. "All young men present are under arrest!" the man shouted. "Walk to the far corner and hand your identification cards to the officer there."

The crowd raced for the doors, but soldiers guarded every exit. Peter winced. In twenty-four hours he'd be at a factory in Germany. As he made his way toward the identification officer, he noticed something out of the corner of his eye: *an unguarded door*! Made of dark wood, it displayed a white cross, perhaps leading the Germans to believe it was not an exit. Remembering the way Mels had "wandered off" when he went to steal bread, Peter affected the same innocent demeanor and headed for it.

No one seemed to notice him as he opened it and slipped into pitch darkness. He felt his way to a flight of stairs, leading down. At the bottom his eyes adjusted and he realized that he was in a basement.

A basement with no exits.

Seeing a furnace against a wall, he crouched behind it and waited. Within a few minutes, he knew, the Germans would search behind every door and discover him.

Up above, chaos reigned as soldiers tossed chairs and heaved furniture.

"Where is that man, van Woerden?" someone shouted.

BACK AT THE Beje, Corrie had her own surprise. In the middle of the night she awoke from someone violently shaking her.

"How many Jews have you hidden here?" a man barked.

Still groggy, Corrie blurted it out.

"Four."

Chapter 8

TERROR

KNOWING HE HAD NO MEANS of escape, Peter waited for the inevitable.

After a few minutes the basement door creaked open, then footfalls down the steps.

"Peter?"

Peter took a breath and stood; the voice was his friend's, the man who owned the building.

"Get out of here quickly, son. The soldiers have gone."

Fortunately, Peter had taken his disguise into the basement so he tied his sister's scarf around his head, donned her jacket, and fled.

He had now dodged two bullets in as many months.

***

Corrie opened her eyes. The man shaking her was not a Gestapo agent, but Leendert. Earlier in the evening, Hans, Henk, and the other refugees had noted that while Corrie was timing their entrance into the Angels' Den, no one was testing *her*. Since she was their first line of defense, her response to any raid had to be flawless.

"Let me take care of that," Leendert had said, and his rude awakening of Corrie revealed that she needed to improve as well.

"You must do this again," she said after the test. "I must get my reactions right."

So Leendert, Hans, and Henk began waking her in the middle of the night with the same treatment. After several runs, she perfected a sleepy response of indignant innocence.

And for the refugees, Corrie kept running raid tests until everyone made it into the Angels' Den in her new time: *seventy* seconds. The combination of the Alpina sign, the alarm system, and the speed of hiding made the Beje virtually foolproof. But further tests awaited.

At the beginning of July the Gestapo stepped up raids and arrests. Corrie and the refugees knew this increased the danger, but they had exhausted all of their defensive precautions.

On the evening of July 5, Hans, Leendert, Henk, and Eusi talked in the boys' room, helping Leendert with some math papers. Just before midnight a car pulled up in front of the Beje carrying men speaking German. Someone hit the light and Hans raced down the corridor to the girls' room and knocked on their door.

"Alarm! Germans around!"

The girls flew into action and the commotion woke Corrie. Hans whispered to her about the Germans and she readied the sliding panel. After all the refugees crammed into the Angels' Den, Corrie closed the panel, slid the sewing boxes into place, and waited. While she heard voices, no one banged on the Beje door. She went down to the parlor and peered through a slit in the window blackout sheet.

A German army truck.

Everyone in the Angels' Den checked their watches. It had been thirty minutes, but they heard nothing suggesting a raid.

Finally, someone came into the room, and then Corrie's voice: "It's a German army truck, apparently with engine trouble. . . . You must stay inside till they are gone, just to be safe."

Not until two in the morning—when the army truck was towed away—did Corrie open the panel and let everyone out.

The practice came in handy, though, because a rumor circulated that the Germans were planning mass arrests in Haarlem over the weekend.

On Friday, July 9, it started. All day German soldiers and army trucks passed back and forth in front of the Beje. The spectacle set nerves on edge since the Gestapo almost always carried out raids outside of Amsterdam. Why was the Wehrmacht here?

Hans, Leendert, and Henk decided to stake out an all-night vigil. Taking turns on the window, each boy observed the streets in two-and-a-half-hour stints. Hans's last watch started at four-thirty a.m. and an hour later German soldiers raced by on motorbikes and patrol cars. He passed word to the others and then returned to his post.

Betsie came down and made everyone breakfast, and at eight Hans saw Henny, the shop salesgirl, speeding toward the Beje on her bike. Corrie went to the back door and Henny couldn't blurt it out fast enough:

"Invasion. Invasion in Italy!"

Henny was close, but when news came that morning on the BBC, they heard that the invasion was of Sicily, not mainland Italy. A little disappointing, but at least the Allies were making progress.

A WEEK LATER the Beje added two more divers: Henk Wiedijk and Jop. At six foot four, Henk was too tall for any bed in the house, so he slept on a mattress on the floor. More significant was his mobility, as everyone wondered whether he could squeeze through the tiny Angels' Den entrance. He agreed to practice, but the worry remained.

Jop was the ten Booms' seventeen-year-old shop apprentice. He traveled from the suburbs daily to arrive at work, and on two occasions he barely escaped arrest in a *razzia*. After the second close call, Jop's parents asked if he could stay at the Beje and the ten Booms agreed.

The new arrivals, however, brought additional risk. While the Angels' Den had been constructed to hide eight—the current number of refugees—passing everyone through the secret entrance in seventy seconds proved challenging. Still, Corrie didn't want to turn anyone away.

When the refugees weren't on edge from suspected raids, loneliness and boredom set in. None of them could go outside, save time on the rooftop, and all longed to see loved ones.

To pass the time they decided that each person should share their talent or knowledge on a subject with the entire group. So for many evenings they took turns: Hans taught astronomy and the constellations; Henk Wessels entertained with magic tricks; Leendert highlighted modern Dutch literature; and Mary gave lectures on Italian culture and language. Since Mary also had an excellent voice and played the piano, she led the group in singing, offering moving renditions of Schubert, Beethoven, Brahms, and Bach. Eusi, who had a strong voice, could always be counted on to rattle the windows.

Thea, though, felt a little out of place. "Most of you know so much and can perform so well," she said one evening. "What can I do that you all can't?"

As it turned out, Thea indeed had a valuable skill, and soon she taught everyone first aid. For an hour the parlor became a field hospital, and everyone practiced applying bandages and dressings on make-believe injuries.

On Sunday evenings Peter would visit, almost always giving

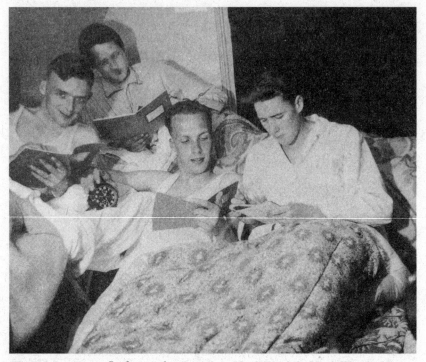

The Beje boys' room. Left to right: *Leendert, Henk Wiedijk, Henk Wessels, Hans.*

the group a concert of favorite hymns and personal compositions. Yet, when Monday rolled around, the tension would return.

One afternoon, as everyone gathered in the dining room for lunch, they heard a scraping sound on the window. "Do not turn around," said Nils, an underground worker visiting that day. His face was pale. "Someone is looking over the curtain."

Corrie couldn't believe it. They were on the second floor and the Beje had no ledge.

"He's on a ladder," Nils added, "washing the window."

"I didn't order the windows washed," Betsie said.

Just then the man peered through the lace curtains and waved.

Everyone froze. This had to be a Gestapo agent or infor-

Ten Booms and the Beje "permanent" refugees, July 1943. Front, left to right: *Mary, Betsie, Opa, Corrie, Thea.* Back, left to right: *Henk Wiedijk, Leendert, Eusi, Henk Wessels, Hans.*

mant, and he clearly could see the ten Booms with a room full of people. Eusi waved back and said under his breath: "Just go on as though everything is normal. In a few moments we'll sing 'Happy Birthday!'"

When the group finished singing, the window washer—still working on the same window—laughed and waved again.

Corrie couldn't stomach the uncertainty. She went downstairs and into the alley.

"What are you doing?" she asked, peering up at the man. "We didn't want the windows washed. Especially not during the party!"

The man pulled a paper from his pocket. "Isn't this the Kuipers?"

Corrie shook her head. Kuiper's was the candy store across

the street, she told him. "But—anyhow, come in and help us celebrate."

The man declined and Corrie watched as he took his ladder and bucket across the street.

Nothing happened later that afternoon, but the mystery about the man made for a miserable evening. At times like these the refugees would escape the pressure by heading up to the roof for fresh air and scenery. The walking space was small—seven feet by twenty—but it provided a needed haven of refuge and solace.

Hans remembered later the respite this little place offered: "Often I went there to peel a bucket of potatoes, and, the job finished, I would lie on my back, watch the clouds sail by, and dream away. I yearned for freedom and for the wide-open skies and the soft late-afternoon light that slanted over the spacious Zeeuwse polders. . . . I was also homesick for my love, so dear, yet so far out of reach. We yearned for a future together and yet we faced such an uncertain and grim tomorrow.

"In the twilight hours, after dinner and dish washing, when the sky was darkening and the stars would slowly appear, some of us would quietly sit there and escape for a short time the prison of our shadowy existence."

The rooftop, though, was more than a restful retreat; it became something of a counseling center, too—the refugees hearing each other's stories and offering comfort or condolences. On the evening of July 18 Hans went to the roof and took in a surreal scene: beneath the drone of countless RAF bombers headed to Amsterdam or Germany, the dark cross of the Roman Catholic Church at the Nieuwe Groenmarkt seemed to glow. "Two searchlight beams flashed towards the southeast," he remembered, "pencils of light searching, intersecting, almost playful against the peaceful night sky."

At eleven o'clock the bell at the old St. Bavo Church tolled, and Hans peered heavenward. As he marveled at the Big Dipper, Orion, and the seven Pleiades, he began thinking about Mies— pondering their situation—when the rooftop door opened.

Mary emerged from the shadow, saying she needed to talk to someone about *her* circumstances. Hans listened with a sympathetic ear as Mary described her love—an Italian named Antonio Sanzo. They had met in the early 1930s, she said, while on vacation in Rome. He had a promising career at the Banco di Roma, and they became engaged. In 1935, however, fascist dictator Benito Mussolini outlawed marriage between Italians and Jews, so they postponed a wedding until things changed.

She told Hans that she hadn't seen Antonio in a year. "I don't know where he is, whether he is in the army or whether he is even alive. Maybe it's too dangerous for him to associate with a Jew. I don't know whether I should try to get a message to him. Hans, I don't know what to do. Sometimes I feel so desperate. And today is the anniversary of our engagement."

"My goodness," Hans said, "why didn't you tell us before? Aren't we willing to share each other's sorrows as well as our joys?"

"What could you or anyone else do?"

"I don't know. I don't have the answers to your sorrows, Mary, but listen, why don't you write a perfectly innocent letter to your sweetheart. At least that will show him you are still alive. We could ask Kik ten Boom to mail it for you somewhere far away from Haarlem the next time he comes to visit. And you could sign it 'Mary d'Italia.'"

She smiled. "Do you really think that would work?"

"Why not? Just take care that no one can trace it to you here."

Hopeful, Mary said she'd try it.

All around Haarlem, however, things worsened. The follow-

Beje refugees catching some fresh air and sunlight on the rooftop while doing chores. Left to right: *Mary, Leendert, Henk Wessels, Hans, Eusi, and Thea.*

ing day Hans learned that friends of his parents had been arrested, together with nine Jews they sheltered. The Beje refugees worried, but Corrie assured everyone that angels protected the house.

That very day Anne Frank recorded what had happened with the RAF bombers Hans had heard the night before: "North Amsterdam was heavily bombed on Sunday," she wrote in her diary. "There was apparently a great deal of destruction. Entire streets are in ruins, and it will take a while for them to dig out all the bodies. So far there have been two hundred dead and countless wounded; the hospitals are bursting at the seams. We've been told of children searching forlornly in the smoldering ruins for their dead parents. It still makes me shiver to think of the dull, distant drone that signified the approaching destruction."

Ironically, Hitler met with Mussolini in northern Italy on the nineteenth, insisting that the Italians increase their war effort.

While they were in conference, seven hundred Allied bombers dropped 1,100 tons of bombs on Rome. Mussolini was arrested by his own people six days later.

The Allies continued the onslaught, and they didn't let up. On July 27 the RAF firebombed Hamburg, dropping 2,300 tons of incendiary bombs. The resulting inferno killed 40,000 residents. Two days later the city received another 2,300 tons of bombs.

All told, RAF Bomber Command dropped 16,000 tons of bombs on targets in Germany, France, and Norway in July, with the U.S. Eighth Air Force adding another 3,600.

THE BEJE, THOUGH, continued in full swing. Near the end of the month Leendert and Henk Wessels left for another safe

A Beje concert. Left to right: *Henny van Dantzig (at the piano), Eusi, Mary, Mr. de Vries (playing the violin), Betsie, Henk Wiedijk, Mirjam de Jong, Corrie, Opa. The inscription on the back states that the photo may have been taken by Hans Poley.*

house, and Corrie took in an elegant and immaculately dressed Jew, Mr. de Vries. A few days later Willem's son Kik arrived with two friends. Learning that the three were active in the underground, the Gestapo had raided their place but they managed to escape. Since all beds in the Beje were taken, they agreed to sleep on the floor in the parlor. The Angels' Den, however, posed a problem: with seven in the space, they only could cram in one more person, not three. Kik and his friends decided that if a raid came, they would rush onto the roof and jump house to house to escape.

As expected, the raids and persecution ground on, especially in Amsterdam. Word traveled back to the Beje that the Nazis were sending Jews to Poland in regular transports, that the Gestapo was continuing mass arrests of eighteen- and nineteen-year-old boys, and that captured Dutch Resistance workers were being executed.

In Haarlem, the Gestapo continued to chase every lead about locals hiding Jews, and the information gap finally closed.

The morning of August 14 they arrested Nollie.

Chapter 9

RESISTANCE

THAT AFTERNOON CORRIE WAS SITTING in the dining room having lunch when she glimpsed something through the window: a lone figure lingered in the alley facing the Beje. Corrie knew there were only two options of who this might be: a Resistance worker or the Gestapo.

She went to the window to get a better look and parted the curtain. The figure was Katrien, Nollie and Flip's maid. Corrie rushed downstairs and threw open the alley door.

"Katrien!" she cried out as she pulled her inside. "What are you doing here? Why were you just standing there?"

"She's gone mad!" the maid said as she began to sob. "Your sister's gone mad!"

"Nollie? Oh, what's happened?"

"They came! The SD! I don't know what they knew or who told them. Your sister and Annaliese were in the living room and I heard her!"

Annaliese was one of two Jews the van Woerdens were hiding at the time, and Corrie's temperature rose. "Heard what?"

"Heard what she told them! They pointed at Annaliese and said, 'Is this a Jew?' And your sister said, 'Yes.'"

Corrie shuddered. This was precisely the scenario that Eusi had feared. Why couldn't Nollie have lied, just this once? Now she and the Jewish woman—perhaps the other Jew they were hiding as well—were certainly in prison.

"And then?"

"I don't know. I ran out the back door."

Flip had been away at the time, Katrien went on, and Peter escaped through the roof. She then confirmed Corrie's fear: not only Annaliese, but the other woman staying with the family also had been arrested.

Corrie rushed to the shop and locked the front door, telling Henny to open it only for customers. She then passed word around the house and Hans began calling underground contacts. "Keep away for a few days," he warned, "we have an outbreak of flu here. Don't contact us." Knowing that Pickwick had lived in the Dutch East Indies, Hans gave him the message in Malay. From then on the phone was off-limits and the refugees, including Thea and Mary, took shifts during the night to watch the street.

Amsterdam

Nollie crouched in the police van in a small, dark compartment, worrying where they were taking her. As the van rolled along, a narrow beam of light shot into her holding cell, flooding the wall. Removing a pencil that she had hidden in her hair, she sketched out: "Jesus is Victor!" It wasn't much, but maybe the next captive would be encouraged.

When they arrived at the police station someone pushed Nollie into a pitch-black basement cell. The Nazis, it appeared, believed that darkness would dispirit a captive, perhaps keeping them more docile. She would have none of it, and began to sing.

"However can you sing?" a voice asked from the shadows.

Before Nollie could answer the woman began to cry.

"Don't lose courage," Nollie told her. "God is still on the throne. We are not alone."

ON SUNDAY A trustworthy Dutch policeman stopped by the Beje to announce that Nollie had been interrogated at the police station. Given her involvement with Jews, he said, and the danger of releasing names under torture, the underground was considering a raid to liberate her.

The Beje refugees shuddered. The Gestapo would stop at nothing, and the thought of Nollie revealing information about them weighed heavily. Everyone gathered in the parlor to discuss the best plan of action and the refugees agreed: they would have to leave immediately. That morning, one by one, they fled: Hans sneaked Mary to his house, Eusi and Thea hid in homes of friends, and Henk disappeared to the home of relatives.

On Tuesday Mary crept back to the Beje for a hurried visit and was touched by what she heard. Independently, Opa, Corrie, and Betsie told her that they missed everyone and wanted them to return as soon as possible.

Hans and the others knew it was too risky to return, though, so Mary and Thea decided to act as couriers, hustling to various places to convey news, messages, and requests.

A week after Nollie's arrest, word came that the Gestapo had raided the home of the de Leeuws, whom the ten Booms and Poleys knew, arresting the family and nineteen Jews they sheltered. Worse, some of the Jews who had been arrested knew Eusi, and the likelihood that one or two knew he was hiding in the Beje gave the refugees cause to stay away for another two weeks.

On August 24 Nollie was transferred to the federal prison in Amsterdam. This news was especially disturbing because the

SS ran prisons controlled by the Germans, which meant that the Gestapo would interrogate her night and day. Stories from underground workers who had gone through the treatment were frightening: with some prisoners the Gestapo would offer freedom in exchange for information; with others they threatened to arrest spouses, children, and parents; with yet others—if the psychological tactics didn't work—the Gestapo would torture them.

Corrie, beside herself, began a campaign to have her sister released, appealing to everyone she knew: police officers, soldiers, underground contacts. Pickwick, it turned out, had the best solution. The German doctor who supervised the prison hospital, he said, sometimes arranged a medical discharge for prisoners.

Corrie unearthed his home address and showed up unannounced. A maid let her in and Corrie waited a few minutes in the foyer while three Doberman pinschers sniffed her. When the doctor came in, Corrie beat around the bush about dogs, apparently the man's hobby.

The doctor seemed pleased to discuss the subject, and Corrie said her favorite was the bulldog.

"People don't realize it," he responded, "but bulldogs are very affectionate."

After ten minutes of the warm-up, Corrie came to the point. "I have a sister in prison here in Amsterdam. I was wondering if . . . I don't think she's well."

"What's her name?"

"Nollie van Woerden."

The doctor checked his records. "Yes. One of our recent arrivals. Tell me something about her. What is she in prison for?"

Corrie said that Nollie had been arrested for hiding a Jew, but she was the mother of six children; if she remained incarcerated the children would become a burden to the state.

"Well, we'll see."

He walked Corrie to the door without further comment.

A week turned into two and Corrie could take it no longer. She returned to the doctor's house.

"How are your dogs?" she asked at the door.

"Miss ten Boom, you do not seem to trust me that I am willing to help your sister. Please leave it to me."

Corrie remained firm. "If she is not with us within a week, I will come again to ask about your dogs."

IN EARLY SEPTEMBER the Allies began bombing northern France, Belgium, and southwest Holland. On the eighth Italy surrendered* and five days later, on September 13, Nollie was released from prison. Back at the Beje, she announced that one of the Jewish girls the van Woerdens had sheltered also had been saved; the underground, apparently, had raided the truck that was carrying her to Amsterdam.

The following week Hans, Mary, Eusi, and Henk returned to the Beje. Thea had found a new place to hide, and her place at the Beje was quickly taken when eighteen-year-old Mirjam de Jong arrived. To everyone's surprise, Eusi already knew her.

"Well, well," he said when Betsie began the introduction, "we wait for the Messiah and look who comes? Is this not the charming Mirjam, the daughter of my good friends?"

"Mister Mossel, I never expected to meet you in these circumstances. Now I feel at home with you around."

Eusi beamed. "This is Mirjam de Jong, daughter of one of the most important men in our *mishpoche*† in Amsterdam."

Mirjam quickly became part of the Beje family and she and

---

* The Italians signed the surrender document on September 3, but the capitulation was not announced until September 8.

† Synagogue family.

Opa, in particular, bonded. That night, when Opa closed the evening with prayer, he commended Mirjam and her family to the Lord's care.

"Thank you," Mirjam whispered in his ear as she kissed him good night.

The joy that came with Mirjam's residence, however, faded after bad news arrived in the morning. Henk Wessels's father had been arrested by the Gestapo, an underground worker informed, along with a Jewish woman and baby he had been hiding. It was yet another blow to the Beje refugees. The Wessels and ten

The ten Boom family with their "guests," September 1943. Front row: *Henk Wiedijk, Mirjam, the father of Henk Wessels.* Second row: *Opa, Hans, Mary.* Standing: *"Verdonck," Tante Kees, Mr. Ineke, Henny van Dantzig, Tante Bep, Eusi.*

Booms belonged to the same Resistance network and regularly exchanged addresses, information, and ration cards.

That afternoon another courier stopped by with an even worse report: Mirjam's parents had also been rolled up in the Amsterdam raid the prior evening. The news was devastating since witnesses confirmed that the Jews were taken directly to the railway station and loaded on cattle cars headed to Poland. Mirjam's parents would be dead within days. Betsie, Hans, and Mary were in the kitchen preparing lunch and overheard the news. Corrie suggested that they not tell Mirjam about her parents, only about the raid in general.

To be expected, Mirjam assumed the worst.

After lunch Opa took her hand and began reading Psalm 23: "Even though I walk through the valley of the shadow of death, I will fear no evil, for You are with me."

Mirjam began to cry and Opa continued to read and clutch her hand. When he finished, he folded his hands over Mirjam's and prayed for her and all of the Beje refugees.

Later that afternoon, as Hans and Mirjam washed dishes, they heard that Henk's mother also had been arrested in the raid. "And he does not yet know," Mirjam said, "that his parents are in the hands of the Gestapo."

Hans turned away, speechless. Here was Mirjam worrying about Henk and his family, when she didn't know that her own parents also had been arrested, and faced a worse lot. Hans collected his thoughts and turned back.

"You don't know where your parents are, and we don't know what will happen to us. You don't even know if you shall arrive safely at your new place, and I don't know whether I'll be arrested tonight. Everything is so insecure for us all. But remember what Opa read to us after lunch? We are never alone, Mirjam. Our God will be with us even in this valley of death. We do have to trust Him for we can't handle this ourselves anymore."

Betsie, who had overheard Hans from the living room, came into the kitchen and hugged Mirjam. "That's the answer," she told both of them. "If you trust Him, God will be with you wherever you have to go, or whatever you have to do. Opa has always told us that God gives us more strength when the burdens grow greater. He'll carry us through on eagles' wings, if necessary, right into His arms."

The refugees were going to need such deliverance as that night everyone had to leave again due to a raid warning. Mirjam planned to head back to the Minnema family's home in Heemstede, Eusi intended to hide with the Vermeers, and Hans and Mary decided to return to his family's home.

Realizing the time had come, Corrie quietly told Mirjam about her parents. Mirjam took it calmly, without a word, and then went upstairs to be alone. Knowing that Mary had suffered through the same torture, Corrie asked her to go to Mirjam's room to comfort her.

After a while they came down and Mirjam kissed everyone goodbye. When she reached Opa, she fell in his arms, crying.

Opa held her as one of his own. "God bless you, my child."

WARNINGS OF RAIDS near the Beje continued, so for two weeks the refugees waited in their temporary accommodations. From their various locations they heard the news and reports: more Gestapo raids in Haarlem, mass arrests in Amsterdam, and rumors of an Allied invasion. Daily air raid signals confirmed that the Allies were indeed sending more planes to bomb German factories.

The beginning of October, though, brought devastating news: in revenge for the killing of two Gestapo agents, the Nazis executed nineteen Haarlem Resistance workers.

Ten days later, another 140 were shot.

Chapter 10

THE CHIEF

IN MID-OCTOBER HANS, MARY, AND Eusi returned to the Beje, but Mirjam—whose host had been forced to go underground—had found another home. While they were away, one of the refugees said, the Gestapo raided a farm where a notorious Nazi police officer had been killed. A shoot-out ensued, the story went, and some fifty Jews were arrested. As a result, the Germans planned another round of raids.

WHILE STAYING WITH his parents, Hans had been reflecting about the fear brought on by the Gestapo, and by his lack of power to do anything. One day he came upon divers who had formed their own Resistance group, and he decided to join them.

The penalty for being caught was death.

Soon thereafter an underground worker borrowed Hans's identity card to falsify it. His birthday would be altered, the man said, as well as his occupation. As Hans Poley, a twenty-four-year-old assistant minister of the Haarlem Dutch Reformed church—complete with a certificate that would come later—he would be less vulnerable to arrest.* When the revised card arrived,

---

* Initially, the Nazis exempted Dutch clergy from being sent to Germany for forced labor.

he informed Corrie of his decision since it would endanger the ten Booms and other refugees. To his surprise she asked him to operate out of the Beje so she could assist. He would be a courier, Hans had learned, and would transport messages and ration cards. And since the Beje would become part of the Resistance network, Corrie could oversee the regular influx of underground visitors and their needs.

Days afterward Hans learned that his father—a Resistance leader—had narrowly missed execution. Mr. Poley's group had been gathering regularly, calling their meetings "The Exchange." On October 13 a network colleague asked him to attend the group's meeting in Hoorn, some twenty miles north of Amsterdam. Knowing that a large gathering brought unnecessary risk, Mr. Poley declined. His instincts proved accurate, as the Gestapo had been tipped off about the meeting and raided it. Worse, every underground member caught was executed.

SOME NIGHTS LATER, as the ten Booms gathered around the dining table, the shop doorbell rang. *A customer after curfew?* Corrie wondered. Who would be so bold?

She hustled downstairs to the front door and listened.

"Who's there?"

"Do you remember me?" a man asked in German.

Corrie asked again who was there.

"An old friend, come for a visit. Open the door!"

Corrie unlocked the door and cracked it open to find a German soldier. Before she could push the alarm buzzer, the man forced his way in. When he took his hat off, Corrie's pulse jumped.

"Otto!"

It had been almost five years since she had seen their Nazi apprentice.

"Captain Altschuler. Our positions are slightly reversed, Miss ten Boom, are they not?"

Corrie saw nothing on Otto's uniform indicating an officer's rank, but kept it to herself.

"Same stuffy little place." Otto reached for the light switch and Corrie stopped him.

"No! We don't have blackout shades in the shop!"

"Well, let's go upstairs where we can talk over old times. That old clock cleaner still around?"

"Christoffels? He died in the fuel shortage last winter."

"Good riddance then! What about the pious old Bible reader?"

Corrie began easing her way toward the sales counter. The nine refugees the Beje now housed would have to squeeze into the Angels' Den before Otto started snooping around. "Father is very well, thank you," she said, depressing the alarm button behind the counter.

Otto wheeled around. "What was that?"

"What was what?"

"That sound! I heard a kind of buzzing."

"I didn't hear anything."

Otto headed toward the back of the shop to go upstairs and Corrie dashed in front of him. In the dining room, Opa and Betsie were finishing their meal.

"Father! Betsie!" Corrie said just outside the room. "I'll give you three—no, uh—six guesses who's standing here!"

Otto brushed her aside and went in. Pulling out a chair for himself, he joined Opa and Betsie at the table. "Well! Things happened just like I said, didn't they?"

"So it would seem," Opa replied.

Corrie asked Betsie to pour Otto some tea and when he sipped it, he blurted: "Where did you get real tea! No one else in Holland has tea."

Corrie winced at the oversight; the tea had come from Pickwick, who obtained it through the underground. "If you must know," she said, "it comes from a German officer. But you mustn't ask any further questions."

Otto seemed to buy it but he lingered, apparently looking for something he could discover about the ten Booms helping Jews or divers. After fifteen minutes he collected his hat and left, satisfied that he had sufficiently humiliated the family.

The ten Booms had avoided disaster, but each day brought further danger. Every arrest, every raid, every visitor ratcheted up the Gestapo's likelihood to discover them.

DURING THE LAST week in October the Beje added another two refugees: Nel, a young woman wanted by the Gestapo, and Ronnie Gazan,* a Jew who had been on the run for fourteen months. The pair fit in immediately. Nel, who would take Thea's old spot in the house, was a slight but industrious woman, ever ready to help with anything.

Ronnie equally impressed. Showing up at the house in a butterfly tie, he quickly revealed he had manners to match. Handsome and quiet, he also offered to help at any time. As a bonus, Ronnie hit it off with Eusi, who reveled in Ronnie's stories and Jewish jokes.

Hans, meanwhile, desperate to help in the Resistance, grew restless and irritated. His false identity papers had yet to arrive, and he missed Mies; the only contact he had had with her the last six months was through letters, and he longed to see her. Mies had a birthday approaching so one night Hans wrote her a letter to celebrate. Mary, whom Hans often had spoken with about Mies, wrote a letter to include with his own.

When Hans went downstairs Corrie asked what he had been

---

* Ronnie also had a Gentile alias: Tom van Sevenhuysen.

Mies and Hans.

doing and he explained his letter to Mies. "That's wonderful!" she said. "I'd like to write her, too!"

Corrie penned a short note on a pad:

Dear Mies,
I look forward to getting to know you. You have a very likeable boyfriend, but don't tell him I wrote you so! We all love him very much. My best birthday wishes. God bless you with good health and at school, but especially with the wonderful assurance that you are Jesus' own.

Warmest greetings from your Tante Kees

Ronnie then took the pad, added his own note, and passed it to Betsie, who penned her greeting and passed it to Opa, who finished with "I also join in sending my sincerest congratulations." Opa then excused himself and went upstairs. After a few minutes he returned and handed Hans a booklet.

"Here, my boy, send this to her, a small present from an old man to your fiancée."

Hans looked at the pamphlet and was touched. It was called *Herinneringen van een Oude Horlogemaker* (Memories of an Old

Memories of an Old Watchmaker, by Casper ten Boom.

Watchmaker), and Opa had written it in 1937 for the one hundredth anniversary of the ten Boom watch shop. Hans stumbled for words. This grandfather whom he loved and respected so much always seemed to offer a kind gesture or word of encouragement at the appropriate moment.

"We love you very much," Opa added, "so we love her, too, and this is my way of saying it."

Hans, like the other refugees, was learning day by day the deep, abiding, and unconditional love of the ten Booms.

THE BEJE, MEANWHILE, went all in on their effort to assist the underground. It became part of the Landelijke Organisatie, now a nationwide network. Ration cards—far more than the hundred Corrie received from Mr. Koornstra—topped the list of needs, followed by homes where refugees could be hidden. Hans took the lead in obtaining more cards, while Corrie searched for other hiding places. Finding ration cards, though, proved exceedingly difficult. The Germans monitored card distribution carefully, and the underground had only one option to obtain a sufficient number: raiding—at gunpoint—the distribution centers.

In November these raiding parties stole 317,000 new cards in North Holland alone. Once obtained, the underground would send out couriers to different areas for distribution. The danger of the robberies was significant enough, but the Nazi reprisals were worse. To counter the raids and countless Jews and divers being hidden, the Gestapo now resorted to threats and torture to root out those involved. The relentless pace and pressure took its toll, and Corrie became overwhelmed. Managing the shop and Beje refugees, along with chasing leads for new homes, she sometimes lost her notes containing names and addresses of Resistance workers.

The first rule of espionage is to put nothing on paper, but Corrie had no professional training. Her notes, if discovered by the Gestapo, would mean certain death for those implicated.

ON NOVEMBER 21 Hans finally received his falsified identity card. The doctoring was flawless; the ink appeared the same as the original, and there was not a trace of tampering. Together with his certificate of clergy, the new identity added one more layer of arrest protection.

Corrie wasted no time taking advantage of Hans's new status; she sent him out immediately to distribute ration cards and messages. Notwithstanding his new credentials, though, he would head out on courier runs dressed as a girl. Soon these missions became more dangerous, requiring him to take refugees to new safe houses, or to notify other underground districts of impending Gestapo raids. In time Hans found a rendezvous spot to meet other couriers—the entrance corridor of the Brouwershofje (home for the elderly).

He was now a Resistance operative.

ONE DAY IN late November an underground worker showed up at the Beje with a British pilot. The airman had been shot down, he told Henny, who had greeted them. Unable to confirm their identity, Henny pressed the alarm buzzer and Corrie rushed down.

Corrie sympathized with the man's plight, but a recent Nazi edict made helping downed Allied pilots a capital crime, and executions often occurred without trial. To bring him in added too much risk. She asked Hans to help and he called the one man always with an answer: Pickwick. Minutes later Hans and the pilot left for Aerdenhout, a Haarlem suburb.

The address Pickwick gave would lead them to an old tennis court, he had said, and next to it was a clubhouse, the door of which would be unlocked. Sneaking a pilot across town, whether by day or night, involved significant risk, and even if they made it, Hans had to run the gauntlet again in his return to the Beje.

They made it to Aerdenhout without incident and found the place Pickwick had mentioned. Hans instructed the airman to stay there for the night. The next day, he said, another underground worker would fetch him and take him to a pilot escape line, which went to Belgium, France, and then to safety in Spain.

With each successful mission, the underground expanded Hans's duties. One morning they asked him to shadow a notorious Gestapo agent, recording his regular appointments and stops. The Resistance, Hans learned, was considering this man's murder.

Days later they gave him a gun.

Things were getting desperate in Haarlem, and available Resistance workers were asked to take the fight to the Germans. That ultimately meant assassinations. But even *possessing* a firearm was punishable by death.

Hans accepted the assignment and risk as part of his obligation. He hid the gun at his parents' home—in the bookcase of his old room.

DECEMBER BROUGHT ANOTHER Beje birthday, this time for the shop sales clerk, Henny van Dantzig. Henny had worked at the ten Boom watch shop now for twelve years and Corrie, Betsie, and Opa wanted to make her day special. On normal workdays, Henny's duties began at eight o'clock, but today the ten Booms asked her to show up at nine. When she arrived, everyone greeted her with the birthday song, "Long May She Live," and Betsie surprised her with a bouquet of chrysanthemums.

Next came Opa's tribute. He began with memories of the day Henny first joined them, and how the ten Booms had come to love her. He then presented her with a certificate of appreciation and a personal gift. Afterward, he hugged her and Henny teared up. Like so many others, she loved the old man.

Over coffee and candies, Opa informed Henny that she had the day off.

Opa's grace and love, his quiet gentleness and consideration, touched everyone around him. On December 23 he sent a letter to Bob van Woerden, one of Nollie's sons.

My greatly beloved grandson . . .
The war continues to rage outside. From that side we are
shaken and plagued by all kinds of sad and troubling rumors.

On the other hand, here inside the house we rejoice in a great many experiences. We are protected and blessed here by a most extraordinary providence.

Your aunts and I are enjoying good health, and we have enough to eat. . . . I have nothing to complain about. I am only sorry that I can do so little work on my watches. I am too weak to work much, and my hands are not always steady. But after all, I have had my time in the shop, and the new life I am now living is also good.

I receive every day as an undeserved gift. I only hope that I will be able to enjoy seeing, with all my faculties, the deliverance of our people and our fatherland. At any rate, I have so much to be thankful for! I am enjoying God's favor, and the future is perfectly clear.

With the approach of Christmas, Hans too received a special blessing: news that Mies was coming. She would stay in Haarlem with his parents during the holiday, they planned, but she would spend each day with him. He picked her up at the train station and introduced her to everyone at the Beje.

"We've heard so much about you," Corrie told her, "we feel you're a part of our crowd already."

Hans gave Mies a tour of the old house, and she noticed every detail—the heavy purple drapes, the sun clock, and most importantly, the large picture of grandfather Willem ten Boom. He then took her upstairs to show her the boys' room and the Angels' Den, where he would sleep that night.

On Christmas Day Hans was touched by the family's celebration. "We shared the good tidings," he remembered, "prayers, and hymns, and celebrated the coming of Light into this dark world, singing about peace on earth, good will toward men, while war raged about us, while so many loved ones were gone, and while we still lived in fear for our own lives."

The Beje, Christmas 1943. Left to right: *Hans, Mies, unknown, unknown, Mr. Hischemöller, Eusi, Nel, unknown.*

After dinner Corrie read Tolstoy's story about the village cobbler Awdjewitsch. The message was clear: where love reigns, there is God. Mary then played the piano, allowing everyone to escape the burden of the occupation for a few minutes.

When the holiday ended Hans took Mies back to the station, kissing her goodbye and watching with pounding heart as her waving hand disappeared with the train.

JANUARY 1944

As the New Year rolled in, the Gestapo edged ever closer to the Beje. Near the end of January a loyal Dutch policeman came by the shop and informed Corrie that the Nazis had planned a raid on an underground home in Ede that very evening.

He asked if Corrie had anyone who could go there to warn the family.

She said she didn't have any available couriers, but Jop—overhearing the conversation—offered to go.

"Then quickly, boy," the officer said. "You must leave immediately."

He gave Jop the address and Corrie helped to disguise him as a woman. Given the distance, the trip to Ede would take all day, but Jop could easily make it back by the seven o'clock curfew.

Seven o'clock came and went, but Jop never returned.

ABOUT A WEEK later Corrie received a letter from the Haarlem chief of police. The paper contained one sentence: "You will come to my office this afternoon."

Corrie assumed the worst. Her work housing and hiding refugees, together with her involvement in ration cards, surely had been exposed. She informed the Resistance workers in the house at that time and one by one they quietly left. The permanent refugees emptied wastebaskets and otherwise prepared the house for a search. Corrie collected incriminating papers and burned them.

She would go to face the music. She took a bath and then collected in a bag what Nollie had suggested for prison: her Bible, a comb, toothbrush, soap, pencil, and needle and thread. She dressed in multiple layers of clothing, hugged Opa and Betsie, and then left for the meeting.

At the station she showed the chief's letter to the attending policeman and he led her to the man's office. Behind the desk a balding man with reddish-gray hair greeted her.

"Miss ten Boom. Welcome."

The chief closed his door and asked Corrie to have a seat. "I know all about you," he said. "About your work."

Corrie stiffened. "The watchmaking you mean. You're probably thinking more about my father's work than my own."

"No, I mean your *other* work."

"Ah, then you're referring to my work with retarded children? Yes. Let me tell you about that—"

"No, Miss ten Boom. I am not talking about your work with retarded children. I'm talking about still another work. . . ."

The chief smiled and Corrie returned a timid grin.

"Now, Miss ten Boom, I have a request."

He rose from his seat and came around the desk and sat on the edge. In a whisper he said he was working with the underground.

Corrie maintained her calm, saying nothing. This was precisely how the Gestapo trapped people.

A betrayer in the police department was leaking information to the Gestapo, the chief went on, adding, "There's no way for us to deal with this man."

Corrie tried not to show any emotion. Again, she thought the best way to respond was to remain silent.

"What alternative have we?" the chief asked. "We can't arrest him—there are no prisons except those controlled by the Germans. But if he remains at large many others will die. This is why I wondered, Miss ten Boom, if in your work *you* might know of someone who could—"

"Kill him?"

"Yes."

Chapter 11

THE MISSION

"LIQUIDATION," DUTCH PATRIOTS preferred to call it.

At first underground leaders disagreed on whether such extreme violence was justified, but as the brutality of the German police intensified, opposition to assassinations diminished. In the first months of 1943 the Resistance had targeted dangerous traitors—Dutch leaders who had thrown their lot in with the NSB*—starting with the liquidation of General Hendrik Seyffardt, the figurehead commander of a Dutch SS unit on the eastern front. Next was Hermannus Reydon, secretary-general of the NSB's Department of Propaganda and Arts, and then F. E. Posthuma, a member of the NSB's Political Secretariat of State.

Later in the year Resistance groups killed a number of German agents, as well as lower-ranking members of the NSB. Between February and September, they eliminated some forty National Socialist leaders, including the police chiefs in Nijmegen and Utrecht.†

Corrie leaned back in her chair. She had stepped into what chess players call a "fork": whatever move she made had devas-

---

* Nationaal-Socialistische Beweging in Nederland (National Socialist Movement in the Netherlands).
† In 1944 the Dutch underground would kill more than three hundred NSB leaders.

tating consequences. If she acknowledged that she had an active role in the underground and the chief worked on behalf of the Gestapo, she'd be arrested and sent to prison. On the other hand, if the chief was a loyal Dutchman and she played along, she'd be setting herself up as an accomplice to murder. With the history of Gestapo torture to wring confessions from underground workers, the likely discovery of Corrie's connection to the killing would result in her own death.

She looked at the chief. "Sir, I have always believed that it was my role to save life, not destroy it. I understand your dilemma, however, and I have a suggestion. Are you a praying man?"

"Aren't we all these days?"

"Then let us pray together now that God will reach the heart of this man so that he does not continue to betray his countrymen."

The chief nodded, and Corrie prayed that the betraying Dutchman would come to realize not only his worth in the sight of God, but the worth of every person. When she finished the chief thanked her, and she returned to the Beje with her prison kit.

She had dodged arrest, but for how long? If the Haarlem police chief knew what she was up to, who didn't?

That very point was brought home when she learned that Jop had been arrested on his courier run. When he arrived at the Ede address, the Gestapo was waiting. So now it was back to the usual risk: if the Gestapo tortured him, he'd likely talk. If nothing else, they would find out where he worked.

The Beje was again hot.

Days later another warning came when Kik, Willem's son, visited. As he and Corrie sat talking on the Beje staircase, the doorbell rang and he stiffened.

"Why are you afraid?" Corrie asked.

Little did she know, Kik was deeply involved with the Resistance, working closely with the British Army. To assist downed

RAF pilots, he had built a cabin in the woods and had been actively hiding them.

"Tante Corrie, you are in far greater danger than you realize."

"Kik, don't you believe that the Lord will protect us with His angels?"

Kik shrugged. "Sometimes yes, sometimes no."

TO COMPOUND MATTERS, two more refugees showed up at the Beje in January. The house was already packed, but Corrie couldn't turn them away. Meta and Paula Monsanto, two sisters who were Lutheran in their theology but Jewish in descent, knew Corrie from church. She had told them they always had a place with the ten Booms, so when a Dutch policeman informed the sisters they were on the Gestapo arrest list, they fled.

Meta, whom everyone called "Tante Martha" because she was about the same age as Corrie and Betsie, was a thin, quiet, and modest woman. Like the ten Booms, she had an unshakable faith and was helpful and kind. Even Eusi, who saw Jewish Christians as apostates, admitted that he liked and respected her.

Paula, on the other hand, was the opposite; she was outspoken and openly frustrated at the loss of her freedom. Nonetheless, she also fit in.

After the arrival of the Monsanto sisters, the floodgates opened. Everyone, it seemed, saw the Beje as their best chance of survival. "Our now widely known shelter attracted those who desperately needed a place to stay or needed food or coupons or money," Hans remembered of the time. "Although the house was overflowing, the ten Booms never turned away anyone who had no place else to go. . . . Every day, it seemed, I guided someone to a new hiding place."

When the ten Booms weren't shuffling people, they stayed busy finding and distributing ration cards. Hans, meanwhile,

Conversation in the Beje parlor, January 1944. Left to right: Eusi, unknown, Mary, Hans, Mr. de Vries, Nel.

plunged deeper into the underground. Because Haarlem desperately needed more ration cards, the Resistance planned an armed raid on the distribution center. Hans—with other operatives—practiced dry runs, explored escape routes, and perfected the robbery plan. At the last minute, however, the raid was called off.

Hans never knew why, but eleventh-hour changes were typical for underground work. Everything, it seemed, was spur of the moment.

ON THE MORNING of January 14 Corrie called her brother. Strangely, the voice answering the phone wasn't Willem's or

Kik's. She mumbled something and then it dawned on her. The *Gestapo*. She had called during a raid.

Without identifying herself she slammed down the phone and ran upstairs.

"Get your things into the hiding place, quickly," she told Hans, Eusi, and the other boys. "And stay upstairs. . . . Get ready to move at a moment's notice."

The boys scrambled to move their belongings into the Angels' Den, and Corrie hurried to notify the girls. She wasn't worried about the call being traced—so far as they knew the Gestapo couldn't do that—but often they raided the homes of relatives at the same time.

For more than twelve hours everyone waited upstairs, all ready to plunge into the Angels' Den. But nothing came of it. Willem, they learned, had talked himself out of danger.

In the midst of the tension caused by rumors, raids, and air alarms, the Beje family had a pleasant January surprise: Eusi's wife, Dora, had given birth to their third son. Eusi bounced off the walls, singing praises, quoting Old Testament passages, and praying for his family. Knowing the dangers of visiting Dora, he begged Hans to go. Hans wasn't thrilled about the idea—he had enough danger from his underground activities—but Betsie and Mary successfully nudged him.

So off Hans went—a courier run to deliver flowers and blessings. He made it back to the Beje without incident, but each courier run dramatically increased his odds of arrest.

On the last day of the month he received the final part of his new identity: a certificate of occupation as a pastor in the Dutch Reformed Church of Holland. With professional credentials and the falsified identification card that he had received earlier, Hans believed he could take on more dangerous work. He didn't have to wait long.

FEBRUARY 5, 1944

Hans felt someone shaking him. He hadn't been asleep for more than a few hours and the cobwebs were slow to clear.

"Hans, Hans, wake up!" Corrie said. "Put your clothes on and come downstairs. You have to go on an urgent mission. I'll prepare some tea and sandwiches for you while you get ready."

Hans dressed and made his way down the dark stairs. As he ate breakfast Corrie filled in the details. The Gestapo had raided the home of a Mrs. van Asch last night, she said. Among her things they found the address of an underground worker from Soest. His name was van Rijn, and the Gestapo planned to arrest him that very morning, unless Hans could warn him first.

"You'd better take the first train to Amsterdam," she said. "Now let's pray for your safe return."

Corrie said a quick prayer and gave Hans the van Rijn address. The four a.m. train for Amsterdam, she added, would bring him to the man's house while it was still dark.

Hans made the train, but in Amsterdam there was no connection to Soest until six.

When it was daylight.

He had no choice but to wait. As he disembarked in Soest, he saw two men in trench coats who appeared to be locals. He asked them for directions to the Vredehofstraat, the road on which van Rijn lived, and they pointed him in the right direction. About fifteen minutes later he rang the man's doorbell. Van Rijn opened the door—still in his pajamas.

"Who are you? What's the matter?"

Hans explained what Corrie had told him, and as he talked van Rijn's wife appeared and began crying at the news. He stressed again that the man needed to leave immediately, and wished him luck.

As Hans made his way down the driveway, he saw two figures.

The men in trench coats.

"Hold it right there!" one of them barked. "Gestapo! Who are you and what are you doing here so early on Saturday morning?"

"I brought these people a message from their relatives in Amersfoort."

The Gestapo agents didn't buy it. They marched Hans back to the door and banged on it. After questioning van Rijn, they arrested and handcuffed both men. Crying again, Mrs. van Rijn said her husband had a heart condition, and she begged them not to take him. She also admitted that Hans had come to warn them.

Cover blown.

On the train back to Haarlem, Hans worked on his story. It would be dicey at best. The agents identified themselves as Willemse and Smit, and the former began the "good cop" routine. He had influence at Gestapo headquarters, he said, and if Hans cooperated, he could get him off. But cooperation meant telling the whole story, including who had given him the message and how he became involved.

Vredehofstraat 23, Soest, where the Gestapo arrested Hans.

"Moreover," Willemse said, "as an associate minister you aren't supposed to lie."

Hans hadn't figured out how to avoid implicating Corrie or the Beje, so he bought time.

"I have nothing to tell."

Willemse chuckled. "You'll certainly change that tune when we start working on you. But you better think twice, while I can still help you. When they get you at headquarters at the Nassauplein, I can't do anything more for you."

Hans held his tongue and the man dropped it.

As the agents escorted him to the Haarlem police station and his cell, Hans thought again about his story. Perhaps he could keep the ten Booms out of it, but what about his parents? Worse, if the agents searched his parents' home, they'd surely find the gun he had hidden behind the books on one of the shelves in his room.

The thought clamored through his brain: *possession of a firearm was punishable by death.*

An hour later Willemse returned to take him to Gestapo headquarters. Hans knew what awaited. The Nassauplein was to Haarlem what the Prinz-Albrecht-Strasse was to Berlin: a torture chamber to extract confessions and names.

Handcuffing Hans to himself, Willemse escorted him into the building. He led him to a large but mostly barren room—the first stop for interrogation. At a long table with chairs on both sides, Smit sat studying some papers.

"Ah, there's our preacher!"

Willemse led Hans into an adjacent veranda, uncuffed himself, and then cuffed Hans to the central heating.

"Oh, when I called to check on his identity papers," Smit said over his shoulder, "I found those idiots at the Citizens Register at City Hall had already left for the weekend."

Hans breathed a sigh of relief. Had the employees been in,

the register would have revealed that Hans's actual birthday was different from what was on his identification card, and that the card had been altered.

After a short while Willemse returned and escorted Hans back to the main room. He handcuffed Hans to a chair, and the agents went to work. Again and again they asked Hans his true identity, how he received the message to warn van Rijn, who his contacts were, what his underground address was, the type of Resistance work he was doing, and for how long. As Willemse and Smit became frustrated over Hans's unresponsive answers, they resorted to shouts and threats.

Hans felt he had his story down, but kept the agents at bay as long as possible; each minute gained might give his parents or those in the Beje time to flee when they realized he had been arrested.

And now the show began. One of the agents flipped a switch and a powerful light shone directly into Hans's eyes, blinding him. With the ceiling lights off, the room was dark but for the interrogation beam. The questions came rapid-fire.

Who are you, really?
Who recruited you?
Who is your underground supervisor?
Who sent you to warn van Rijn?
Who else is involved with you?
Where is your underground headquarters?

Though hungry, tired, and lightheaded, Hans stuck to his evasive answers.

Frustrated, the agents warned Hans that he would be tortured, and that his relatives would be arrested. Assuming the effectiveness of their pressure, Willemse and Smit alternated to rain down more questions. Hans continued to stall despite the realization that torture—and probably death—hung only minutes away.

He said a quick silent prayer for guidance and an idea struck him. When the opportunity presented itself, he pretended to break down, collapsing under the pressure, and begged the agents to stop. Willemse and Smit, taken aback, stopped asking questions. They left the light in Hans's face, however, as he told the story he had conjured up.

He had this friend, he told the agents, whom he had approached in December about getting involved in the underground. For reasons he didn't know, the man never reestablished contact. Then last night someone rang his doorbell and when he went to the door, he found only a note telling him to warn van Rijn. He memorized the address, he said, and then burned the note.

On cue, the agents asked him for his contact's name and Hans was ready: Evert van Leyenhorst. Leyenhorst was in fact an underground worker, but the Gestapo had killed him in December, Hans knew, and so Willemse and Smit would come to a dead end. The agents asked a few more questions but Hans stuck to his story, telling them he knew nothing more.

"You do realize we're now going to your home to verify your story?" Smit asked.

Hans nodded and Willemse took him back to his post—handcuffed to heating pipes—and the two agents departed.

"Thus began the darkest hour of my life," Hans remembered. "I knew that my parents' comments or story might expose mine as a set of lies. I knew for sure that they would ransack our place to search for incriminating material. I knew they would find my gun, and I knew that would be the end, because possession of a gun . . . invariably meant the firing squad. I had come to the end of my possibilities. The shadow of death fell over me."

In a span of a few minutes, Hans had lost everything: Mies, his parents, his future. Dread and anguish swept over him and he prayed that God would be with him during the trial that followed. A moment later a remarkable calmness and confidence washed over him.

"The peace that came over me conquered the other emotions—sheer terror and anger at myself—that were whirling inside. Whatever might happen now, I was His and in His hands, safe and secure. Nobody could hurt me anymore. I felt lifted out of my worries and agony and set up on a rock where no worldly power could reach me. . . . I was still handcuffed to the central heating but I felt free, more free than I had ever felt before."

BACK AT THE ten Booms', Corrie and the refugees flew into action. When Hans didn't return they suspected he had been arrested, and a raid on the house could come at any time. Once again they purged the place of incriminating papers and guests' personal effects. Eusi, Mary, Tante Martha, and Ronnie all fled to other homes and the ten Booms did their best to make the shop and house appear "normal" again.

That afternoon a friendly Dutch policeman stopped by and informed Corrie that Hans had indeed been arrested and was at the police station. Corrie, Betsie, and Opa finalized preparations for the Gestapo visit that was sure to come.

HANS WAITED ALL day and well into the evening before Willemse and Smit returned. When they did, his anxiety peaked. *Had they arrested his parents? Perhaps they were locked up in the Haarlem jail at this very moment.*

Willemse uncuffed him and took him back to the table in the main interrogation room.

"Well, you probably know what we found," Smit said. "And you also know what this means for you."

Chapter 12

SIX HUNDRED GUILDERS

HANS LOOKED AT SMIT WITH acquiescence, his fate a fait accompli. End of the road. He would be executed and never know what happened to his parents. Or Mies.

He lifted up a quick prayer: "God, be with me, give me courage!"

Smit set a briefcase on the table and retrieved what they had found during the search: a few underground papers and a Boy Scout knife.

Hans looked at the items in disbelief. This was too good to be true. The papers would of course mean prison or a concentration camp, but not execution. *How did Willemse and Smit not find my gun?* he wondered. Did they not search his bookcase?

In fact, the Germans *had* searched his bookcase. It contained twenty-four shelves and they had thrown the books off of twenty-one. His gun remained behind one of the three untouched shelves.

Hans's heart swelled. God had indeed delivered him from the lion's den. For the Gestapo agents, though, he feigned guilt and bowed his head.

"What your parents admitted to us corroborates your story," Willemse said. "That makes it easier for us."

For Hans this was a double win: neither his parents nor the

ten Booms had been arrested. With a grateful heart, he accompanied the agents back to the police station.

***

On Sunday morning Hans heard footsteps approaching his cell. He couldn't see anyone, but he heard a quiet voice: "Hans, greetings from Tante Kees."

He froze. *Is this a trap?* Why would Corrie risk her life by coming to visit him? If the voice belonged to a woman operating for the Gestapo and he acknowledged her, it would implicate Corrie, Betsie, and Opa. He decided to play it safe.

"I don't know who you are talking about."

Then another voice: "She asks whether she can do anything for you."

Hans's mind raced. If Corrie was there, why did she need someone else to speak for her? And why couldn't she just appear in front of him so he could see her? It made no sense.

"Leave me alone!"

The footsteps retreated.

In the afternoon Smit and Willemse showed up and took him back to the interrogation room at the Nassauplein. Again and again they tested his story, trying to find any inconsistency. He repeated what he had already told them, and eventually the agents were satisfied; they returned him to the police station.

An hour or so later, Hans heard the voice again. *The stranger's whisper.*

He considered what the Gestapo might know. As far as he could tell, neither the ten Booms nor the Beje had been implicated or exposed. He waited without answering and the soft voice continued. He still couldn't tell if the woman was Corrie, but whoever was speaking mentioned underground names and details that only Corrie or an underground insider would know. Still, there was risk.

"Tell them not to worry about me," he said. "I'm OK, but ask Grandfather to pray for me."

The footsteps retreated.

FROM THAT POINT on, Hans was left alone. Alone with alternating emotions of hope, despair, fear, and loneliness. Gnawing at his stomach constantly was the thought that his parents, Corrie, and Mies were at risk of being interrogated—perhaps even tortured—over his activities.

Days later the first shoe dropped: Willem's son Kik was arrested.

Not long after that a guard came by to inform Hans they were transporting him to prison. He took it as a victory. If they had arrested his parents, Corrie, or Mies, he reasoned, they would have kept him at the station to undergo further interrogation. The Gestapo had apparently closed his case.

What he couldn't know at the time was that the Gestapo had more on their hands than a few upstart Dutch Resistance workers. From the time Hitler came to power in 1933, German military leaders had plotted to do away with him—either by assassination or by arrest and trial. In 1938 the so-called Generals' Plot to oust or kill Hitler involved the highest leaders of the German army. In March 1943 they tried to assassinate Hitler twice, and another six times between September 1943 and January 1944.

Now, though, in early February 1944, the conspirators had picked up considerable speed and organization. While three civilian plotters—Pastor Dietrich Bonhoeffer, lawyer Hans von Dohnanyi, and diplomat Dr. Josef Müller—had been arrested ten months earlier, the Gestapo lacked concrete proof of a conspiracy to do away with the Führer. They had suspicions, too, about General Hans Oster, Admiral Wilhelm Canaris's second in command at the Abwehr. Realizing that the Gestapo might raid his office, Oster destroyed incriminating papers in the nick of time. In December 1943 the Gestapo forced him to resign from the Abwehr and placed him under house arrest.

Canaris himself—also deeply involved in the conspiracy—was mistrusted by the Gestapo as well, but not arrested. And so the plot of the military leaders gained momentum.*

In January 1944 the conspirators had added their biggest gun: Field Marshal Erwin Rommel—the most popular man in Germany. That very month he had been appointed commander of Army Group B in the west, tasked with defeating an Allied landing in France. As part of his new work Rommel spent considerable time with two old friends, General Alexander von Falkenhausen, military governor of Belgium and northern France, and General Karl-Heinrich von Stuelpnagel, military governor of France. Both generals were part of the anti-Hitler conspiracy, and they encouraged Rommel to join.

Near the end of February, Rommel met with another friend, Dr. Karl Stroelin, mayor of Stuttgart, at Rommel's home in Herrlingen. Stroelin also was one of the conspirators, and he informed Rommel that a number of senior army officers in the east proposed to arrest Hitler and force him to announce via radio

---

* By the end of 1943, those organizing the movement to oust Hitler included General Ludwig Beck, former Army General Staff chief; General Friedrich Olbricht of the General Army Office; General Hellmuth Stieff, head of the Army High Command's (OKH) Organizational Branch; General Eduard Wagner, first quartermaster general of the army; General Erich Fellgiebel, Armed Forces High Command (OKW) chief of signals; General Fritz Lindemann, head of the Ordnance Office; General Paul von Hase, chief of the Berlin *Kommandantur;* and Colonel Freiherr von Roenne, head of the Foreign Armies Section.

that he had abdicated. Rommel said he approved, but Stroelin wanted more.

"You are the only one," he told the field marshal, "who can prevent civil war in Germany. You must lend your name to the movement."

Rommel reflected for several moments, and then said, "I believe it is my duty to come to the rescue of Germany." He opposed assassinating Hitler, though, stressing that the Führer should be arrested by the Wehrmacht and tried before a German court for crimes against his own people, and those in occupied lands.

In Germany and in all occupied countries, it seemed, a fuse was burning.

✳ ✳ ✳

In Arnhem, Audrey Hepburn and her family had been waiting for some time for the Germans to commandeer their house; they had already taken more than a hundred villas in the Arnhem-Velp area.

German soldiers did pound on their door one day, not to move in, but to place a radio monitoring station in their attic. While Audrey and her family were relieved not to be homeless, having a radio in their house meant soldiers coming in and out at all hours.

THE THIRD WEEK of February brought a frightening yet uplifting spectacle to the cities of Arnhem, Nijmegen, Haarlem, and Amsterdam. Commencing February 20 the U.S. Strategic Air Forces in Europe, together with Britain's RAF Bomber Command, began Operation Argument—better known as "Big Week"—the six-day series of bombing raids to knock out the German aircraft industry, including fighter pilots. By day the U.S. sent some 3,800 bombers with fighter escorts, and by night the RAF sent 2,351 bombers. Since the Luftwaffe had a fighter base not far from Audrey's home in Velp, she and her family witnessed some of the most vicious dogfights of the war. In Haarlem, too, everyone at the Beje saw countless waves of Allied planes overhead, with either German antiaircraft guns or fighters chasing them. Each day flaming American, British, and German planes fell from the sky, a parachute often trailing. On the twenty-third, due to inclement weather, U.S. bombers accidentally bombed Nijmegen, killing some two hundred civilians.

But the campaign was successful: by the end of the week the U.S. Air Force and RAF had dropped nearly 20,000 tons of bombs on German fighter and munitions factories, wiping out nearly 40 percent of their aircraft. For the month they killed 434 enemy fighter pilots. But the Allies suffered terrible losses as well—more than four hundred aircraft, the parachuting crews of which were either captured by the Germans or hidden by the Dutch underground.

Many of the wounded pilots ended up in the Velp hospital— not far from where Audrey lived—which had become a makeshift Resistance headquarters. All of the doctors working there, it turned out, hid Jews in their homes.* One physician especially active in the underground was thirty-nine-year-old Dr. Hendrik Visser 't Hooft, whom Audrey began to assist. Only fourteen at the time, most of her tasks were menial. Not long after her fifteenth birthday, though, she decided to contribute more to the Resistance. A ballet prodigy, Audrey began giving private dance performances in nearby homes, donating the proceeds to the underground.

---

* Dr. Wim Op te Winkel hid thirteen Jews and Dutch divers in his home, for example, while Dr. Willem Portheine and Dr. Vince Haag also hid Jews.

***

By February 26 the Beje was relatively quiet. Too quiet, almost. Several of the regular refugees—Eusi, Mary, Ronnie, and Martha—had returned, and the house was once again a Resistance center.

One afternoon several underground workers met in the parlor, among them Reynout Siertsema (alias "Arnold")—leader of the Haarlem Resistance—to discuss their plans. As they spoke, Corrie burst into the room.

"Listen, we've run out of money. There are some people here who need it desperately. Will you join me in praying for that money?"

The Resistance workers looked at each other. This was not normally how they solved problems. Yet they were in the Beje, and Corrie was free to help in her own special way. They bowed their heads.

"We do this work as Your servants," Corrie prayed, "and in Your service. If we can't do it for lack of money, it is Your cause which suffers."

As Corrie continued to pray, the doorbell rang and Martha left to answer it. About the time Corrie finished, Martha returned holding an envelope that someone had dropped off.

It contained five hundred guilders.

That money, though, would soon have a surprise recipient.

THE MORNING OF February 28, a cold and bleary day, Corrie lay sick in bed with the flu and everything hurt—her head, her joints, her throat. Eusi came in to store bedding and pajamas in the Angels' Den, followed by Mary and Thea with their things. When they left, Corrie tried to fall back asleep, but Betsie appeared with hot tea.

"I'm sorry to wake you, Corrie. But there's a man down in the shop who insists he will talk only to you."

"Who is he?"

"He says he's from Ermelo. I've never seen him before."

Corrie sat up to sip the tea. After a minute she dressed and headed down. At the top of the stairs, though, she felt a wave of vertigo. Clutching the rail, she stepped gingerly until she made it to the shop, where a small, sandy-haired man stepped forward.

"Miss ten Boom!"

Corrie tried to meet his eyes but he was looking at her mouth. "Yes? Is this about a watch?"

"No," he said, "something far more serious!"

Corrie again tried to catch his eyes but they were now circling her face.

"Miss ten Boom, my wife was arrested in Alkmaar. We've been hiding Jews, you see. If she is questioned, all of our lives are at stake."

"I don't know how *I* can help."

"I need six hundred guilders. There's a policeman at the station in Ermelo who can be bribed for that amount."

The story seemed odd. The towns of Alkmaar and Ermelo are some seventy miles apart. If his wife was arrested in Alkmaar, how could a policeman in Ermelo help?

"I'm a poor man," he went on, "and I've been told you have certain contacts."

"Contacts?"

The man said nothing and Corrie asked if he could provide references to assure that she could trust him.* He couldn't.

_____

* When underground workers met there were two safety precautions to assure that the newcomer wasn't a Gestapo agent or informant. First, a secret code phrase or sentence was typically expected. Diet Eman, a young female Resistance agent in Amsterdam, recalled a meeting she was called to in the spring of 1943: "When I first showed up at that place, I had to give some code sentences

"Miss ten Boom! It's a matter of life and death! If I don't get it right away she'll be taken to Amsterdam and then it will be too late."

Corrie paused. If his wife had been caught for hiding Jews, she *would* be taken to Amsterdam, and once there, it *would* be too late. She told him to come back in half an hour and she'd have the money.

The man thanked her and Corrie sent a courier to the bank to withdraw six hundred guilders and give it to the man when he returned. With that she made the slow climb back up the stairs. Unfortunately, though, her fever had now turned to cold chills. She undressed, refilled her vaporizer, and crawled back into bed.

Once again she had been called on to make a snap judgment to assist the underground, and now she just wanted to sleep. Tomorrow was another day, and she could get back to obtaining ration cards. In the meantime, she likely had saved that man's wife.

But everything he told her was a lie.

---

to identify myself as someone who could be trusted. I rang the bell and said the correct words, and a woman . . . invited me in. Her dwelling was very small, a one-person apartment. . . . She had a small living room, a tiny bedroom, a kitchenette, a shower, and a toilet. . . . And in that little place . . . she had hidden twenty-seven Jews."

In the absence of code words, references of other underground names could be given. Corrie received neither from the man in front of her.

Chapter 13

TRAPPED

ZZZZZST. ZZZZZST. ZZZZZST. A buzzer.

As Corrie was processing between dream and reality, she heard the rustling of feet, and then a whisper: "Hurry! Hurry!"

She sat up to find refugees racing past her bed. Martha and Ronnie were crawling into the Angels' Den when Eusi arrived. His face was ashen, his pipe and ashtray rattling in his hand. Mary then rushed in, followed by two visiting Resistance agents, Arnold and Hans*. She did a quick count—six—and closed the sliding panel. Below she could hear doors slamming, and then footsteps on the stairs.

Scanning the room she saw her briefcase, which contained names and addresses of underground workers. Snatching it, she yanked up the sliding door, flung it in, and slammed the door shut again. Her "prison bag" lay beside her so she tossed it in front of the panel, threw off her housecoat, and jumped into bed.

Seconds later her bedroom door burst open.

"What's your name?" a tall, heavyset man shouted.

He wore a blue suit and Corrie assumed he was Gestapo. "What?" she asked, sitting up.

"Your name!"

---

* Hans van Messel was an underground operative assisting Siertsema.

"Cornelia ten Boom."

"We've got one more up here, Willemse," the man yelled toward the door. He turned back to Corrie. "Get up! Get dressed!"

Corrie reached for clothes and the agent looked at his notes. "So you're the ringleader! Tell me now, where are you hiding the Jews?"

"I don't know what you're talking about."

The agent laughed. "And you don't know anything about an underground ring, either. We'll see about that!"

Corrie pulled on her clothes over her pajamas and the agent barked again. "Where is your secret room?"

Once again, Corrie pleaded ignorance.

"Never mind. We know you have Jews hidden in this house and we'll get them. We'll search and turn this house inside out. We'll guard the house till we starve them out or till they turn into mummies!"

Corrie was about to grab her prison bag, but since it rested in front of the secret panel she decided not to draw attention to it. She left the room without anything for the ordeal she knew was coming. Still feeling the effects of the flu, she again began descending the stairs slowly. The Gestapo agent pushed her from behind, though, and she stumbled on.

When they arrived downstairs the living room was packed: Opa, Betsie, Willem, Nollie, Mr. Ineke, and Henny van Dantzig, along with guests who had come for Willem's Bible study. Willemse, the Gestapo agent who had interrogated Hans Poley, was busy rifling through silver and jewelry he had put on the dining table.

Glancing to her right, Corrie noticed that the Alpina watch sign—the Beje's "all clear" code to the underground—still sat in the alley window. Pretending to trip, Corrie knocked the sign off the sill. Willemse heard it hit the floor and came over.

"It was a signal, wasn't it?" He returned it to the ledge.

The trap would remain open.

The agent who had walked Corrie down then said to Willemse: "My information says she's the leader of the whole outfit."

Willemse glanced at Corrie and back. "You know what to do, Kapteyn."

Kapteyn clutched Corrie's arm and hustled her down the steps leading to the shop. A soldier stood guard at the front door, and Kapteyn ordered her to take off her glasses. When she did he shoved her against the wall.

"Where are the Jews?"

"There aren't any Jews here."

Kapteyn slapped her. "Where do you hide the ration cards?"

"I don't know what you're—"

Kapteyn struck her again, harder. Corrie's knees buckled. She regained her bearing leaning against the astronomical clock, but before she could utter a word he slapped her again and again and again.

"Where are the Jews?"

Another strike.

"Where is your secret room?"

Corrie could taste blood in her mouth and the beating, together with her flu, was causing her to lose consciousness. Her ears rang from the blows and she cried out, "Lord Jesus, protect me!"

Kapteyn, about to deliver another slap, stopped midair: "If you say that name again I'll kill you!"

Corrie's head pounded as she struggled to remain standing. Kapteyn gave up on the interrogation, mumbling about a "skinny one" who would talk. He pushed her back up the stairs and into a chair in the dining room. Kapteyn then grabbed Betsie and took her out of the room.

Upstairs Corrie could hear knocking and scraping as the Gestapo agents searched the home. Then the alley doorbell ringing. Willemse ran down to answer it and Corrie heard the exchange.

"Have you heard?" a woman asked. "They've got Oom Herman!"

Corrie sat back. Pickwick. They had the leader of the Haarlem underground, and a dear friend of the ten Booms.

Willemse played along to entice the woman to provide details, then arrested her and brought her upstairs.

Just then Betsie stumbled into the room. Her lips were swollen and a bruise showed on her cheek.

"Were you beaten?" Nollie asked from across the room.

"Yes," Betsie said, dabbing at the blood on her lip, "and I do so pity the man who beat me."

"Prisoners will remain silent!" Kapteyn shouted.

A moment later another German brought in from the shop a box of watches belonging to Jews, and then two more agents appeared coming down the stairs with the radio that had been hidden in the steps.

"Law-abiding citizens, are you?" Kapteyn smirked. "You!" he said, pointing to Opa. "I see you believe in the Bible. Tell me, what does it say in there about obeying the government?"

He was referring to Paul's admonition to the Romans* to obey the governing authorities, Opa knew, but there was more to it than that.

"Fear God; honor the queen."

"That's not true; the Bible doesn't say that."

"No, it says 'Fear God and honor the king,' but in our case that is the queen."

Just then the phone in the hall rang and Willemse yanked

---

* Romans 13:1 provides: "Everyone must submit himself to the governing authorities, for there is no authority except that which God has established" (NIV).

Corrie up by the wrist and dragged her to it. "Answer!" he commanded, holding the phone between their ears.

Corrie tried to say it as stiffly as possible: "This is the ten Boom residence and shop."

"Miss ten Boom," the caller blurted, "you're in terrible danger! They've arrested Herman Sluring! They know everything! You've got to be careful!"

No sooner than the caller hung up, the phone rang again. Willemse continued to hold her and the phone and Corrie repeated the stiff greeting.

"Oom Herman's been taken to the police station," this caller said. "That means they're on to everything."

Corrie hung up and Willemse returned her to the dining room. Another Gestapo agent, one Corrie had not seen before, came in and said: "We've searched the whole place, Willemse. If there's a secret room here, the devil himself built it."

Willemse glared at Betsie, then Opa, then Corrie. "There's a secret room. And people are using it or they would have admitted it. All right. We'll set a guard around the house till they've turned to mummies."

Willemse ordered everyone to their feet and another agent brought in Willem and those who were in his Bible study. Together, Willemse informed, the arrested group would walk to the police station in the Smedestraat, about a hundred steps from the Beje.

Outside in the bitter cold, Corrie shivered in the walk to the station. When they arrived, she noticed a significant number of German soldiers in the lobby, apparently waiting to transfer the arrested to prison. Willemse herded the group into a large room once used as a gymnasium and told them to sit on the tumbling mats scattered about. Huddled in various groups around her, Corrie saw a number of her neighbors, but not Pickwick.

***

"Who's here?" someone asked.

One by one, Martha, Mary, Eusi, Ronnie, Arnold, and Hans whispered their names. After a few moments they checked for supplies and it was pitiful—blankets, sheets, and a few crackers. No water or real food. They tried to get comfortable but the space was so cramped that two had to stand while the other four sat.

So back and forth they went, shifting and changing places for hours. And there was another thing they had neglected: with all of their test runs scrambling into the hiding place, they had never anticipated being cooped up for hours, or how they would address bodily needs without a toilet.

As night fell desperation set in. How would they ever get out? Corrie, Betsie, Opa, and everyone in the house during the raid would have been arrested, and no one else knew they hid in the Angels' Den.

Just then the Beje's alley doorbell rang. It came in the code planned for when a trusted underground worker visited: three short rings. Every person who came to the house this way would be arrested by the waiting Gestapo, but there was no way to warn them.

PETER RELEASED THE doorbell and stepped back into the shadows.

A man with a deep voice opened the door and invited him in. Peter didn't know him, but Resistance workers often answered the alley entrance. The man led him up the stairs and into the living room. On most occasions when he visited, Peter found the ten Booms and several Jews reading or listening to the radio. In front of him now, though, was a group of strangers. One by one those present introduced themselves as members of the underground. They invited Peter to sit and join the conversation.

"We have very sad news," one of them said. "Part of the organization has been uncovered, and our plans have been shattered in many places. The Nazis have found out about our work, and to make matters worse, Uncle Herman has been captured."

Peter glanced around the room. Everyone seemed to be looking at him, waiting for his response. Something was wrong. He remembered that they had not even vetted him as an underground member. He said nothing and showed no reaction.

"We have to do something quickly!" another added. "What do you think about a holdup of the prison where Uncle Herman is being kept?"

Peter maintained his silence.

"There's just one hitch to trying to get Uncle Herman from prison," the first speaker said, turning to Peter. "We don't have enough weapons to successfully manage such an undertaking. Perhaps you could help us in securing some?"

Peter played the part. "I'm sorry, sir. Are you sure there hasn't been some misunderstanding? I'm an assistant to a minister. Now if I could help you with something along that line, I'd be glad to be of service. I really am sorry I can't help you. Now if you'll excuse me, I should leave. I have some work to do."

Peter jumped to his feet and made his way toward the door when a man stepped in front of him, revolver at the ready.

"I think you'd better sit down, fellow. You're a prisoner."

Peter took a seat and grimaced as he heard the alley doorbell ring again and again with the secret code—more underground workers who would be arrested. Later that evening he and several other Resistance members were transported to the police station. Looking around, he saw Opa, Corrie, Betsie, Willem, and then some thirty other friends who had been nabbed in the

Beje raid. Another glance and he shivered; his *mother* had been arrested.

"Let's have it quiet in here!" a Dutch policeman shouted. He said something privately to Willem and then barked out again: "Toilets are out back. You can go one at a time under escort."

Willem went over to Corrie and sat down. "He says we can flush incriminating papers if we shred them fine enough."

Corrie checked her pockets but all she found were a few scraps of paper and some money in her wallet.

One by one, individuals made their way to the bathrooms. For Henk van Riessen, an underground leader arrested in the raid, his turn could not come soon enough. His pockets were filled with Resistance notes and, astonishingly, he had not been searched at the Beje. Once inside the restroom he closed the door and began dumping his contraband into the toilet. But he put too much in, and the toilet clogged. He flushed several times to clear it.

When he came out, a policeman outside the door asked him if he had been able to get rid of everything. Realizing the officer was a loyal Dutchman, Henk checked his pockets and found he had missed one paper—a Hitler joke.

"Give it to me quickly," the officer said, "and I will throw it away for you."

Henk did, and Peter was next up for the men's room. When he closed the door, he noticed that some of Henk's papers had resurfaced and floated on the water. He tried flushing again but they wouldn't go, so he pushed them through with his hand.

LATE THAT EVENING, before everyone tried to sleep, Opa called the ten Booms to gather around him and asked one of the guards for the Bible they had taken from Willem. The guard returned it and Opa asked Willem to read Psalm 91 aloud.

"He that dwelleth in the secret place of the most High," Willem began, "shall abide under the shadow of the Almighty. I will say of the Lord, He is my refuge and my fortress: my God; in him will I trust. . . ."

When Willem finished Opa prayed, as calm and peaceful as ever. He asked God to stay close to each of them, anticipating that they would soon be separated.

Corrie, though, remained shaken and inconsolable. They had been doing the Lord's work, after all, so where were the protecting angels? She began to weep and Betsie, sitting beside her, reminded her that God does indeed protect those who trust in Him, but such protection is of their *souls*, not of their lives or physical well-being. Betsie assured Corrie that God would be with them—even in the deepest hell—and would give them courage to face prison.

Betsie then prayed for Corrie, and for everyone in their group.

❋ ❋ ❋

The trapped six sat and stood as the St. Bavo Church chime sounded twice: it was two a.m. Between hunger and the cramped arrangement, no one could sleep.

From somewhere in the house they heard German voices.

A few moments later Germans came into Corrie's room and began pounding on everything: the walls, the floor, and finally on the false linen closet. Seconds later the trapped six heard the most frightening sound they could imagine.

Splintering wood.

Chapter 14

PRIVILEGED

SPLINTERING WOOD MEANT ONE THING: the Gestapo was tearing through the linen closet. Everyone inside the Angels' Den held their breath. They didn't know the depth of the wood in the main part of the closet, but if the Germans tried the panel door, all was lost.

Eusi began to pray, half aloud in Hebrew: "I will trust in Adonai, who can harm me?"

Someone smothered his mouth.

"Hush, Eusi!" another whispered. "Your noise will betray us."

They waited while the breaking of wood continued, but the Angels' Den entrance remained intact. As time passed they realized the Gestapo was breaking up the floor in Corrie's room. That was good news, but for how long? When the Germans realized there was nothing under the floor, the linen closet was probably next.

* * *

At first light the next morning a policeman brought in rolls for everyone in the gym. Because she had slept so little that night, Corrie tried to doze off again with her back against a wall. At noon soldiers entered the room and ordered everyone to their

Linen closet with brick cutaway revealing Angels' Den.

feet. All of the arrested group were to board a bus out front, a German officer said.

Outside, a large group of Haarlemers had assembled around the police barricade. Corrie, Betsie, and Opa walked together and when the crowd saw the town's "Grand Old Man," a rumbling of gasps, murmurs, and weeping swept through them. In front of Corrie idled a green bus with soldiers in the back. She and Betsie clutched Opa's arms to help him down the station steps and then paused.

Stumbling past them—between two soldiers—was Pickwick. His coat and hat were gone, and bruises and dried blood covered his face.

..

AS PETER MADE his way down the bus aisle, he found Pickwick and sat beside him. He was relieved to sit with a friend and kindred spirit, but the man he knew as Uncle Herman wasn't his jovial self. Pickwick put his hand on Peter's—a touch of consolation and assurance.

"Peter, I've suffered much. They beat me many times; you know how they work. It finally got so bad that I prayed in my moment of weakness that the Lord would let me die. Then I realized that that was no prayer for me, a Christian, to pray, and I asked the Lord to forgive me."

While he spoke Pickwick turned toward Peter. His face had been so brutalized that he was almost unrecognizable. Herman reached for something in his pocket and when he opened his hand, Peter gasped.

There were several of Uncle Herman's teeth.

Roots intact.

***

At the Beje, things had become unbearable for the trapped six. Day two and the Angels' Den seemed more like a punishment cell. Everyone was thirsty and hungry, but the worst was the lack of facilities. To prevent seepage down the walls, they had been urinating on bedsheets they had shredded. For the other, they had a small bucket—which Ronnie had accidently kicked over. The stench was nauseating.

Tension and frustration heightened the anxiety to a dangerous level, but Eusi and Martha calmed everyone. "If you trust the Almighty," they said, "He will be with you and He will protect your soul."

Still, the thought lingered in everyone's mind: how long could they last?

* * *

Corrie, Betsie, Opa, Nollie, and Peter watched through the windows as the bus headed south, away from Amsterdam—where the prison was—but to where?

Two hours later they arrived at The Hague, and the bus stopped in front of a new building. Whispers passed among the prisoners that this was the Gestapo headquarters for all of Holland. Everyone filed out and Corrie noticed that Pickwick wasn't with them.

"*Alle Nasen gegen die Mauer!*" someone shouted. "All noses to the wall."

The ten Booms complied, facing a gray stone wall, and a soldier gave Opa a chair. Hours went by and the group remained in their spots without moving or talking.

"Peter, pray for me!" Nollie said beside him. "I don't think I can stand any longer."

Keeping his nose and eyes to the wall, Peter reached over to take his mother's hand and then prayed.

"It's all right now," she said moments later. "Thank the Lord."

Late in the afternoon a guard herded them into a processing room and Corrie noticed that the officers handling the administration were Willemse and Kapteyn. One by one the prisoners were taken to them, and again the requested liturgy: name, address, occupation. As each person finished, Willemse or Kapteyn dictated to a third man at a typewriter.

Supervising the room, the Gestapo officer in charge saw Opa and pointed.

"That old man! Did he have to be arrested? You, old man!"

Willem helped Opa to the desk and the officer said, "I'd like to send you home, old fellow. I'll take your word that you won't cause any more trouble."

"If I go home today," Opa said calmly, "tomorrow I will open my door again to any man in need who knocks."

The Gestapo agent scowled. "Get back in line! *Schnell!*"

The processing of prisoners continued well into the evening, and then everyone was escorted into the back of a large army truck. Opa was too weak to manage the climb onto the truck bed so two soldiers lifted him.

Darkness had fallen by the time they reached their destination: Scheveningen prison. Huge iron gates closed behind the bus, and then the drill repeated—everyone was marched inside and told to put their nose to the wall. Corrie stayed close to her father, who once again was allowed to sit on a chair.

Bending forward, she kissed him on the forehead. "The Lord be with you."

"And with you."

Opa had an angelic look about him, and Corrie remembered her father's earlier exchange with someone warning him about harboring Jews. "If you persist . . . you will eventually end in prison, and in your delicate condition you could never survive that."

"If that should come to pass," Opa had replied, "I shall consider it an honor to give my life for God's ancient people."

Just then Corrie heard the guards assigning the ten Booms to cells: Betsie to 314, Corrie to 397, Opa to 401, and Nollie to an undetermined cell.

"Women prisoners follow me!" a harsh voice cried out.

Betsie grasped Corrie's hand and together they walked behind a guard down a long corridor, the end of which had yet another processing desk. Here an attendant took their remaining personal items and Corrie handed over her watch, wallet, and guilders. The guard motioned to the gold ring Corrie wore—which had been given to her by her mother—and she gave that up as well.

Another guard then led the line down the hall and read from a list the cell each inmate would occupy. Betsie was among the first called, and before Corrie could say goodbye the door slammed shut. Nollie was next.

The line continued on and they reached 397.

"Ten Boom, Cornelia."

Corrie stepped into the small cell, where three women sat on straw mats and another reclined on the lone cot.

"Give this one the cot," the guard said. "She's sick."

"We don't want a sick woman in here!" one of the inmates shouted.

Ignoring the comment, the guard closed the door.

"I'm sorry that I must share your very limited space," Corrie told her cellmates.

Surprisingly, the women were considerate—offering bread and water—and allowed her to use the cot. Corrie ate and then reclined with her coat wrapped tightly around her. She fell asleep in minutes.

IN THE HOLDING area Peter and Opa waited their turn. Assuming he would be searched, Peter thought about the pocket New Testament he had smuggled in. He couldn't take it into his cell, but he didn't want to let go of the one precious thing he needed for prison. When the guard was preoccupied with another prisoner, Peter slipped his hand into his back pocket and ripped a handful of pages from the text. The guard's attention was still elsewhere so Peter squeezed the pages into a ball and—pretending to scratch his foot—inserted the wad under his arch.

Minutes later he heard his name announced and he said a quick prayer: "O Lord, may they forget my shoes."

The guard searched each of his pockets, turning them inside out. Slipping out Peter's New Testament, the officer sneered and tossed it in a corner.

He then chained Peter to another prisoner and they started down the corridor behind the guard. Before they came to the cell area Peter saw Opa—sitting as peacefully as if he were at home in his favorite chair—and he tugged on the chain to draw the other inmate over.

He kissed Opa's head and whispered, "I'm going to my cell now. Goodbye."

Opa looked up with a calm smile. "God bless you, my boy. Aren't we a privileged family?"

Peter struggled to see prison life as a privilege, but he was still learning from Haarlem's Grand Old Man. At the moment, though, all he could concentrate on was the wad in his shoe making it painful to walk. When he finally came to his cell and the guard shut the door, Peter pulled it off to find out which pages he had removed. Straightening the papers, he discovered that he had taken the first twelve chapters of the Book of Acts. Fitting, he thought, since that section contained stories of the persecution of first-century Christians as they sojourned among people who scorned their faith.

Opa's turn was next, and a guard took him to cell 401. Like Corrie, he had cellmates, all of whom were immediately inspired by his composure and peace. For Opa, prison was like a bridge, and he spoke of death as "going home."

WEDNESDAY, MARCH 1, 1944
The Beje, Haarlem

The trapped six had reached their wits' end. They had been entombed in the Angels' Den now for three days. They were hungry, dehydrated, sleep deprived, and claustrophobic, and their little box now reeked like an underground sewer. They had to do something. Much longer in this hellhole and every-one would die.

The Jewish refugees wanted to try an escape. They would go to the roof, the plan went, and make the eight-foot jump from the Beje onto the gutter of the adjacent house. Arnold questioned whether the women in the group could make the leap and, be-lieving the underground would rescue them at any moment, thought it better to wait.

So they came to a compromise. If help didn't arrive before evening, they would make their break when it turned dark.

At four-thirty that afternoon they heard footsteps coming up the stairs, then into Corrie's room. Everyone remained quiet and suddenly they heard a tap. It wasn't clear where the tap was made—on the false wall, or on the linen closet? Then a voice.

"Siertsema . . . Siertsema!"

Chapter 15

PRISON

THE SIX WHISPERED QUICKLY. The person in the room had said "Siertsema"—Arnold's real last name—not the alias he had been using for underground work. But while those on the other side could be their rescuers, they could just as easily be Gestapo agents who had bribed or tortured someone into giving up Arnold's real name. If they remained silent, they could still make the break that night, but the jump to the other house would be noisy and some might fall in the attempt. It was a gamble either way.

"It's okay," Arnold whispered. The odds were greater, he felt, that the voice came from an underground worker.

He lifted the panel door.

On the other side waited two policemen.

The officers leaned in to get a look and then jerked back, reeling from the stench. Arnold recognized one of them as a man named Jan Overzet,* a loyal Dutchman, and crawled out. One by one the others followed, and the policemen warned them to be silent as enemy guards remained downstairs.

The officers gave them all water, and Eusi—after his first desperate swallow—in a loud voice began praising God.

---

* The other officer was Theo Ederveen.

"Sh, Eusi," one of the others whispered. "Don't betray us after all of this."

The policemen gathered them close and explained the plan. They would take Arnold and Hans to the roof to make the jump to the house next door, and both would come down through a skylight into the attic. Once inside, they would make their way to the ground floor and make their exit onto the street through an empty shop.

The officers would then wait until dark and try to slip the four others out the alley door without giving away their presence to the guards. Once the Jews were outside, an underground worker would take them to new hiding places. If the guards heard them and came up, the policemen would use their guns.

With that the Dutchmen escorted Arnold and Hans to the roof and they made the leap and followed the escape route. Meanwhile, the Jews sat in Corrie's room, praying that the plan would work. Minutes passed as days, but they remained silent and hopeful.

For two hours they waited. Finally, at seven o'clock the policemen returned and said it was time. One by one Eusi, Mary, Martha, and Ronnie tiptoed down the staircase to the alley exit. So far, so good.

Slowly they opened the door and slipped out to awaiting underground workers.

They were free.

※ ※ ※

At dawn Corrie awoke to a guard shuffling in metal plates filled with some kind of watery porridge. Still suffering from influenza, she gave hers to one of the others.

Sometime midmorning a guard came to collect the cell's "sanitation bucket" and returned clean water for the basin. When she left, Corrie engaged her cellmates in conversation, discovering a bit about each.

The youngest—only seventeen—was a baroness. To overcome boredom, she paced the twelve-by-twelve cell up and back for hours.

Another cellmate had been in Scheveningen prison for two years and knew every detail of the place. She could tell by the footsteps who was coming down the corridor, and knew exactly how many times neighboring prisoners had been called for hearings.

Corrie was surprised to find that another of her mates was an Austrian woman who had been part of the Wehrmacht. German prisons and concentration camps were run not by the Wehrmacht, however, but by Hitler's Nazi Party. As such, all guards and officials were members of the SS—a makeshift political police force despised by the professional military.

The conversation brought Corrie's thoughts to her family and friends. Throughout her first week in prison, she worried constantly about her father, Betsie, Willem, and Pickwick. Opa, in particular, posed a serious concern. Could he even eat prison food? Her own condition, too, was severe. Her flu seemed to have migrated to something worse; she found it hard to sit up during the day, her head pounded, her arms hurt, and she began to cough up blood.

PETER, OPA, BETSIE, Nollie, Flip, and Hans, meanwhile, languished in their own cells. Like the others, Peter was surrounded by four cold gray walls, but he could see a bit of the sky through the window above. For a while he anguished over his plight, but one afternoon he noticed that the sun would set at an angle where its rays shone directly into his cell. He took out his loose pages of the Book of Acts and began to read in the light.

He marveled at how the early Christians waited for power from above, and when the Holy Spirit came they boldly proclaimed the Gospel to those around them. There was a balance, Peter saw, in the waiting and going.

"In the quietness of my cell," he remembered, "I waited on the Lord. I prayed about where and how He wanted me to go."

Luke 14:33 kept coming to mind and Peter wrestled with the text: "So likewise, whosoever he be of you that forsaketh not all that he hath, he cannot be my disciple."

All. It seemed too much. Could he forsake his home, his parents, and all he held dear, if that was the cost?

He had come to the crossroads that Dietrich Bonhoeffer had written about in his 1937 book, *The Cost of Discipleship.* "When Christ calls a man," Bonhoeffer had written while fighting the Nazis, "he bids him come and die."

Like Bonhoeffer, Peter had joined the Resistance to fight Hitler, and both were currently incarcerated in SS prisons. But he and the pastor also shared the same source of power and release: their faith in Christ.

Peter knelt by the stool in his cell and prayed: "Lord, whatever you want, wherever you want, whenever you want—I'll go."

He stood and an indescribable happiness overcame him. He remembered the passages where Paul and Silas sang in prison, and he began to do the same.

Amstelveenseweg Prison

In Amsterdam, Hans Poley was making the best of quartering with four others. There were only three beds, however, so he slept on the floor on a straw mattress. The daily meals were inadequate, too: breakfast consisted of bread and water, lunch of either stew or a watery gruel of grits, and dinner of four slices of thin bread. To stave off hunger pains he consumed as much water as he could.

Fortunately, every other Friday the Red Cross provided each prisoner a brown paper bag containing wheat or rye bread, cheese or butter, chocolate or candy, and cigarettes. "The packages were the highlights of my stay in that prison," he wrote later, "and did wonders for our morale. Many times I blessed the Red Cross for that invaluable and visible signal of hope."

Scheveningen Prison

On March 8 Corrie was called to her first hearing, but the officials asked few questions and she was soon back in her cell. Meanwhile in cell 401, Opa's fragile health slipped away by the hour. His mind began to wander and his cellmates cried out for medical help. The following day the prison staff finally took him to the Ramar clinic, but he fell unconscious by the time he arrived. On a stretcher in the corridor, Opa received the honor of giving his life for the Jews.

Casper ten Boom, Haarlem's Grand Old Man, died on March 9, 1944.

They buried him in an unmarked grave in Loosduinen cemetery.*

THE FOLLOWING TUESDAY guards noticed Corrie's deteriorating condition and announced that she would be taken to the "consultation bureau." Minutes later she was escorted outside to a waiting car, and two other ill prisoners joined her for transit to

---

* After the war Casper's grave was located and he was reinterred at the National Cemetery of Honors in Loenen, Netherlands—a resting place designed to honor World War II resistance fighters, political prisoners, and soldiers.

The Hague. The driver stopped at an office building and a guard ushered them into what appeared to be some kind of clinic.

Corrie asked the nurse behind the reception desk if she could wash her hands and the woman led her down the hall, and then followed her into the restroom.

"Quick, is there any way I can help?"

Corrie asked if she could provide soap, a toothbrush, and a Bible.

"I'll do what I can."

After a short wait the doctor saw Corrie, and he announced that she had pleurisy* with effusion,† pre-tubercular. He wrote something down and put his hand on her shoulder.

"I hope that I am doing you a favor with this diagnosis."

Corrie assumed the paper was a hospital pass.

As she left, the nurse she had seen rushed over and slipped a small wrapped item into her hand. When Corrie was back in her cell, she found in the package two bars of soap and copies of the four Gospels.

Two days later a guard came by in the evening.

"Ten Boom, Cornelia. Get your things."

Relieved that she was going to the hospital, Corrie grabbed her coat and said goodbye to her cellmates. The guard marched her down the hallway, but not toward the main entrance. They came to an empty cell and the guard motioned her to go in.

Number 384. Solitary confinement.

Corrie looked around. The cell, similar to the one she had left, contained four cold, gray stone walls and a cot, but there was an icy draft, apparently from a brewing storm outside. As she

---

* An inflammation of the pleura—the tissue separating the lungs from the chest wall—that causes stabbing chest pains, difficulty breathing, and coughing.
† Effusion occurs when fluid builds up between the pleura and the chest wall. When both conditions occur, simply inhaling and exhaling causes pain, and this pain often is felt in the shoulders and back.

stepped closer, she noticed that the cot reeked of something—mildew perhaps. Keeping her coat on, she sat and reached for the blanket.

Someone had vomited on it.

Immediately nauseous, Corrie lunged for the bucket by the door to make her own deposit. Just then the overhead light went out and the cell turned pitch dark.

Welcome to a Nazi prison.

IN THE MORNING Corrie's fever worsened and she couldn't eat. For three days attendants brought food to her cot, but her appetite was meager.

One day an orderly brought her medicine and Corrie asked, "Is my father still living?"

"I don't know," the worker said, "and if I did I would still not be permitted to tell you."

Minutes after the orderly disappeared the *Wachtmeisterin** threw open her door.

"If you ever dare do such a thing again as ask the *Sanitäter*† about another prisoner you will get no medical attention at all as long as you are here."

This was the hardest part—the hatred. Over ensuing days Corrie tried to be nice to the woman, but to no avail. "She seemed to be entirely devoid of human feeling," Corrie recalled, "and altogether hard, hostile, and wicked. These women were so hard and cruel, and they were the only human beings I saw. Why should they always snap and snarl at us? I always greeted them with a pleasant 'Good morning,' but everything seemed to glance off their impenetrable armor of hate."

---

* Female head guard.
† Orderly or Red Cross worker.

To overcome boredom and worries, Corrie began to sing. Prison rules, however, prohibited singing. When a guard heard her she threatened Corrie with *Kalte-kost*—the loss of that day's one warm meal, which meant that the day's sustenance would be only a small piece of bread.

What was worse—her hunger or the stench of her filthy blanket and pillow? On top of that, her straw mattress seemed to be fermenting. About four times a night she would get up to adjust the straw, but that brought up dust, which brought on her cough and more blood.

Despite the conditions, though, this cell had one distinct advantage over her prior one: a window. It had seven iron bars and was too high to see anything outdoors, but by looking through it Corrie could see the sky. On overcast days the clouds showed traces of white, pink, and gold, and for hours she would watch them float by. It seemed a slice of heaven, and if the wind blew from the west, she could hear the sea.

Over ensuing days her illness faded and she began reading the Gospels, which put her incarceration in a different light. Was it possible, she thought, that the war, the prison, and her cell were part of God's plan? The suffering and persecution she read about in these pages of Scripture, were they the pattern of God's activity and purpose? "We are all at school," Spurgeon had observed almost a century earlier, "and our great Teacher writes many a bright lesson on the black-board of affliction."

Still, it seemed peculiar. Looking around her cell, Corrie wondered how victory could be around the corner.

Nollie, too, was reading. She had smuggled into her cell—hidden in her hair—the twelfth chapter of Hebrews. As Corrie was encouraged by the Gospels and Peter the Book of Acts, Nollie's spirits lifted from the famous Hebrews passage: "Therefore, since we are surrounded by such a great cloud of witnesses, let us throw off everything that hinders and the sin that so easily entangles, and let us run with perseverance the race marked out for us. Let us fix our eyes on Jesus, the author and perfecter of our faith, who for the joy set before him endured the cross. . . . Consider him who endured such opposition from sinful men, so that you will not grow weary and lose heart."

When he wasn't reading, Peter tried to make the most of his time. One day something in his cell caught his eye—a piece of metal reflecting the sun's rays—which turned out to be an old rusty nail. Prying it from the cement, he began using it to scratch on the wall each day. Before long he had carved out Romans 8:31: *"Zo God voor ons is, wi ezal tegen ons zijn?"*—"If God be for us, who can be against us?"

At night, when guards were less apt to check on cells, he would use the nail to dig a small hole in the floor beneath his table. After a while he broke through, saw light on the other side, and bent down to take a look.

An eyeball peered up at him.

Chapter 16

LIEUTENANT RAHMS

HIS NAME WAS GERARD, the man in the cell below said, and he had been charged with espionage, a capital crime. He would be executed soon, he added, so Peter began sharing the Gospel with him. Before long Peter was rolling his Acts pages into the shape of a straw and passing them down.

"In this manner, as well as many others," he remembered, "the Word of God traveled on in what seemed to be a hopeless prison. It brought strength and help to the desperate, assurance to the doubtful, and awakened faith in the fearbound heart."

Amstelveenseweg Prison

Near the end of March, Hans Poley was told to grab his things; he was being transferred. As guards gathered prisoners and escorted them to the train station, word traveled about their destination: Amersfoort.

Hans cringed. Amersfoort, a Gestapo transit camp notorious for starvation and atrocities, required prisoners to remain outside at attention for hours, regardless of the weather. Other stories were worse. Sometimes prisoners were forced to crawl on their stomachs while SS guards jumped on their backs and hammered them with rifle butts. And anyone caught trying to escape or found in violation of prison rules was sent to solitary confinement in the "Bunker"—a pitch-dark cell belowground. Here a prisoner might sit in complete darkness for a month, two months, even three months.*

At the moment, though, Hans had other matters on his mind. He had previously written two letters—one to Mies and one to his family—and this was his opportunity to have them delivered. When the train slowed as it approached a crossing, he tossed them out the window, praying that someone would find and deliver them.

When they arrived at the Amersfoort station, Hans and the others marched to the prison. The place was chilling, with a double barbed-wire fence, watchtowers with machine guns, searchlights, and soldiers patrolling with dogs.

"Johannes Poley!" someone shouted.

Hans stepped forward and a guard thrust into his hand a strip of cloth with a number. From that point on, Hans Poley didn't exist.

He was simply prisoner 9238.

Scheveningen Prison

On April 11 Corrie sent a letter home, addressed to "Nollie and all friends."[†]

"I am fine," she told everyone. "Have severe pleurisy but have improved much, except that I am still coughing. I have miracu-

---

* At Ravensbrück, SOE spy Odette Sansom was confined to a Bunker cell for three months, eight days. The light in her cell would be turned on for five minutes a day; otherwise, the cell was pitch dark.

† Nollie was still in Scheveningen prison at this time, and wasn't released until April 20. Corrie may have rightly assumed that her sister would be released soon, since there was less evidence of her or Flip's involvement with the underground.

lously adjusted to this lonely life, but I am in communion with God."

Unaware that her father had already died, Corrie continued: "The most difficult thing for me has been my worries about Betsie and especially Father. . . . I do worry about our customers' watches [Jews hiding in the Angels' Den] left in the empty house, but the Savior is all the time averting all worry and fear and homesickness so that the doctor said to me, 'You are always cheerful.' I sing inside nearly all day long and we do have much to be thankful for—an airy cell . . . three Red Cross sandwiches, half a pan of porridge extra, and then that continuous communion with the Savior.

"Life's dimensions here are very strange," she wrote in closing. "Time is something to be waded through. I am surprised that I can adjust so well. . . . Please never worry about me. Sometimes it may be dark, but the Savior provides His light and how wonderful that is."

That same day Betsie penned a letter to Nollie's daughter Cocky. "The rush of great waters came at me," she told her niece, "but I did not despair for one moment. The Lord is close to me as never before in my life. Even in those first terrible days I felt His nearness. . . . From the first moment on, I have been able to adjust to my cell and to prison life. I sleep well, and do not suffer from cold. . . . Due to nervousness, my stomach could not tolerate the prison food. I hardly ate anything and was suffering from hunger. After 4 weeks of that I asked to see the doctor and now I am getting delicious porridge and things are going better.

"I am longing so much for you and for news from Willem, Peter, [and] Corrie."

On April 15 Corrie turned fifty-two. For her entire life a birthday meant a party, especially at the Beje. But she lay in sol-

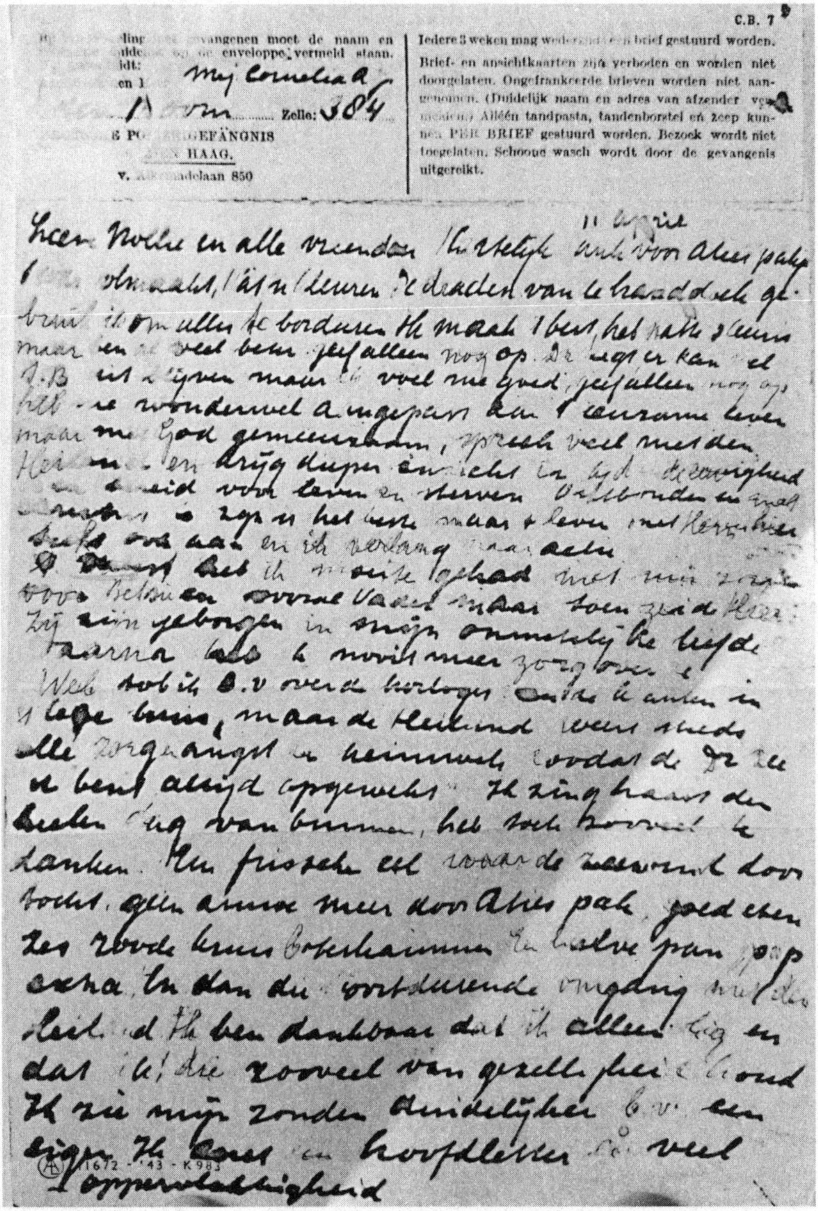

C.B. 7

[illegible] gevangenen moet de naam en [illegible] op de enveloppe vermeld staan. [illegible]idt: [illegible] en [illegible] Mej Cornelia A. Boom Zelle: 384

[illegible] POLIZEIGEFÄNGNIS [illegible] HAAG. v. [illegible]adelaan 850

Iedere 3 weken mag wederzijds een brief gestuurd worden.

Brief- en ansichtkaarten zijn verboden en worden niet doorgelaten. Ongefrankeerde brieven worden niet aangenomen. (Duidelijk naam en adres van afzender vermelden.) Alléén tandpasta, tandenborstel en zeep kunnen PER BRIEF gestuurd worden. Bezoek wordt niet toegelaten. Schoone wasch wordt door de gevangenis uitgereikt.

11 April

Lieve Nollie en alle vrienden Hartelijk dank voor alles pakje [illegible] De draden van de handdoek gebruik ik om alles te borduren. Ik maak 't best, [illegible] Ik ben wonderwel aangepast aan 't eenzame leven maar met God gemeenschap, spreek veel met den Heiland en krijg dieper inzicht in tijd en eeuwigheid [illegible] bereid voor leven en sterven. Verbonden in gebed [illegible]

[illegible] Zij zijn geborgen in mijn onmetelijke liefde [illegible] Ik zing haast den heelen dag van binnen, heb toch zooveel te danken. Een frissche cel waar de [illegible] geen armoe meer door Alles pak [illegible] en dan die voortdurende omgang met den Heiland. Ik ben dankbaar dat ik alleen lig en dat ik [illegible] zooveel van gezelschap [illegible] Ik zie mijn zonden duidelijker b.v. een eigen [illegible] hoofdletter [illegible] veel oppervlakkigheid

(A) 1672 - '43 - K983

Corrie's letter to Nollie on April 11, 1944.

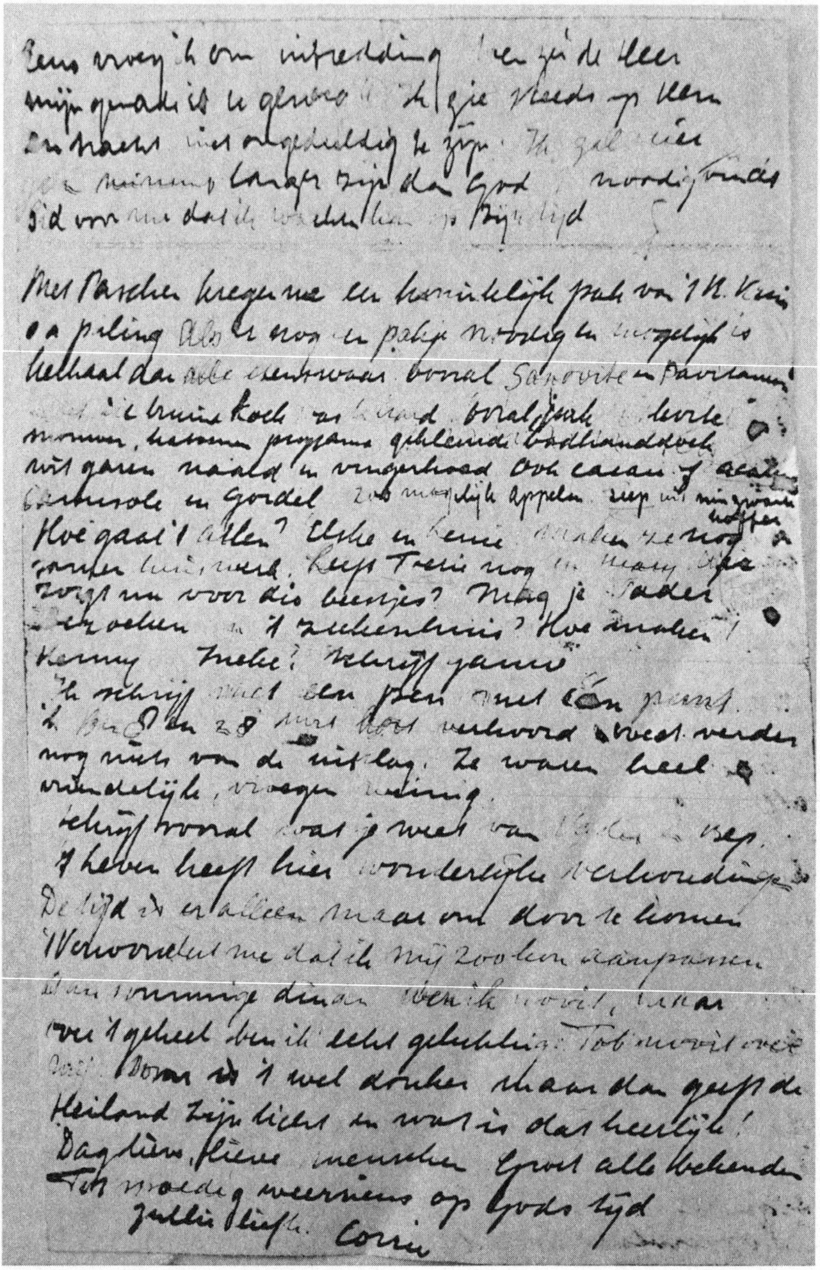

Eens vroeg ik om uitredding [illegible] de Heer
mij gemaakt is te genoeg [illegible] Ik zie steeds op Hem
en tracht niet ongeduldig te zijn. Ik zal niet
een minuut langer zijn dan God [illegible] noodig vindt
Bid voor me dat ik wachten kan op Zijn tijd

Met Paschen kregen we een heerlijk pak van 't N. Kruis
[illegible] piling. Als er nog een pakje noodig en mogelijk is
herhaal dan alle eetwaar vooral Sanovite en Davitamon
[illegible] die bruine koek [illegible] vooral [illegible] korte
mouwen, katoenen pyjama, gebloemde badhanddoek
wit garen, naald en vingerhoed. Ook cacao of [illegible]
[illegible] en Gordel. Zoo mogelijk appelen, zeep [illegible]
Hoe gaat 't allen? Elske en Kennie [illegible] ze nog
[illegible] werk. Heeft Tresie nog [illegible]
Zorgt nu voor die beestjes? Mag je Vader
bezoeken in 't ziekenhuis? Hoe maken 't
Kenny [illegible]? Schrijf gauw
Ik schrijf met een pen met een punt.
'k Ben den 28 Maart [illegible] verhoord. Weet verder
nog niets van de uitslag. Ze waren heel
vriendelijk, vroegen [illegible].
Schrijf vooral wat je weet van [illegible] en Bep.
't Leven heeft hier wonderlijke verhoudingen.
De tijd is er alleen maar om door te komen.
'T Verwondert me dat ik mij zoo kon aanpassen
aan sommige dingen. Went ik nooit, maar
over 't geheel ben ik echt gelukkig. Tob nooit over
ons. Soms is 't wel donker maar dan geeft de
Heiland zijn licht en wat is dat heerlijk!
Dag lieve, lieve menschen. Groet alle bekenden.
Tot weerziens op Gods tijd
Jullie liefh. Corrie

Corrie's letter to Nollie (continued).

Bij briefwisseling met gevangenen moet de naam en
voornaam duidelijk op de enveloppe vermeld staan.
Het adres luidt:
Aan Mevr./den Heer

E ten Boom   Zelle: 314.

DEUTSCHE POLIZEIGEFÄNGNIS
DEN HAAG.
v. Alkemadelaan 850

11-4-'44

Lieve Cocky,   [Wijf vraag van mij bidden]

Betsie's letter to her niece Cocky on April 11, 1944.

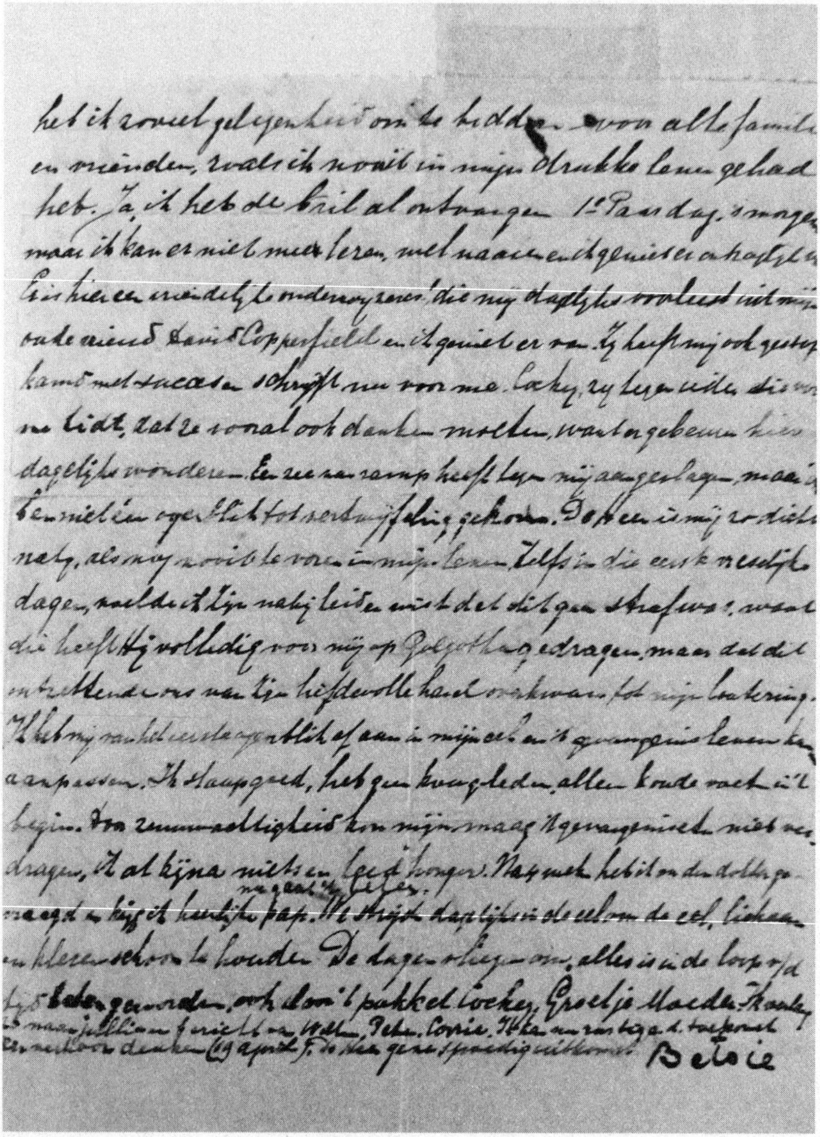

heb ik zoveel gelegenheid om te bidden voor alle familie
en vrienden, zoals ik nooit in mijn drukke leven gehad
heb. Ja, ik heb de bril al ontvangen 1e Paasdag 's morgens
maar ik kan er niet meer lezen, wel naaien en ik geniet er [illegible]
Er is hier een vriendelijk [illegible] die mij dagelijks voorleest uit mijn
oude vriend David Copperfield en ik geniet er van. Zij heeft mij ook [illegible]
kamt met succes en schrijft nu voor me. Cocky, zij lezen ieder die [illegible]
me lijdt, dat ze zoveel ook danken moeten, want er gebeuren hier
dagelijks wonderen. Een zee van ramp heeft tegen mij aangeslagen, maar ik
ben niet één ogenblik tot vertwijfeling gekomen. De Heer is mij zo dicht
nabij, als nooit te voren in mijn leven. Zelfs in die eerste vreselijke
dagen, voelde ik Zijn nabijheid en wist dat dit geen strafweg was, want
die heeft Hij volledig voor mij op Golgotha gedragen, maar dat dit
ontzettende uit Zijn liefdevolle hand voortkwam, tot mijn loutering.
'k Heb mij van het eerste ogenblik af aan in mijn cel en 't gevangenisleven kunnen
aanpassen. Ik slaap goed, heb geen [illegible], alleen koude voeten in 't
begin. Door zenuwachtigheid kon mijn maag 't gevangenisbrood niet ver-
dragen, at bijna niets en leed honger. Na 4 week heb ik om den dokter ge-
na gaat 't beter
vraagd en krijg ik heerlijke pap. We krijgen dagelijks de gelegenheid om de cel, lichaam
en kleren schoon te houden. De dagen vliegen om, alles is in de loop v/d
tijd beter geworden, ook door 't pakket Cocky. Groetjes Moeder. Ik [illegible]
[illegible] maar jullie [illegible] Willem, Peter, Corrie. Ik [illegible]
[illegible] (19) april [illegible] de Heer geve spoedig uitkomst. Betsie

Betsie's letter to Cocky (continued).

itary confinement. No family or friends. No cake. No gifts. No singing. Just four gray walls and silence.

She'd have a party by herself, Corrie decided. She began singing a children's song, "Bride of the Haarlem Tree," but almost immediately someone pounded on her door.

"Quiet in there! Solitary prisoners are to keep silent!"

For Corrie, the restriction was especially painful; for fifty years she had enjoyed noise, singing, and laughter at the Beje. Today, though, her birthday would pass in silence. Two days later, however, she experienced the best luxury she'd had since her arrest: a shower. The room was large, but, as always, silence was observed. Still, Corrie reveled in just seeing other faces.

"The shower . . . was glorious," she remembered, "warm clean water over my festering skin, streams of water through my matted hair. I went back to my cell with a new resolve: the next time I was permitted a shower I would take with me three of my Gospels. Solitary was teaching me that it was not possible to be rich alone."

A week later Corrie received her second special treat: time outside. It had been nine weeks since she enjoyed fresh air and sunshine, and she made the most of it. When the guard opened the gate, Corrie strolled through, absorbing colors as fast as she could—red flowering shrubs, bright primroses, the brilliant blue sky.

As she strolled along her walk, though, an oblong pit at the end of the garden caught her eye. She continued toward it and realized it was a freshly dug grave. Her heart sank. Beyond the pit a high stone wall with shards of glass across the top loomed ominously. She peered around and noticed that this wall encircled the garden.

Then she smelled it. Burned bones. She remembered that Kik had said Scheveningen had three crematoria, and the stench suddenly overwhelmed her. Seconds later she heard beyond the wall the blistering rattle of a machine gun.

It all became clear. Scheveningen was a city of the condemned and the dead.

Almost immediately, though, she remembered Genesis 5:24: "And Enoch walked with God." She was not alone after all; God was with her. Ignoring the misery around her, she continued on the walk, again enjoying the shrubs, flowers, and sky. What she was absorbing around her, Corrie thought, was a metaphor: the earth was like the prison garden, and heaven was the free outdoors, full of light and life.

❋ ❋ ❋

The last days of April brought better fortunes for the ten Booms. Willem, Nollie, and Flip had been released from Scheveningen, and Peter, Corrie, and Betsie were due to start hearings with the officer who could free them.

One morning a guard escorted Peter to a small office where a German in full uniform awaited. His name was Lieutenant Hans Rahms, the prison's *Sachbearbeiter* (judge). Peter understood the man's power immediately: Rahms determined whether prisoners were released or sent to concentration camps.

"He might have been part of an ad in an American magazine," Peter wrote later. "He was nice looking, with regular features and blond hair. His strongly molded hands, his broad shoulders and massive build might easily have put him into the category of an athlete."

"Sit down, won't you?" Rahms asked in a deep, pleasant voice.

He asked Peter to recount what had happened the night of his arrest and Peter explained that he had gone for a simple visit to see his grandfather. Once inside the Beje, however, a group of Gestapo men arrested him and took him to prison.

Rahms held Peter's gaze, seemingly looking into his soul. "Did you know that your grandfather was harboring Jews in his home?"

Peter prayed for wisdom. This was going to be tricky.

"Well, I knew that my grandfather always had an open door for anybody who was in need. He helped anyone, whether it was a German or a Dutchman, a Nazi or a Jew, simply because he counted this as his duty as a Christian."

"Are you a Christian, too?"

"Yes sir, I am."

Rahms shook his head. "I can't understand it. I can't figure out what advantage there is to your being what you call a 'Christian.' I'll admit that you are good people. Many of you have sacrificed much for others. But just look at the results of it. In the end, you suffer for all of your work. Take, for instance, what has happened to your family. Your grandfather, your mother, as well as your aunts, have all been imprisoned. Do you still feel that it really pays to be a Christian?"

Peter smiled. The hearing was supposed to be about his culpability in assisting the hiding of Jews, but before him now was the witnessing opportunity of a lifetime.

"We do not expect to have an easy life here on earth," he told Rahms. "God has never said anywhere in the Bible that everything would be easy or go smoothly. Trouble serves only to prove and test us, strengthening us for what lies ahead. We are looking forward to the day when Jesus Christ will come again. He has promised to set up his kingdom. . . . In the meantime, our hearts have the peace which He supplies, and we can be happy even in times of suffering and persecution, because we have the assurance of salvation that comes with believing and accepting Christ as our personal Savior."

Rahms looked perplexed. This was apparently the first time he'd actually heard the Gospel, and he had many questions. Back and forth they went over what the Christian believed and why.

Hours passed.

"Do you really, really believe that Christ will come again?" Rahms asked.

"Yes sir, I certainly do!"

"Do you think that He will come during my lifetime?"

"I can't answer that for certain. It says in the Bible that we can't know the hour or the day; but it has also prophesied many things which we can see being fulfilled as history is being made today. . . . But, if he did come, would you be ready?"

The question caught Rahms off guard and with a nervous gesture of his hands he changed the subject.

Peter and the German had been going at it so long that a guard had to interrupt to bring in the lieutenant's lunch.

Rahms motioned to Peter. "Bring another portion for the prisoner."

Peter cherished the hearty food and they made small talk while Rahms picked at his plate.

"I don't seem to feel very hungry. . . . Would you like to finish what I have left?"

Peter couldn't believe his good fortune. A prisoner on starvation rations, and now before him were two nutritious and delicious meals. As Peter devoured both plates, Rahms turned to his typewriter and began a report. "My time for an interview is almost over," he said. "Quickly dictate to me your story."

Peter finished off the string beans and potatoes and recited his innocent story once again. Rahms typed it up exactly as Peter described, without a single challenge.

That afternoon Peter was released from Scheveningen prison.

NEXT UP FOR Lieutenant Rahms were the ten Boom sisters, starting with Corrie. For two months she had dreaded a hearing because an intense interrogation would lead directly to details about her hiding of Jews and divers, ration cards, and countless names of underground workers.

On a cold and drizzly morning she dressed and followed a guard down long corridors to the inner gate of the prison. Here another guard led her along a row of small rooms built along the outer wall, and into an office.

Behind a desk sat a young but distinguished officer.

"I am Lieutenant Rahms." He pulled out a chair for Corrie and closed the door. "Does it seem cold to you here? Just a minute and I'll have a fire going. You are ill, and we must not let you take cold."

Rahms reached into a small coal scuttle with his bare hands and shuttled several pieces into a potbellied stove. "I hope we won't have many more days this spring as cold as this one."

Suspecting the German's kindness might be a trap, Corrie prayed that God would guard her lips.

Instead of diving into the interrogation, though, Rahms seemed to want small talk, a politeness perhaps before getting to the business at hand. For a while they talked about flowers, and how Rahms had planted tulips against the prison wall. "The best I've ever grown," he said. "At home we always have Dutch bulbs."

Everything about this man appeared gentle and honest, but Corrie kept worrying that it was all a psychological ploy.

"Tell me, now," he said, "exactly what you have done. It is possible that I may be able to do something for you, perhaps a great deal. But then you must not hide anything from me."

Rahms probed about her involvement with the Resistance, and what role the Beje had. After a few minutes Corrie realized that the Gestapo believed the Beje was headquarters for raids on ration offices. For almost an hour the lieutenant asked pointed questions about it, but Corrie's ignorance of details seemed to convince him of her innocence.

"Your other activities, Miss ten Boom. What would you like to tell me about them?"

"Other activities? Oh, you mean—you want to know about my church for mentally retarded people!"

Before Rahms could answer Corrie plunged into her work with Haarlem's handicapped.

"Isn't that a waste of time?" he asked. "It certainly is of much greater importance to convert a normal person than a feeble-minded one."

Rahms had been indoctrinated with the National-Socialist philosophy that the elderly, weak, and handicapped were to be set aside and done away with and Corrie saw an opening.

"May I tell you the truth, Lieutenant Rahms?"

"This hearing, Miss ten Boom, is predicated on the assumption that you will do me that honor."

Corrie swallowed and plunged ahead. "The Lord Jesus has other than human standards. The Bible reveals Him as one who has great love and mercy for all the lost and despised, for all who are small and weak and poor. It is possible that in His sight a mentally deficient person is of greater worth than you or I. Every human soul is valuable to Him."

Rahms sat silently for a minute, reflecting, and then stood.

"That will do for today."

The following morning Rahms came by Corrie's cell and escorted her not to his office, but to the garden. "You get far too little sunshine," he said. "We can go on with the examination here as well as inside."

Corrie, touched by his kindness, watched as Rahms leaned against a wall, pensive.

"I did not sleep all night," he said, "but thought constantly of what you told me about Jesus. Tell me more about Him."

The tables had turned, Corrie thought. Gone was the German judge who had godlike authority to set people free or send them to the gallows. Before her now was a man—just an ordinary man—who for the first time was confronted by his own spiritual barrenness.

"Jesus Christ is a Light," she said, "come into the world in order that everyone who believes in Him need not remain in darkness. Is there darkness in your life?"

Rahms nodded. "There is great darkness in my life. When I go to bed at night I dare not think of the moment that I must awaken in the morning. When I awaken, I dread the day. I hate my work. I have a wife and children in Bremen, but do not even know if they are alive. Who knows, a bomb may have shattered them last night."

"There is One who has them always in his sight, Lieutenant Rahms. Jesus is the Light the Bible shows to me, the Light that can shine even in such darkness as yours."

Rahms mumbled it so low Corrie could barely hear: "What can you know of darkness like mine. . . ."

They went back to Corrie's cell and Rahms asked one more question. "I cannot understand how you can believe that there is a God, for if there is, why should He permit you, a brave woman, to be imprisoned?"

"God never makes a mistake," Corrie replied. "There is much that we shall not understand until later. But this is not a problem to me. It is God's will that I should for a time be alone with Him."

A day or so later Rahms called Corrie to yet another hearing, this one again in his office. To her surprise, he had not one question about her involvement with hiding Jews or assisting the underground. Instead, he wanted to know about her childhood, her parents, and her aunts.

She told him that her father had died in Scheveningen and Rahms was incensed; the file he had said nothing of it. Corrie asked why she was in solitary confinement and he read it back to her: "Prisoner's condition contagious to others in cell."

"But I'm not contagious now! I've been better for weeks and weeks, and my own sister is so close. Lieutenant Rahms, if I could only see Betsie! If I could just talk to her for a few minutes."

Rahms weighed her request and Corrie could see compassion and anguish in his eyes. "Miss ten Boom, it is possible that I appear to you a powerful person. I wear a uniform. I have a certain authority over those under me. But I am in prison, dear lady from Haarlem, a prison stronger than this one."

Later in the week Rahms called Corrie for one more hearing, again to talk about spiritual matters. He struggled with cognitive dissonance over why Christians suffer. "How can you believe in God?" he asked. "What kind of a God would have let that old man die here in Scheveningen?"

Corrie remembered what her father had said about tough questions—"Some knowledge is too heavy . . . you cannot bear it . . . your Father will carry it until you are able"—but before she could tell him, a guard came in.

Rahms stood.

"Prisoner ten Boom has completed her hearings," he told the guard, "and will return to her cell."

As Corrie slipped past Rahms for the door, he said under his breath: "Walk slowly in Corridor F."

Chapter 17

BONES

CORRIE FOLLOWED THE GUARD AND when they turned down Corridor F, they came upon Betsie's cell. Among several women, Betsie stood facing away from the hallway, but Corrie saw her and that was enough.

A few days later Lieutenant Rahms called for Betsie. Since she was not active in the underground, he went back to his spiritual curiosity, asking about her Christian faith. They talked for a while and then Betsie said, "Mr. Rahms, it is important to talk about Jesus but it is more important to talk with Him. Would you mind if I prayed with you?"

Rahms nodded and bowed his head.

Four more times he called her to his office and each time they closed in prayer. Independently, Peter, Corrie, and Betsie saw it: God was working on this man's heart. And for Rahms, he couldn't get away. He had to interrogate everyone at Scheveningen, and the ten Booms kept God before him. With each interview he became more haunted, perplexed, and comforted by what they said.

Perhaps there was something to what they believed.

✳✳✳

One morning Rahms called Corrie to his office again. On his desk lay a number of papers—*her* papers. They included ration cards and her notes for underground activities that contained the names and addresses of friends, Jews, and Resistance workers. The Gestapo had found them during a search of the Beje and apparently had just given them to Rahms.

"Can you explain these pages?" Rahms asked.

Corrie's heart raced. Aside from incriminating her for several capital crimes, every name on that list was in danger. If the Gestapo hunted them down, underground workers would be arrested and transported to concentration camps or shot. Jews named in the papers would be rounded up for shipment to a death camp. But what could she tell the lieutenant—that those were not her notes? No, this was the end. For her, for everyone.

"No, I can't."

Rahms said nothing and stared at the papers for several moments.

Then he crouched forward, gathered them into a pile, opened the stove door, and tossed them into the fire.

Corrie was speechless. Rahms had spared her life, and the lives of countless others. As she watched the flames consume her Gestapo trespasses and sins, Colossians 2:14 came to mind: "Blotting out the handwriting of ordinances that was against us, which was contrary to us, and took it out of the way, nailing it to the cross."

ON MAY 3 Corrie received a letter from Nollie*:

"How happy we were with your letter. When I heard you were alone, I was so upset. Darling, now I have to tell you something

---

* Nollie had been released from Scheveningen on April 20.

very sad. Be strong. On the 10th of March,* our dear father went to Heaven. He survived only 9 days. He passed away in Loos- duinen. Yesterday I fetched his belongings from Scheveningen. I know the Lord will help you bear this."

Corrie burst into tears. It was not that his death was unex- pected, but the loss of the man who had been the ten Boom spiritual anchor for almost sixty years broke her heart. Corrie pressed the emergency bell and a minute later a humane guard named Mopje appeared.

"Please stay with me a few minutes," Corrie pleaded. "I have just received word that my father has passed away. Please do not leave me."

Mopje told her to wait and came back with a sedative, which Corrie declined. Sitting next to Corrie, Mopje didn't know what to say and remained silent. After a few minutes she reminded Corrie that the ten Booms were in prison for what they had done.

"You really shouldn't cry," she added. "You should be happy that your father lived so long. My father was only fifty-six when he died."

Mopje didn't provide quite the comfort Corrie longed for, but she did have a point: Corrie should be grateful for the many years she had spent with her father.

The next day Corrie wrote a letter to Nollie, expressing her emotions about the loss.

"His death has left a great void in my life," she wrote. "For the love and help I gave to him, the Lord will provide another outlet. What I received from him cannot be replaced. But what a privilege it is that we have enjoyed him, consciously and in- tensely, for so many years! I was upset for a few days, but that is

---

* Nollie is unaware at this point that their father had died on March 9 rather than March 10.

past. . . . How good the Savior is to me! He not only helps carry my burden; He carries me also."

NOT LONG THEREAFTER Betsie heard the news that Willem, Flip, and Peter had been released and she penned her own letter to Nollie:

"Everything is fine with me," she told her sister. "My soul is very peaceful."

She informed Nollie about her hearings with Lieutenant Rahms, adding: "It was not an interrogation but a wonderful witnessing, telling the motives for our acts. Because of this, I could constantly witness of the love and the redemption of our Savior, which I always do in the cell.

"I heard that Peter and Willem are free and that Father was liberated on March the 10th. . . . I am longing so much for you, for freedom, and for work. I sleep as I have never slept in my life. . . . The friendship in the cell is such that one by one I have invited my cell mates to come to our house."

※ ※ ※

Meanwhile in Amersfoort, Hans Poley adjusted to prison life. His head had been shaved and he lived in one of ten barracks, each with about six hundred men—all on starvation rations. Each morning half of the inmates would be marched to town for forced labor in a factory, the rest remaining in the camp for cleaning or working in the repair shop.

Three things, however, Hans found especially difficult. The first was an SS deputy commander named Kotälla, who called roll each morning. Known as the "executioner of Amersfoort," he regularly kicked prisoners in the groin, and as he strolled through the ranks, he would shout and intimidate as much as possible.

"Häftlinge, Die Augen, links!" (Prisoners, eyes left!)
"Augen gerade, aus!" (Eyes front!)
"Abzählen!" (Count!)

The odors, too, were unbearable. Each morning the stench of laundry cooking on the stove—not just to clean it, but to kill lice—filled the air. On Fridays the Red Cross delivered food, and prisoners either ate too much, or too fast. Each Saturday morning, then, the latrines reeked from vomit and feces.

Most disturbing of all, though, was the piercing sound at dawn: firing squads.

Yet, amidst the terror and deprivation, the camp received an unusual blessing from a woman the prisoners called the "Angel of Amersfoort." Mrs. Loes van Overeem was the area's Red Cross commander and she provided the food packages each Friday. She also supervised the distribution so that guards wouldn't confiscate anything. More than that, by browbeating, threats, or blackmail, she reached a compromise with the SS commandant. She would regularly inspect the camp for hygiene and have access to all prisoners, including those in sick bay. While she couldn't prevent the executions or routine beatings, her efforts warded off much of the violence and starvation.

※ ※ ※

Near the end of May a guard opened Corrie's cell door and admitted Lieutenant Rahms. Corrie wanted to greet him with a pleasant smile and word, but Rahms was all business.

"You will come to my office. The notary has come."

"Notary?"

"For the reading of your father's will. It's the law—family present when a will is opened."

Corrie followed Rahms down the corridor, perplexed at the comical notion that the Nazis gave one whit as to what Dutch

law said about wills. She wasn't familiar with such a procedure, and her father had never spoken of it. And what was with
Rahms's stiff upper lip?

The guard walked with them to the courtyard and then left in
another direction. Rahms led Corrie into the brilliant sunlight,
and then four huts down he opened a door.

Corrie's heart swelled. Standing before her were Willem,
Tine, Betsie, Nollie, and Flip.

Willem reached her first and clutched her tightly. "Corrie!
Corrie! Baby sister!"

It had been fifty years since he had called her that. Nollie and
Betsie then joined the embrace, and Corrie was struck by Willem's appearance: his face was gaunt, yellow, and haunted. Two
of the eight men in his cell, she found out, had died of jaundice,
and her brother didn't look far off.

Betsie's pale face and thin body, too, were disturbing.

Corrie glanced back at Rahms, who seemed to be having his
own private moment staring down at an unlit stove. Again she
was struck by his kindness. The Gestapo never would have allowed such a reunion, and Rahms's serious demeanor in fetching
her seemed to be for the benefit of the guard.

Nonchalantly, Nollie pressed a small Bible into Corrie's hand.
It was enclosed in a small pouch that had a string so that it could
be hung around the neck. Quickly, Corrie slipped it over her
head and let it fall down her back under her blouse.

Willem came close and explained that the refugees trapped
in the Angels' Den had been rescued by loyal Dutch policemen.
He added that the underground had found new hiding places for
the Jews, and Corrie asked: "And now? They're all right now?"

Willem paused to meet her eyes. "They're all right, Corrie—
all except Mary." Mary van Itallie, he explained, had been arrested while walking down the street one day.

Lieutenant Rahms then stepped forward. "The time is up."

A notary joined them and began reading Opa's will. The only significant asset he owned was the Beje, which he left to Corrie and Betsie. Any money derived from the sale of the watch business or house, it read, would be distributed as Corrie and Betsie determined. When the notary finished, the room fell silent and Willem began to pray.

"Lord Jesus, we praise You for these moments together under the protection of this good man. How can we thank him? We have no power to do him any service. Lord, allow us to share this inheritance from our father with him as well. Take him too, and his family, into Your constant care."

Back in her cell, Corrie summarized her emotions on a scratch pad.

"Now I really know what it means to cast my anxieties on the Lord when I think of Father. Is there still a future for the Beje here on earth or are we going straight towards the return of Christ? Or are we going to die? How wonderful it is to know that the future is secure, to know that Heaven is awaiting us. Sometimes I have self-pity, especially at night, then my arm hurts very badly. This has to do with the pleurisy, but then I think of how much Jesus suffered for me and then I feel ashamed."

Corrie had cause for further anxiety several days later when a new head guard appeared at her door. The woman, known as "the General" by prisoners, had been head of a prison in Berlin, someone said, and then another in Oslo. Apparently she was transferred to Scheveningen—to bring "order."

The General had a tall, rigidly erect posture, with cold and piercing eyes in a hard and cruel face. Corrie thought this woman was the most evil-looking person she had ever seen.

Corrie followed the normal protocol—jumping up and standing at attention—while the General inspected her cell. Without a word the woman ripped off Corrie's makeshift lampshade, and then moved on to the small canisters that Corrie had received in a care package from home. One by one the General turned them upside down—apparently looking for contraband—spilling out vitamins, cookies, and sandwich spread. Fearful of the woman's wrath, Corrie attended to the jar of apple butter herself, turning it over as well.

Next the General inspected Corrie's bed. She pulled off the covers, then looked under the mattress but, surprisingly, missed the Gospel tracts that Corrie had tucked away. Then, still without a word, the General turned on her heels and left.

Over ensuing days the General said little, except to issue sharp, biting commands. In a cell not far from hers, Corrie heard the General scold an elderly woman for not jumping to attention when she arrived.

"Whether there was anything good," Corrie recalled, "anything human, in her character would always remain a mystery to me."

✳✳✳

"Get your things together!" someone shouted one morning. "Get ready to evacuate!"

Corrie's spirits lifted. *Evacuate?* Were the Allies close, perhaps even about to liberate the prison? It was June 6, after all, and perhaps an American or British division had crossed into Holland. Corrie had no way of knowing about the D-Day landings, but the frantic demeanor of the guards suggested that the Germans had been given an emergency order.

She packed her few possessions and waited on her cot. An hour went by. Then two. Three. Not until the late afternoon did a sudden ruckus reveal it was time. Cell doors banged open and the guards went to work.

"Everybody out! *Schnell!* All out! No talking!"

Someone opened her door and Corrie stepped into the corridor and, for the first time, saw the women from cells around her.

"In-va-sion," everyone silently mouthed.

The guards hustled the prisoners into ranks of five, and then began herding the group onto awaiting buses and vans. Corrie boarded the third bus and hoped to find Betsie, but to no avail. Inside the bus the seats had been removed, forcing everyone to stand, and the windows had been painted over so no one could see out. Whispers swept across the coach that they were headed to Germany.

After an hour or so the convoy of transports arrived at their destination: a train station outside The Hague. Everyone deboarded and fell into ranks. Across the platform Corrie finally saw Betsie but couldn't get her attention. The prisoners remained in formation for hours, and when the train arrived it was well after dark.

While the group was being funneled onto railcars, Corrie held back so that she could find and board with Betsie. She did, they found seats together, and as the locomotive pulled out they held hands and wept. Bad as everything was, though, Corrie was grateful to be reunited with the person who had been her lifelong soulmate.

For twelve hours Corrie sat with her sister. At four a.m. the train finally stopped in Vught, a town in southern Holland some sixty miles inland from The Hague. There seemed to be a bit of chaos, with not enough guards to handle the crowd. In the confusion, several prisoners escaped into the darkness.

The Germans began shouting, cursing, and shoving as they disembarked the women and herded them toward their new destination. Corrie later recorded what she saw and experienced:

"Ahead of us is a forest with many, many soldiers with helmets and machine guns all aimed at us prisoners. . . . Many floodlights are aimed at us and shine on the trees, helmets, and guns—it all seems like a gruesome movie. After waiting a long time, we are ordered to start walking in rows of five. . . . We are being hurried on through darkness. Swearing, raging, and yelling is all we hear. One soldier kicks several women in their backs because they try to avoid a big puddle. Oh, night of terror. . . ."

And terror it was. Unlike Scheveningen, an existing Dutch prison, Vught was a concentration camp built specifically for political prisoners and Jews.

The guards marched all one hundred fifty women to a large hall just outside the camp where they waited another twelve hours—now twenty-four hours since any prisoner had eaten or slept—and soldiers called them in groups of twenty to shower. The Germans stared at the naked bodies as the women undressed, and Corrie and Betsie cringed.

"Oh Lord, not that."

After a few groups had gone through the soldiers realized there were not enough prisoner gowns and they halted the procedure. Just then a young Jewish girl came up to Corrie.

"Can you comfort me? I am so frightened."

Corrie did, and then Betsie prayed for her.

Soldiers then led everyone to Barrack 4, outside the concentration camp, but the rules and activities matched those inside the camp. Roll call began at five a.m. the next morning, and when Corrie heard the shrill voice barking out orders, she shuddered.

The General.

Even more so than at Scheveningen, the General ruled here with an iron fist. With her cruel face and merciless punishments, she kept prisoners in a constant state of fear. To add to their misery, the General kept them at attention for hours. During one morning assembly a pregnant woman collapsed, hitting her head on a bench as she fell to the ground. The General scarcely noticed and continued reading off names.

AFTER NINE DAYS in Barrack 4, Corrie, Betsie, and a dozen others were summoned forward during roll call. The General gave them some forms and told them to report to the administration barrack in three hours.

"You're free!" a worker in the mess hall told them at breakfast. "Those pink forms mean release!"

Corrie and Betsie couldn't believe it. *Free?*

The administration barrack, they found out at nine, was a labyrinth of procedures: stamping of forms, shuttling from office to office, questioning, and fingerprinting. Hours it took, and Corrie noticed that the number of prisoners in their group had reached forty or fifty. They went into another office where prisoner valuables were returned—Corrie's Alpina watch and her mother's ring—and then the group marched outside, through circular rows of barbed wire, and into the camp. At a registration desk a clerk told them to give up the possessions they had just received.

They were not being set free, Corrie realized; they were becoming documented prisoners in the camp. Once again soldiers brought them together and began marching everyone down a street lined with barracks. Corrie clutched Betsie's arm as the group made their way to a featureless gray building. Their new home.

Inside it was much like the barrack they had stayed in outside the camp—one large room with tables and benches—but this one also had bunk beds. No one was allowed to sit, though, as yet another attendant began checking everyone's papers.

Corrie had had enough standing for one day. "Betsie, how long will it take?"

"Perhaps a long, long time. Perhaps many years. But what better way could there be to spend our lives?"

Corrie looked at her sister. "Whatever are you talking about?"

"These young women. That girl back at the barracks. Corrie, if people can be taught to hate, they can be taught to love! We must find the way, you and I, no matter how long it takes."

Corrie could only shake her head. This sister of hers—perhaps really an angel—wore altruism as a necklace. Betsie, she realized, had taken the place of their father as her spiritual leader and guide.

With Betsie's vision and direction, the ten Boom camp ministry officially began. Corrie recognized the responsibility, recording in a note: "We now had association with many people. We would have to share in their grief, but we would also be privileged to help and encourage them."

Because the prisoners had nothing to do all day, they grumbled, bickered, and criticized. Betsie had the cure: an encouragement society.

"Whoever wishes to become a member," she told Corrie, "must promise to do her utmost not to grumble or complain, or speak ill of anyone, but only to speak encouragingly to others. Next, she must resolve to obey all orders of the corridor attendants."

Before long they had a small group, and the women prayed that the atmosphere in the barrack would improve.

A few days later a physician came by to examine prisoners. He had a surprising diagnosis for Corrie: "You have tuberculosis; you must stay abed from now on."

What Corrie didn't know was that the designation often meant a one-way ticket to the gas chambers.

Chapter 18

MRS. HENDRIKS

SINCE NAZI DOCTRINE DESPISED the sick and weak, many concentration camps used tuberculosis as an excuse for execution. Whether Vught observed the penalty remained to be seen.

After roll call the next morning Corrie went to see the General. Given the doctor's orders, she asked if she might lie close to a window.

"You are going to work today," the General snapped, "and work hard, then your tuberculosis will disappear."

Corrie didn't feel like she had tuberculosis, but the General's callous answer stung. The hatred of so many of the SS guards was inexplicable and beyond the pale. Yet, while it seemed the Nazi antagonism could not be worse, someone was working behind the scenes to have her freed.

Lieutenant Rahms.

On June 20 Nollie sent an encouraging letter to Corrie: "After we were together in Scheveningen, the notary and a few others went to see the gentlemen who are now in charge of your case, and the result was that the house and the shop were released."

More importantly, Nollie wrote, Rahms had called her on June 9 to notify the family that he was still working on Corrie's case, and that he had sent a letter to higher authorities that would result in her being freed. A few days later he called again to tell

Nollie that he was unable to locate Corrie's caseworker, but he reiterated that his letter requesting release had been mailed.

Nollie reminded her sister that providence might be at work. "You wrote once, 'I won't stay here one moment longer than God wants me to.' I think that maybe, you may still be a blessing to others or, perhaps you still have to learn something yourself."

Nollie was right, Corrie knew, but it was refreshing to know that Lieutenant Rahms was working on her freedom, and probably Betsie's as well.

In the meantime, Corrie and Betsie did their best to enjoy the small things—a walk together between the barbed wire, a piece of bread given by a fellow prisoner, a brilliant sky. One Sunday, though, they received a pleasant surprise when a girl came up to them and invited them to a worship service. The "church," a small plot of grass between barracks, inspired the ten Booms about worshipping with fellow believers.

The service started as one woman read a passage from the Bible, and then another came up to read a sermon. Singing followed, and after that one of the leaders asked Corrie if she would close them in thanksgiving.

"As I prayed," Corrie remembered later, "a great joy filled my heart. How wonderful it was to speak to the Lord together, to give expression to our common need! Never before had I prayed as now. There was so much sorrow among these prisoners, who had had to leave husbands and children and other loved ones behind, and above whose heads still hung so dire a threat. And I spoke to One who understood, who knew us and loved us. On Him I cast all our burdens."

Corrie led the next Sunday's service, and also coordinated a discussion group for the evening.

Betsie, meanwhile, tried to keep everything in perspective. On June 30 she wrote in her diary: "Yesterday, many blessings. . . . Went to doctor and dentist. Jan gave me butter and cheese. Red

Cross sandwich with bacon. . . . Evening devotions. . . . Corrie is doing well at Philips.* Together we enjoy the beauties of nature, the skies, very much. The weather is cold. Just right. Every day some sunshine. We receive amazing strength for this harsh life. I am suffering much from hunger. Corrie brings me a warm meal of Philips' mash for me and I eat it while we stand at roll call."

Two weeks later Corrie sent a letter to Nollie and other family members, expressing strength and joy:

"Bep and I are well. Life is heavy, but healthy. . . . Please don't find it terrible that we are here. We can accept it ourselves. We are in God's training school and learn much. It is ten times better than being in a prison cell. Bep is aging fast, but fights her way courageously. . . . We are so happy to be together, especially when we grieve over Father. My lungs are healed. Write us how the children are going on. . . .

"We long much for freedom, but are unusually strengthened. . . . At the roll call often a skylark comes and sings in the sky above our heads, so we try to lift up our hearts. There is much fellowship of the saints here. . . . Great sadness we bear with God."

In another letter to everyone back home, Corrie revealed a bit of the other side: "We sometimes hear shooting in the barracks at night. We know what that means. Then we pray for the bereaved relatives, and also for those who may be next in turn. . . . Much has happened these last days. Men were called out of ranks during roll call and shot a few minutes later. . . . Mrs. Boileu works in the same factory with me. She is a splendid person, a real aristocrat. She has sacrificed everything. Her two sons have been shot to death."

Privately, Corrie was alternating between homesickness,

---

* Many Vught prisoners, including Corrie, worked at the Philips factory located inside the camp.

grieving over her father's death, hope, and joy. A few days after her letters to family she wrote in her journal:

"It's hot and the blankets are terribly itchy. I close my eyes and dream of a bed with sheets. I am walking in our house in the Beje. I stroke the railing post at the foot of the stairs. Then I look at Father's portrait and my closed eyes fill with tears. I think again of the 9 days which Father had to spend in that cell, but quickly I switch over and lose myself in thoughts of the glory of Heaven, which he is now enjoying. I am saturated with joy. We will meet again in God's time."

*** *** ***

Meanwhile in Amersfoort, Hans Poley received an unexpected assignment. In mid-July he was asked to join the *Schreibstube*, or camp administration, to maintain prisoner counts and movements. While it was monotonous work, the tracking determined the critical distribution and allocation of food and Red Cross parcels. The personal benefit was that he was given a uniform, allowed to grow his hair into a crew cut, and avoided dangerous situations. It seemed to be the safest job in the camp.

One day while tabulating numbers he intercepted a list of prisoners scheduled to be transferred to Germany for forced labor. Scanning down the names he suddenly stopped. There, included with the other prisoners who would suffer this death sentence was the last name he expected.

Poley, number 9238.

Hans hustled to the infirmary and explained his predicament to Dr. Kooistra, a physician and friend.

"Report to sick parade for doctor's check tomorrow morning," Kooistra said.

Hans understood it to mean the doctor intended to help, and

the next morning Dr. Kooistra completed a form for signature by the camp's medical chief.

It said that Hans had been diagnosed with tuberculosis.

* * *

In Germany the chaos could not have been greater. On July 20 the conspirators who had been plotting the assassination of Adolf Hitler came close to their goal, but the bomb that Wehrmacht officer Count Claus Schenk von Stauffenberg had placed in Hitler's Wolf's Lair* failed to kill the Führer. Virtually every high-ranking general or field marshal had either been involved or gave explicit or tacit approval,† but the leaders of the putsch, not surprisingly, were devout Christians. It was their duty, they felt, to do away with the evil causing the deaths of millions, and leading their country into ruin.

Among the conspirators were General Franz Halder, chief of the Army General Staff; his predecessor, General Ludwig Beck; Major General Henning von Tresckow, chief of operations for Army Group Center; Admiral Wilhelm Canaris, head of the Abwehr; Field Marshal Erwin Rommel; and von Stauffenberg, a devout Roman Catholic.

When the explosion failed to kill or even severely injure Hitler, the Gestapo began a ruthless investigation that included torturing many into confessions. By the time the wrath and vengeance ended, some five thousand German officers were either executed or had committed suicide, including twelve generals and three field marshals.

---

* The Wolf's Lair was Hitler's Eastern Front headquarters in Rastenburg, Prussia (now Ketrzyn, Poland).
† Hitler sycophants Field Marshal Wilhelm Keitel and General Alfred Jodl were the two notable exceptions.

It was Germany's last chance to save itself.

The Allies were closing in on Paris, and in the east the Wehrmacht had been steadily losing ground to the Red Army. Now, with Hitler's unchallenged control of the military, Germany was doomed.

CORRIE, MEANWHILE, SUFFERED some of the most degrading and despicable aspects of life in a concentration camp. Just three days after the Wehrmacht's ill-fated putsch, she penned an entry called "Slave Market."

"We are ordered to appear before the personnel in charge of the Philips factory prison squad. In Barrack #2 we are waiting in the hallway to learn what kind of work we will be selected to do. The younger women have already been called up. The rest are over 40 and some are even 50 or older. The Germans despise the elderly. . . .

"A group of men enter and keep us standing in the center. One of them is the *Oberkapo*, or boss. He has thick lips and the lower lip protrudes, giving his face a cruel expression. He has beaten many Jews to death. Before the war he was a professional killer and was himself sentenced to sixteen years."

Factory managers then evaluated each woman's strength for labor. The youngest women, and those appearing strongest, were more highly valued than the older, weaker prisoners.

"I feel suddenly like a slave on the slave market,"* Corrie continued. "They point at me and I am commanded to come to the front. A light shiver goes down my spine and, still, I experience this as something totally unreal. . . . This moment on the slave market I will remember for a long time."

---

* Viktor Frankl, reflecting on his time in a concentration camp, similarly wrote: "We were practically sold as slaves: the firm paid the camp authorities a fixed price per day, per prisoner."

On July 27, however, Corrie experienced something worse. In a journal entry called "Mrs. Hendriks," she wrote: "In the washroom of Barrack 42 lies a bag with sandwiches. Mrs. Hendriks prepared them this morning to give to her husband who works in the same barrack as she does. She is a delicate woman with an unusual, fine, intellectual face. She also carries a baby under her heart, her first one.

"Last night Mr. Hendriks was shot to death."

Chapter 19

SUMMARY JUSTICE

AS THE SUMMER ROLLED ON, Corrie and Betsie adapted to working as slave laborers. The Philips factory—where prisoners sorted screws or assembled parts—was the principal destination for most women, while others were given chores such as sewing. Yet, regardless of work location, danger was ever present. On July 28 Betsie wrote in her diary that Corrie had been caught earlier in the week talking to a nonprisoner laborer, an activity strictly forbidden. A derogatory note was put in her prison file and the sisters worried that Corrie would be sent to the Bunker. The next day Corrie was called to the administrative office, but fortunately she received only a warning.

Betsie also noted that her entire barrack had to join the prisoners next door, in Barrack 23B. With one hundred sixty women crammed into one room, the atmosphere was suffocating. Yet, despite the hardship, she could write: "We are continually protected by the most extraordinary Providence so that we can hold out in spite of the hard life."

On most days Corrie would be sent to the Philips factory, while Betsie typically worked in the sewing room, mending a hundred shirts and undershirts a day. The factory, located in another barrack inside the camp, had been arranged with work tables and benches from one end to the other. On the tables lay thousands of small radio parts, each prisoner being given an individual task.

Her first day on the job, Corrie measured small glass rods and arranged them in piles according to length. Tedious and mind-numbing work, but not backbreaking.

For now, at least, Corrie and Betsie had safe, easy jobs, and they settled into a daily routine.

Amsterdam

In the Dutch capital the Gestapo continued to round up Jews who had thus far escaped capture. On August 4 a large sedan parked in front of 263 Prinsengracht, the location of the annex in which the Frank family was hiding. An SS officer, along with several Dutch members of the Security Police, went inside and arrested eight Jews, including Otto and Edith Frank and their daughters, Margot and Anne.

All were sent to concentration camps.

Vught

The second week of August Corrie sent a letter to Nollie to share more glimpses of life under Nazi incarceration. "There is so much bitterness and communism,* cynicism, and deep sorrow," she wrote. "The worst for us is not that which we suffer ourselves, but the suffering which we see around us." She assured her family that she and Betsie were in good spirits. While her hair had turned gray, Corrie noted, she had *gained* twenty-two pounds. But she didn't share everything.

In a personal entry the following day she summarized the be-

---

* Most camps included Russian prisoners, many of whom were Marxist adherents.

havior of the prison's prostitutes: "Pretty but nondescript faces, loud voices, saucy mannerisms. . . . They never seem afraid. When everyone is standing in utter silence, listening to the threats and raging of our superiors, they call out daring replies. They know they are safe if the guards are men. They are the last to report for roll call."

Amersfoort Prison

On August 15, while working in the administration office, Hans came across a list of prisoners to be released. He couldn't believe it, but there it was: *Poley, number 9238*. Dr. Kooistra had been right; the SS refused to allow prisoners with tuberculosis into Germany, and rather than executing Hans for relatively minor offenses, he was to be discharged.

The following day, exactly six months after his arrest, he walked out of the camp as a free man.

Vught

On Corrie's third day in the Philips factory, a prisoner-foreman named Mr. Moorman came by her bench. He had heard, he said, that Corrie had gone down the entire assembly line to learn what eventually became of her little rods. "You're the first woman worker who has ever shown any interest in what we are making here."

"I'm very interested. I'm a watchmaker."

Moorman thought for a moment and then escorted Corrie to the opposite end of the factory, where prisoners assembled re-lay switches. More intricate work, Moorman promised, but not nearly as complex as watch repair. Still, Corrie enjoyed it and the eleven-hour workday went faster.

From time to time Moorman would check on her, and he

seemed more like a big brother than a supervisor. He often counseled and encouraged distraught prisoners, and found easier jobs for the weary. His kindness meant even more when Corrie found out that his twenty-year-old son had been shot at the camp the week she and Betsie arrived. Not once did she see bitterness, sadness, or tragedy in his eyes. But he *was* a patriot.

One day he came by her bench and observed the row of relay switches she had completed. "Dear watch lady! Can you not remember for whom you are working? These radios are for their fighter planes!"

Corrie observed as he began sabotaging her work, yanking a wire from its housing or twisting a tube from an assembly. "Now solder them back wrong. And not so fast! You're over the day's quota and it's not yet noon."

Noon was a significant hour. Unlike Scheveningen, the camp here actually *had* a lunch—a tasteless gruel of wheat and peas—but it was filling and nutritious nonetheless. After eating, prisoners had a half hour to stroll around the compound to enjoy fresh air and sunshine. On most days Corrie would stretch out by the fence and try to sleep. "Sweet summer smells came in the breezes from the farms around the camp," she remembered. "Sometimes I would dream that Karel* and I were walking hand in hand along a country lane."

After almost forty years, Corrie had not forgotten her first and only love.

When work ended at six o'clock, there would be another roll call and then the prisoners would trudge back to their barracks. Without fail Betsie would be waiting for Corrie in the doorway, and one day she had news from another prisoner in the sewing room. The woman was from Ermelo and she, her husband,

---

* As a teen Corrie had fallen in love with a handsome young Dutchman, Karel, hopeful that one day they would marry. That dream was shattered when he showed up at the Beje one day to introduce his fiancée.

and her two brothers had been arrested for Resistance work. The man responsible for betraying the ten Booms, the lady told Betsie, was the same man who had tricked Corrie about the six hundred guilders. His name was Jan Vogel, and he had worked with the Gestapo from the first day of the occupation, eventually teaming up with Willemse and Kapteyn.

Corrie fumed. "Flames of fire seemed to leap around that name in my heart," she recalled later. "I thought of Father's final hours, alone and confused, in a hospital corridor. Of the underground work so abruptly halted. I thought of Mary Itallie arrested while walking down the street. And I knew that if Jan Vogel stood in front of me now I could kill him."

That evening, as women gathered for the prayer meeting around their bunk, Corrie asked Betsie to lead it, saying she had a headache. But it was more of a *heart*ache. That night she couldn't sleep. She now could affix a name—*Jan Vogel*—to the treachery that had led to her father's death, and to the incarceration of her family.

For days Corrie's stomach churned, and one night she asked Betsie how she could be so peaceful. "Don't you feel anything about Jan Vogel? Doesn't it bother you?"

"Oh, yes, Corrie! Terribly! I've felt for him ever since I knew— and pray for him whenever his name comes into my mind. How dreadfully he must be suffering!"

That Betsie, always teaching by quiet and humble example. She seemed to be from another order of beings. And what exactly was Betsie teaching? That Corrie was as guilty as Jan Vogel? "Didn't he and I stand together before an all-seeing God convicted of the same sin of murder?" she wondered. "For I had murdered him with my heart and with my tongue."

Convicted, she prayed, telling God that she forgave Jan Vogel, and asking that she be forgiven. "I have done him great damage," she went on. "Bless him now, and his family."

That night she had her first restful sleep in a week.

Meanwhile, concentration camp life ground on. Wake-up time at five in the morning for roll call at six, but if a single prisoner had been late for check-in the prior evening, or any other minor infraction, the entire barrack would be roused out of bed for roll call at three-thirty or four a.m., often standing in the rain for hours. At half past five, breakfast consisted of black bread and ersatz coffee. After roll call they marched off to the Philips factory at six-thirty. When prisoners returned to their barrack, time outside required a "walking permit."

Then there was the latrine, located inside the barrack. It contained ten toilets, three of which were usually out of order. "In the camp," Corrie wrote in a note, "the latrine is the place where we have our most interesting political discussions. . . . You meet acquaintances in the latrine. You pass on dangerous news to others. . . . Sitting next to each other in the latrine are communists, criminals, Jehovah's Witnesses, Christian Reformed, liberals, prostitutes."

When a guard was on the way to the factory, the barrack, or the latrine, the code words "Thick clouds," or "Thick air" rang out so that everyone could pretend to be busy or hide any contraband.

Most disheartening was the camp's *summary justice*. "If anybody passes on news or a notice," she wrote in a journal entry on August 19, "he gets the bullet."

Later that month, though, Corrie and Betsie witnessed the first signs of possible Allied victory. For several days a rumor spread in the camp that the Princess Irene Brigade—part of the Dutch forces that had escaped to England before Holland capitulated—was closing in on Vught. Not long after that they awoke one night to the thunder of thousands of planes overhead. Moments later bombs exploded very close to the camp, the Allies apparently targeting nearby bridges. The concussions were so great that prisoners kept their mouths open to protect their eardrums.

Then, on August 23, the battle for the skies came directly over the camp. At lunchtime hundreds of planes flew overhead, joined by the crackle of machine gun fire as a dogfight raged at low altitude. Prisoners watched with high hopes and Corrie reclined on the ground to take it in. When bullets and shell fragments kicked up dirt all around her, she dashed for the cover of a barrack, but remained outside to continue watching. Others were less fortunate: five wounded women had to be hospitalized.

Indeed, the Allies were advancing. On August 25 General Dietrich von Choltitz, the Prussian who was Germany's military governor of Paris, disobeyed Hitler and refused to destroy the city before retreating. Instead he surrendered and handed the city over to the Free French forces with only sporadic shots being fired. For that he would be dubbed the "Savior of Paris."

But the Allied victories had devastating consequences to prisoners in concentration camps. Heinrich Himmler, who supervised all camps, ordered mass executions—first of sick and elderly prisoners, then of the healthy—to lighten the travel of retreating.

Vught would not be spared. On the morning of September 3 Corrie was working at the Philips factory when in midmorning the prisoners were ordered to return to their barracks. When they arrived back at Barrack 35, Betsie was waiting outside.

"Corrie! Has the Brigade come? Are we free?"

"No. Not yet. I don't know. Oh, Betsie, why am I so frightened?"

Just then the loudspeaker boomed in the men's camp next door. Oddly, the men were ordered to report for roll call, yet the women were not. Then one by one prisoners were called out. The women around Corrie—many of whom had husbands or relatives in the men's camp—anguished at the sound of every name.

Women climbed on benches or window frames to see what was happening.

"I can see my husband," one woman said, her face ashen. "Do you suppose this will be the last time?"

Several moments passed and another said: "Now men are being called forward out of the various groups. . . . Now they are marching out of the gate. Oh, they are certainly being transported to Germany."

There were so many men the women could hear the shuffle of their footsteps, and after a few minutes it fell silent.

Suddenly a rifle volley pierced the air. Then another. And another. Women in the barrack began to weep. Every shot meant the death of a husband, father, son, or brother. The executions carried on for two hours before the shooting ended.

The SS had slaughtered one hundred and eighty Dutchmen.

Chapter 20

RAVENSBRÜCK

CORRIE LAID HER HEAD ON her sister's shoulder.

"Betsie, I cannot bear it. Why, O Lord, why dost Thou permit this to happen?"

She didn't respond, but Betsie was composed, her face serene.

That night Corrie couldn't sleep, yet her heart was at peace. "God makes no mistakes," she concluded later. "Everything looks like a confused piece of embroidery work, meaningless and ugly. But that is the underside. Some day we shall see the right side and shall be amazed and thankful."

With each tragedy, it seemed, Corrie was becoming more like her sister.

AT SIX THE next morning, guards instructed everyone in the barrack to collect their personal effects. Corrie and Betsie still had the pillowcases they had brought from Scheveningen, and into them went the few belongings they had: toothbrushes, needle and thread, vitamin oil that they had saved from a Red Cross parcel, and a sweater. As she had done previously, Corrie put their Bible in the small pouch with the looped string and hung it so that it fell between her shoulders.

Outside, prisoners collected blankets and then marched out

of the camp. As they progressed through the woods along a dirt road, Corrie noticed that Betsie was breathing heavily. It wasn't the first time, as Betsie labored any time she had to walk even a short distance, but this was more disturbing.

Corrie stretched out her arm under her sister's shoulder and together they shuffled with the others another quarter mile to the train station. When they arrived on the platform, they found at least a thousand women in their group. Up ahead male prisoners gathered, although it was difficult to identify the number. Corrie noticed their transportation; it was not a passenger train, but a *freight* train, and atop every few boxcars were mounted machine guns. Soldiers began sliding open the doors, but it was impossible to see what was inside; with no lighting or windows, the boxcars were dark.

Guards prodded women forward and Corrie helped Betsie aboard. When her eyes adjusted to the dimness, she could make out in a corner a large stack of bread.

They were headed to Germany.

The addition of more prisoners pushed the ten Boom sisters to the back of the car, and Corrie figured the most it could hold was forty women. The guards kept shoving, though, cursing and shouting, until they had packed in *eighty*. The door slammed shut and women began to weep, some fainting. After a few minutes the temperature in the boxcar began to soar, the reek of body odor spoiling the trapped air. While the car had two small grill ventilators, they were insufficient to provide fresh air. Corrie felt nauseous.

"Do you know what I'm thankful for?" Betsie suddenly asked. "I'm thankful that Father is in heaven today!"

Betsie. Only *she* could find joy in a time like this.

Hours passed and the train never moved. Many women had worked out an arrangement where some could sit if they passed their legs around the person in front, while others frantically worked to poke holes in the wood to let in air. A woman next to Corrie found a nail and began to use it as a pick to create a hole. Eventually enough holes were made to allow in a little air, and women began taking turns in front of them.

The boxcar had no restrooms, however, and soon the stench overpowered what fresh air came through the holes. They also had no water.

The train lurched and began to crawl forward. Throughout the day and into the evening it would come to a stop, they'd wait an hour, and then it would move out again. Corrie and Betsie managed to sit, reclining on the person next to them, and Corrie felt a woman leaning against her; she was kind, changing her position so that Corrie could stretch out her legs. They struck up a conversation and Corrie found out that the woman was a prostitute who had been arrested for infecting a German soldier with venereal disease.

Corrie told her about Jesus and said: "If you ever need my help, will you come to me? I live—"

Her voice broke off. Was the Beje still her home? Would she ever see it again?

She leaned back, closed her eyes, and dozed off. Soon she dreamed that she was in the Beje and could hear hailstones hitting the windows. She awoke to what sounded like hail hammering the boxcar.

"It's bullets!" someone shouted. "They're attacking the train!"

The German machine guns began returning fire, and Corrie wondered if the Dutch Brigade was rescuing them. Bullets continued to strike the train and she reached for Betsie's hand. After a few minutes the shooting trailed off and the train sat motionless for an hour before again moving out. In the boxcar in front of them Corrie heard someone singing: "Adieu beloved Netherlands, Dear fatherland, farewell."

Then it dawned on her—none of her family knew where she

and Betsie were headed. She found a small piece of paper and put their names on it, adding that they were being transported to Germany. She asked the finder to forward the note to Nollie, and then forced it through a crevice in the boxcar wall. Perhaps a patriotic Dutchman would pass it on.

After a while she dozed off again, waking at dawn when someone announced they were passing through Emmerich, a town on the western side of the Rhine.

They had entered Germany, but were not nearly close to their destination. The following day women began to beg for water. When the train next stopped a soldier passed in a pail, but the prisoners closest to the door drank it all. In the evening and next morning, guards passed more water into the boxcar, but each time the women at the front consumed everything. It was now day three and Corrie and Betsie had received not a drop. Corrie's thirst left her delirious.

The next time the train stopped, water finally made it to the back and Betsie held a mug to Corrie's lips. She drank deeply, gulp after gulp, and then decided that she had better save some for that evening. Moments later she fell into a stupor, imagining that she was in a hospital.

"Nurse, please give me some water," she was trying to say.

Corrie slept and didn't awaken until the morning of the fourth day. The train had stopped in a town called Fürstenberg, about forty miles north of Berlin. After a considerable delay the boxcar door opened and the prisoners were ordered out. One by one, women crawled and stumbled to exit. The fresh air and sunshine, combined with what looked like a verdant oasis before them, raised their spirits. When Corrie jumped from the train she saw a beautiful blue lake, and on the far side, amidst syca-mores, a small church and abbey.

After everyone had disembarked, guards shouted for them to assemble in ranks of five. Corrie looked at the mere dozen or so soldiers—most of them no older than fifteen—guarding a thousand women. But they were weak, frail, and severely dehydrated, so opposition was not much of a risk. The women began to march and when they reached the lake, buckets were passed around for the prisoners to drink from it.

Corrie swallowed her fill and then collapsed on the lush grass. As she observed the resplendent lake and fields beyond, the opening of Psalm 23 came to mind: "The Lord is my shepherd, I shall not be in want. He makes me lie down in green pastures, he leads me beside quiet waters. . . ."

The psalm was apt, as Corrie and Betsie were about to walk through the valley of the shadow of death: Ravensbrück. For women, the most feared name in all of Europe. A concentration camp for female prisoners, it was notorious for cruelty, brutality, and executions.

After a short while the boy soldiers called the women back into formation and they again marched. For about a mile they circled around the lake and then began ascending a hill. They passed a number of villagers, mostly families, and Corrie delighted in the sight of young, wide-eyed children. The adults, however—apparently warned not to talk to prisoners—looked the other way.

Corrie and Betsie supported each other in the climb and when they reached the summit, they saw it. Amidst beautiful surroundings, endless rows of gray barracks were surrounded by a tall concrete wall with guard towers. At one end, a grayish smoke rose from a smokestack.

"Ravensbrück," someone in the front line cried out.

Word filtered back through the group: they had arrived in hell.

As they approached the camp, the massive iron gate swung open and everyone marched in between rows of SS guards. No sooner than they had cleared the gate, a Dutch prisoner began to sing:

> *We never let our courage lag;*
> *We hold our heads up high;*
> *Never shall they get us down,*
> *Though they be ever so sly.*
> *O yea! O yea! you Netherlands women,*
> *Heads up, heads up, heads up!*

Observing the procession was none other than Fritz Sühren, the camp's commandant. Seemingly too young to be running a camp—midthirties—Sühren's baby face and clear blue eyes belied his penchant for cruelty.

"I don't understand these Hollanders," he remarked to an aide. "You pack them into boxcars for three days, and then they came marching into my camp with their heads up as if to say, 'It doesn't hurt me at all; you'll never get me down.'"

INSIDE THE ENTRANCE Corrie took in her surroundings: tall walls, watchtowers, and ubiquitous barbed wire strung across the top of every wall and on the ground. Every few yards skull-and-crossbones signs indicated that the wire was electrified.* Dull, gray barracks extended for acres, with nothing between them except sand or cinder. Incredibly, the camp contained no trees, shrubs, plants—or even color.

Corrie and a number of prisoners noticed a row of spigots and they rushed over to drink and wash up. In seconds a team of

---

* The most common form of suicide at Ravensbrück was throwing oneself onto the electric wire.

SS guards—women in dark blue uniforms—appeared, shouting and swinging their crops. No one was allowed to break rank, they yelled, and Corrie and the others hustled back to the main group.

The guards led them down a street between barracks and skeleton hands reached out from everywhere, begging for food. Corrie and others began tossing them bread they had saved from the train, but guards beat the emaciated prisoners away.

Starvation was part of the Ravensbrück plan to maintain servility.

Soon they ended up before a massive canvas tent with a makeshift floor of straw. They would stay here for now, they were told, and Corrie and Betsie sank down into the straw. At once, though, they were on their feet, scratching themselves.

Lice! Fleas!

They spread out their blanket over the infested straw and sat on top of it. To keep the lice from their heads, women passed around scissors to cut each other's hair. A pair came to Corrie and as she cut Betsie's hair, she wept.

After a while guards called everyone out and led them to a sandy area away from the tent and barracks. They were told to line up in formation again, but by the late afternoon some began to sit. At dusk the guards disappeared and it became apparent that the Dutch women were to sleep on the ground under the stars. Corrie and Betsie stretched out on the bare ground and pulled their blanket over them.

Corrie admired God's handiwork in the stars for a few minutes, and then she and Betsie dozed off.

At midnight it began to rain.

WHEN SHE AWOKE, Corrie and Betsie found themselves lying in puddles of water. The blanket was soaked through and as they were wringing water from it, a guard called everyone to fall in line for ersatz coffee. Each prisoner also was given a small piece of black bread.

Ravensbrück breakfast.

That afternoon they received a ladle of turnip soup and a small boiled potato. Then it was back to the area where they had slept to again fall into rank. If someone needed a bathroom break, they had to ask a guard for permission to use the facilities: a ditch.

For hours they waited outside, only to find out at dusk that they would again be spending the night here. Their blanket was still damp, though, and Betsie began to cough.

The next morning she had intestinal cramps and had to ask permission to use the "sanitation facilities" several times. Then it was more of the same—standing around for hours waiting for their next orders. When evening fell and the women prepared for their third night outside, guards ushered them into a processing center. Corrie and Betsie inched along in a line leading to a desk and pile of personal belongings. Here every prisoner had to give up her blanket, pillowcase, and every item brought into the camp. Corrie looked beyond and gasped. At a second desk women were undressing—giving up every stitch of clothing— and walking naked past a dozen male SS guards into the shower room. Coming out they were given a prison dress, undershirt, and pair of wooden shoes.

Betsie began to shiver and Corrie saw that her face was ashen. Pulling her sister close, Corrie prayed: "O Lord, save us from this evil; Betsie is so frail."

She then asked Betsie if she was prepared to offer this sacrifice if God should ask.

"Corrie, I cannot do it."

Corrie again prayed, asking God to provide strength. Next to them, an elderly woman wept.

Seconds later a voice behind them boomed: "Do you have any objections to surrendering your clothes? We'll soon teach you Hollanders what Ravensbrück is like."

"I cannot," Betsie repeated.

Corrie prayed yet again and Betsie finally said she was ready. Before it was their turn to undress, Corrie asked a guard where the toilets were.

He nodded toward the showers. "Use the drainholes!"

Corrie led Betsie inside. "Quick, take off your woolen underwear." Betsie did and Corrie removed the Bible hiding inside her dress, wrapped it in both pair of undergarments, and set it in a corner. They couldn't survive without their Bible, she felt, and she hoped she could sneak back in after receiving the dress and retrieve it.

They returned to the line and disrobed and showered. After receiving the prisoner dress—each marked with an X—Corrie lingered over to where she had hidden the Bible. Quickly slipping it around her neck and under her dress, she prayed: "Lord, cause now Thine angels to surround me; and let them not be transparent today, for the guards must not see me."

At the exit, guards frisked all prisoners to see if they had placed anything under their clothing. Corrie and Betsie watched the hands roaming over every woman—front, back, and sides. Ahead of Corrie, a guard found a woolen vest hidden beneath a woman's dress and made her remove it.

Corrie was next. She knew the Bible made a visible bulge, but proceeded forward with confidence. Inexplicably, the guards ignored her. She was neither searched nor spoken to, and simply strolled through the gauntlet. Behind her, a guard carefully searched Betsie.

Outside, though, female guards searched every prisoner a second time. Again, Corrie remained calm and sauntered through, untouched.

She and Betsie then made their way to Barrack 8, the quarantine building. Inside, they were aghast at the sleeping arrangements: bunk beds in tiers three high, two wide, each bed only 27.5 inches wide. For one person it wouldn't be a problem, but five to seven women were assigned to each two beds. When they found their bed in the center of the room, three women already occupied it. Now there would be five, sharing only three blankets.

That night sleep became impossible because the bunkmates couldn't find an arrangement that worked. First they tried sleeping lengthwise, but the straw mattress sloped down on one side, causing the two on that edge to fall off. So crosswise they slept, so close that if one turned over, the other four had to as well.

"EVERYBODY OUT!" A guard shouted in the darkness. "Fall in for roll call!"

At four-thirty a.m., the daily abuse started. To begin the dehumanization, prisoner names were not used in SS camps, only prisoner numbers; Corrie's number was 66730.*

On most days, especially when work assignments had not yet been delegated, Corrie's group of some hundred women stood in ranks for hours. Often they heard hideous wails coming from a punishment barrack next door. This building was a particularly heinous aspect of Ravensbrück, a hell within hell itself.

When a woman was caught in any "major" infraction—an offense that seemed to vary by guard—she was told to report to a specified punishment barrack at a certain time. Here she

---

* "A man counted only because he had a prison number," Viktor Frankl remembered about Auschwitz. "One literally became a number: dead or alive— that was unimportant; the life of a 'number' was completely irrelevant. What stood behind that number and that life mattered even less: the fate, the history, the name of the man."

was ordered to step up to a rack where her feet would be shackled in a wooden clamp. She would then be bent over across the rack, strapped down, and her dress would be pulled over her head. A blanket also would be placed over her head to help muffle the screams, and she would be ordered to count out the blows. The typical number of lashes across her bare buttocks was twenty-five. If she could not count out the strokes, they would be counted for her. If she fainted during the procedure, a bucket of cold water would be thrown in her face to revive her, and the punishment would continue. So that no SS guards would be personally implicated in the beatings, other prisoners—bribed with cigarettes or food—would do the deed.

Sometimes the beatings occurred during roll call, and Corrie and the others could hear every scream, every cry. With trembling hands at their sides—covering one's ears was prohibited—they experienced every blow. At the completion of roll call, everyone raced back to the barrack to lessen the intensity of the nightmare.*

Were this intimidation and horror not enough, medical examinations brought a unique humiliation. Every Friday prisoners were taken to the infirmary in groups and told to undress. As they stood nude in front of leering guards, the exams occurred in an assembly line: one doctor examined each prisoner's throat, another looked between her fingers, and a dentist examined her teeth. The ordeal was especially painful for the ten Boom sisters, but Corrie found comfort in knowing that Jesus had hung naked on the cross, already sharing their burden.

While Ravensbrück prisoners suffered physically and mentally, the Allies struggled with their own setbacks. On September 6 and 7, forty-seven SOE agents who had been captured

---

* The trepidation and chilling effect brought on by mere mention of the punishment barrack was possibly George Orwell's inspiration for "Room 101" in *1984*.

after parachuting into Holland were sent to the Mauthausen concentration camp and executed. Then, from September 17 to 25, British field marshal Bernard Montgomery's Operation Market Garden—the colossal operation to capture bridges at Nijmegen and Arnhem*—was a dismal failure.

A rescue would not be coming.

But the consequences were far greater for Hollanders. As part of Market Garden, London had called for the Dutch to implement a railway strike to hamstring Wehrmacht transports. When the operation failed, the Germans retaliated by blocking shipments of food from Holland's rural east to the industrial west. For residents in places like Amsterdam and Haarlem, food disappeared. All that was left to eat, which they did, was tulip bulbs and sugar beets. This blockade went on for months, the time becoming known as Holland's Hunger Winter.

DURING THE SECOND week in October, Corrie, Betsie, and other women in their group were transferred to a permanent home, Barrack 28. Every other window, it seemed, had been broken and replaced with rags. Inside, some two hundred women knitted.

A prisoner led them to the next room, the sleeping area. The pungent odors Corrie had remembered from the train were suddenly back. Somewhere in the building the plumbing was malfunctioning, and on every bunk the bedding was soiled and rancid.

Like Barrack 8, beds were stacked three high, but there were more—far more—crammed side by side and end to end. To-

---

*   The goal of Market Garden was to land Allied paratroopers in the Netherlands to capture various bridges to allow passage over the Rhine, thus creating an invasion route into northern Germany. The operation was detailed in Cornelius Ryan's *A Bridge Too Far*, which was made into a movie in 1977.

gether they had the appearance of a mouse maze. The guide found the bunk Corrie and Betsie would share and motioned across to a middle row. Because bunks had been set abreast, they had to crawl over several other beds to get to their own. Corrie scrambled up and Betsie followed.

"Fleas!" Corrie cried. "The place is swarming with them!"

Betsie prayed and then asked Corrie to take out her Bible and read aloud the passage they had studied that very morning, 1 Thessalonians 5:14–18: "Encourage the timid, help the weak, be patient with everyone. Make sure that nobody pays back wrong for wrong, but always try to be kind to each other and to everyone else. Be joyful always, pray continually; give thanks in all circumstances, for this is God's will for you in Christ Jesus."

That was to be their response to Barrack 28, Betsie said. "We can start right now to thank God for every single thing about this new barracks!"

Corrie looked around and back to Betsie. "Such as?"

"Such as being assigned here together. . . . Such as what you're holding in your hands."

Corrie glanced at her Bible and nodded. Indeed, the cramped spacing would mean that more women could hear when Corrie or Betsie read, or perhaps read it themselves. Corrie thanked God for that, and then Betsie went on, giving thanks even for the fleas.

Corrie couldn't believe her ears. *Fleas?* Surely Betsie was wrong about that.

AS EVENING FELL the women of Barrack 28 began returning from their work assignments. They poured in by the hundreds—sweat-soaked and filthy. Their barrack had been designed to house four hundred, but because prisoners were being transferred from Austria, Poland, France, and Belgium, *fourteen hun-*

dred had been assigned to it. And to serve all residents there were only eight toilets, several of which were backed up.

At bedtime, Corrie and Betsie discovered that seven other women would be sharing their particular space. Everyone made the best of it, though, and managed to get some sleep.

That morning at four a.m., a piercing whistle awoke the women. Breakfast—the small ration of bread and coffee—awaited them in the middle of the room. After that everyone had to be outside for the four-thirty roll call. With 35,000 other women from surrounding barracks, Corrie and Betsie hustled outside and into rank. Prisoner numbers were read off and work crews announced. The ten Boom sisters, with thousands of other women, received the worst of it: the Siemens factory.

Guards marched them out of the camp and down the road a mile and a half, where they came upon a complex of mills and railroad terminals. Here Corrie and Betsie were ordered to push a massive handcart to a railroad siding, where they would unload heavy metal plates from a boxcar, load them into the cart, and then wheel it to a receiving gate at the factory. The work was grueling and exhausting for the young and fit; for two weakened sisters in their fifties, it was torture.

At it they went for eleven hours, pausing only at noon to eat a boiled potato and ersatz soup. By the time they returned to the barracks they were bruised, blistered, and beat. Their swollen legs testified that Siemens was "hard labor." So exhausting were the Ravensbrück conditions that seven hundred women died or were killed each day.

After several weeks Corrie knew that she and Betsie had to find another job. From a fellow prisoner she learned that they could report to the knitting crew—the women she had seen making socks on the first day. Sure enough, when Corrie and Betsie reported, they were given knitting needles and wool and set to work. It was a lifesaving respite.

A few nights later a clerk came by their bunk and told them that they'd have to report to the Siemens factory in the morning.

"But that's impossible," Corrie replied. "We are both in the knitting commando."

The worker scratched their names off the list and gave them each a red card. The cards classified them as unfit for heavy labor, she said.

In the morning Corrie found out from another prisoner what the clerk didn't say.

When the camp became overcrowded—*as it was now*—those holding red cards were gassed.

Chapter 21

MURDER

Haarlem

One morning in October, Hans Poley heard a commotion in the street. Given that he had been released from Amersfoort only six weeks earlier, it seemed best to stay inside. He peered through a window and saw soldiers gathered in the Westergracht, only a thousand feet from his parents' home. The Poleys soon learned that a Gestapo officer had been shot there only hours before.

As the Germans scoured the neighborhood to find the Resistance operatives who had done the deed, Hans and his parents quickly hid everything that might be incriminating.

That afternoon Hans saw billows of smoke rising from buildings down the street.

Unable to find the perpetrators of the killing, the Gestapo had taken revenge by setting several houses on fire. The Poleys hoped theirs would not be next.

Ravensbrück

Dinner in Barrack 28 meant a ladle of turnip soup. Afterward, when the guards had left, Corrie and Betsie held worship services in their bunk area, typically starting with singing. Dozens of women from all nationalities attended, and on any given night it might be a hymn sung by Lutherans, the Magnificat sung in Latin by Roman Catholics, or a simple chant by the Eastern Orthodox. When the singing ended, Corrie or Betsie would read from the Bible, first in Dutch, then in German. With each verse they would pause, allowing their words to be translated into French, Russian, Polish, and Czech as it passed through the crowd. Over ensuing days the worship attendance grew, and oftentimes they held a second service after evening roll call.

On November 1 the women in Barrack 28 heard encouraging news. For some reason—perhaps because it had been bombed—there were no more work crews for the Siemens factory. In its place the guards created other work: leveling ground. While their red cards exempted Corrie and Betsie from heavy labor, the guards apparently viewed shoveling as mild labor and sent them off to work near the camp wall. Why the ground needed to be leveled was a mystery, and the work was actually exhausting.

Betsie grew weaker by the day, and one morning she could hardly lift even a small chunk of sod. Screaming at her to work faster, a female guard snatched her shovel and began showing the handful of dirt on it to other crews.

"Look what Madame Baroness is carrying! Surely she will overexert herself!"

Other guards and some prisoners laughed and Corrie felt a rage coming over her. She looked at her sister and, remarkably, Betsie was laughing, too.

"That's me all right," Betsie said to the guard. "But you'd better let me totter along with my little spoonful, or I'll have to stop altogether."

The guard drew her leather crop and slashed Betsie across the chest and neck. "I'll decide who's to stop!"

Corrie seized her shovel and rushed toward the guard, but Betsie stepped in front of her.

"Corrie!" she cried, pulling down the weapon. "Keep working!"

Corrie clutched the wood tightly, seething. Betsie grasped the handle, tugged it from her, and buried the blade in the ground. Looking at her sister's neck, Corrie noticed a crimson welt on Betsie's skin, and blood stained her collar.

Betsie covered the injury with her palm. "Don't look at it, Corrie. Look at Jesus only."

IN EARLY NOVEMBER the guards gave prisoners winter coats, apparently all taken from dead Russian soldiers. By the middle of the month, though, fall rains came and the extra clothing did little to offset the cold. During the four-thirty morning roll call it often poured, but prisoners were forced to remain outside in their ranks of ten. For hours they would wait in their designated spot, even if a large puddle of water had formed. On many mornings Corrie stood in ankle-deep water.

But Betsie had the worst of it. Her cough started to bring up blood, and Corrie took her to the camp infirmary. Betsie's temperature was only 102°, though, insufficient for her to be admitted for care. Her condition continued to worsen, and Corrie kept taking her back until Betsie's temperature met the 104° threshold. While she was admitted to a room, Betsie received no medical attention or medicine. When she returned to the barrack three days later, Corrie could feel that she still had a temperature.

The ten Boom "church services" continued, though, and to it Corrie and Betsie added a personal, one-on-one ministry: they began visiting sickly women in the barrack and prayed for them. Then they prayed for all Ravensbrück prisoners and, at Betsie's urging, even the guards.

One evening as Corrie lay beside her sister, Betsie began

talking about what their ministry would be after the war. There had to be a place where people could recover and heal, she felt—physically, emotionally, and spiritually—at their own pace.*

"We have learned so much here," she said, "and now we must go all over the world to tell people what we now know—that Jesus' light is stronger than the deepest darkness. Only prisoners can know how desperate this life is. We can tell from experience that no pit is too deep, because God's everlasting arms always sustain us.

"We must rent a concentration camp after the war," Betsie went on, "where we can help displaced Germans to get a roof over their heads. I have heard that 95 percent of the houses in Germany are bombed out. No one will want these concentration camps after the war, so we must rent one and help the German people to find a new life in a destroyed Germany."

Not only that, Betsie said, but they also must have a house in Holland to receive Dutchmen who had been in concentration camps. They, too, needed to put their lives back together.

A day or so later Betsie described her vision in greater detail. "It's such a beautiful house," she told Corrie. "The floors are all inlaid wood, with statues set in the walls and a broad staircase sweeping down. And gardens! Gardens all around it where they can plant flowers."

---

* Viktor Frankl, a psychiatrist who had been a prisoner at Auschwitz and Dachau, wrote upon his release in 1945: "It would be an error to think that a liberated prisoner was not in need of spiritual care any more. We have to consider that a man who has been under such enormous mental pressure for such a long time is naturally in some degree of danger after his liberation, especially since the pressure was released quite suddenly. This danger . . . is the psychological counter-part of the bends. Just as the physical health of the caisson worker would be endangered if he left his diver's chamber suddenly . . . so the man who has suddenly been liberated from mental pressure can suffer damage to his moral and spiritual health."

Aside from the danger of the "bends," Frankl observed, liberated prisoners also had to be healed from, or protected from, bitterness and disillusionment.

Corrie tried to process Betsie's elaborate plans. "Must we stay in that camp, or will we be able to stay in the house for the ex-prisoners at home in Holland?"

"Neither. You must travel all over the world and tell everybody who will listen what we have learned here—that Jesus is a reality and that He is stronger than all powers of darkness. Tell them. Tell everyone who will listen! He is our greatest Friend, our hiding place."

The dream seemed unrealistic, but it filled Corrie with hope. Eventually she came to believe they would do it. In the meantime, they had to endure the camp.

Near the end of the month Barrack 28 received a new *Aufseherin*. It was always tenuous when new guards or camp police were brought in, each with their own temperaments and cruelty. This one made her mark early.

On her first day she beat a prisoner to death.

DECEMBER BROUGHT COLDER temperatures, making roll call torturous. At morning and evening lineups, prisoners stamped their feet, creating almost a marching cadence. To add warmth to their meager coats, Corrie and Betsie stuffed newspaper inside them. Sleeping, too, was hazardous as the broken windowpanes allowed in icy wind gusts. Someone had thrown a blanket over most of the bare windows, but it did little to block out the cold.

One frigid night Corrie wrapped her arms around Betsie to warm her and was startled at what she felt: Betsie's pulse was weak and rapid.

THE SECOND WEEK of December guards gave every prisoner an extra blanket, but for the ten Booms, this didn't last long. The next day prisoners arrived from Czechoslovakia, one of them assigned to Corrie's and Betsie's area. The woman had no blanket, and Betsie insisted they give up one of theirs.

During roll call an evening or so later, Corrie saw a group of docile women coming out of the *Nacht-und-Nebelbarak*, the "Night-and-Fog" detention barrack next door. The innocuous name masked the terror those inside faced. In this barrack were women condemned to death, some of whom were used as *Kanienchen* ("guinea pigs") for medical experiments. Every corner of Ravensbrück, it seemed, was constructed to create terror and shock, from the Siemens factory to the punishment rooms, the Bunker to the *Nacht-und-Nebelbarak*.

The next morning Corrie, Betsie, and the other women in the knitting group walked past a peculiar building. While all barracks were dreary and gray, this place looked far worse; constructed like a guardhouse, it had a courtyard fenced in by iron bars. An outdoor cell, essentially. These women performed the hardest work, Corrie learned: building roads, carrying coal, or chopping wood.

One day Corrie noticed a young girl—skeletal and sickly—alone in the courtyard. Like a wounded animal, she huddled against the side of the building. She was dying, Corrie knew, and likely very soon.

No one was allowed to speak to those in the courtyard, so Corrie prayed silently:

"O Savior, full of mercy, take this poor child into Your arms; comfort her, and make her happy." It was a prayer she could offer for so many at Ravensbrück.

Like old Mrs. Leness. Deathly sick and weak, she could not make it out for roll call one morning and remained in bed. The *Lagerpolizei*—prisoners who served as camp police—appeared and yanked Mrs. Leness to her feet. She could not stand, though, so the *Lagerpolizei* beat her. When the Barrack 28 prisoners returned, they found Mrs. Leness lying on the ground. Corrie and others rushed over to lift her to her bed, and Corrie asked if they could get a stretcher to carry her to the hospital. None came, so a group of Dutch women decided to assist Mrs. Leness to the restroom.

On the way, though, Mrs. Leness soiled herself and a guard beat her mercilessly. Again and again the blows rained, one after another, until Mrs. Leness stopped moving.

She was dead.

IT NEVER STOPPED, this cruelty. A few mornings later Barrack 28 roll call commenced at three-thirty a.m.—an hour early—because three women had been late the day before. As Corrie waited in the freezing dark, she noticed a pair of headlights bouncing across the snow. They were flatbed trucks heading toward the camp hospital. Whispers circulated through the lineup.

Moments later the hospital door opened and a nurse came out with someone leaning on her arm. The woman helped the patient up and into the first truck, and then other nurses followed with more patients. From what Corrie could tell, these were elderly, infirm, or mentally impaired patients, and the nurses gently helped each one in. Soon orderlies joined in bringing out more patients, one of whom Corrie knew—a mother with a small son also in the camp. She wasn't sickly or infirm, however, and Corrie reckoned she had been taken to the hospital because of her incessant requests to have her son near her.

After a few minutes a hundred or so were packed in, and then came stretchers with patients so ill that they had to be carried to the trucks. But where were they going? To a real hospital?

"Sick transport!" someone near Corrie whispered.

Gasps passed through the crowd, but Corrie couldn't make sense of it. If these elderly and sick were not being transported to a hospital, then why were the nurses so tender and gentle with them?

She watched as the trucks started up and drove directly to the crematorium.*

---

* On December 16, 1946, Odette Sansom—who had been transferred from Ravensbrück's Bunker to a cell near the crematorium—testified at the Ravensbrück war crimes trial in Hamburg that she heard the screams of women being dragged to the crematorium. Doors were opened and closed, she told the judges, she heard more screams, and then silence.

Viktor Frankl described a similar scene upon his entrance to Auschwitz: "For the great majority of our transport, about 90 percent, it meant death. . . . Those who were sent to the left were marched from the station straight to the crematorium."

Chapter 22

THE SKELETON

THROUGHOUT THE LATE FALL and into December—as the Allies closed in—Heinrich Himmler visited a number of concentration camps to order an increase in executions. Some camps would have to move to new locations, he knew, and many prisoners were incapable of travel. At Ravensbrück he met with commandant Fritz Sühren and instructed that prisoners who were sick, old, or incapable of work were to be eliminated. To expedite the killings, he ordered the construction of a second crematorium, as well as a gas chamber.

At Ravensbrück and other camps, prisoners knew their chance of survival diminished with each passing day. Everyone saw the dead bodies hauled away each morning, followed by smoke rising from the crematorium. Many committed suicide.*

Corrie never contemplated taking her life; rather, she considered what she had seen in fellow prisoners and looked deep within her own soul. "Distress teaches some to pray," she later wrote. "It hardens others. Hardness is a defense mechanism which had at times its temptations for me also. If one cannot

---

* Viktor Frankl wrote after the war that nearly all prisoners contemplated suicide. "It was born of the hopelessness of the situation," he remembered, "the constant danger of death looming over us daily and hourly, and the closeness of the deaths suffered by many of the others."

endure the sight of suffering about him he tries to build a cloak of armor about his heart. But that makes people insensitive to good influences also."

Even Betsie was not immune to despair. One morning, as Barrack 28 suffered with another three-thirty a.m. roll call, everyone shivered in the darkness. When the siren came for the group to fall out, women rushed back to the relative warmth of the barrack, only to discover that it was locked. The suffering in the bitter cold would continue.

One woman tried to climb in through a window but a camp policewoman caught her and beat her. Perhaps distraught from seeing the beating, a mentally handicapped girl just in front of Corrie lost control of her bowels and soiled herself. Guards brutally beat her. Then an elderly woman appeared at the barrack door begging to be admitted. When the guard refused, the woman fainted and fell to the ground.

Betsie leaned into her sister's arms.

"Oh, Corrie, this is hell."

FOR CORRIE, LIVING in hell had one windfall: a field ripe for spreading the Gospel and providing hope. In particular, she felt a special obligation to minister to young girls. The bunks in Barrack 28 were stacked so high that on the top bed one could not sit up without hitting the ceiling. The youngest, most agile girls would typically occupy these bunks, and they began to loosen and remove boards so that one could sit upright. This platform became Corrie's Areopagus,* allowing her to teach and witness

---

* The Areopagus was a rocky hill in Athens dedicated to the god Ares (or Mars), and was also the name of the group of Epicurean and Stoic philosophers who met there. From this lofty mount the Apostle Paul preached, taught, and debated. See Acts 17:19–34.

to the dozen or so who would gather around her for guidance and wisdom.

The ubiquitous suffering, Corrie knew, forced every prisoner to contemplate the larger questions in life. Why does God allow evil to exist? How could God allow such a heinous place as Ravensbrück to be created? What essentials of life are necessary for happiness?

Betsie saw the big picture—God's providence—and told Corrie one day: "Your whole life has been a training for the work you are doing here in prison—and for the work you will do afterward."

Corrie saw this providence at work in the camp, too. One day a girl said to her: "It has certainly been no mistake that God directed my life by way of Ravensbrück. Here, for the first time, I have really learned to pray. The distress here has taught me that things are never entirely right in one's life unless he is completely surrendered to Jesus. I was always rather pious, but there were areas of my life from which Jesus was completely excluded. Now He is King in every sphere of my life."

Another girl echoed the sentiment, saying, "I had never before realized the seriousness of life until I came here. After I am released, my life will be different. . . . I have thanked God for sending me to Ravensbrück."

When that girl left, another asked if Corrie could give a Bible message to a group of girls in a different part of the barrack. Corrie did.

That Sunday she preached nine times.

WHILE CORRIE'S MINISTRY flourished, Betsie's health plummeted. By the second week of December the severe cold had done something to her legs. Oftentimes in the morning she could not move them, and Corrie and another would carry her to roll call. Betsie had lost so much weight, though, that she scarcely had the build of a child. As names were read, Betsie couldn't stamp her feet to keep blood flowing, so when they returned inside, Corrie would rub her feet and hands.

A few days later Betsie awoke unable to move her arms as well, and Corrie rushed up to a guard. "Please! Betsie is ill! Oh please, she's got to get to the hospital!"

"Stand at attention. State your number."

"Prisoner 66730 reporting. Please, my sister is sick!"

"All prisoners must report for the count. If she's sick she can register at sick call."

Another woman helped Corrie carry Betsie out. They trudged across the snow and by the time they were halfway to the hospital, Corrie could see that a line had formed at the door, stretching around the corner of the building. Alongside one wall three prisoners lay in the snow, likely dead. Corrie couldn't leave her sister to suffer the same fate, so they carried her back for roll call, then tucked her again into bed.

Corrie tried to comfort her but Betsie's speech became faint and labored. "A camp, Corrie . . . But we're . . . in charge. . . ." Betsie rested a moment, and then went on: "It will be so good for them, watching things grow. People can learn to love, from flowers."

Corrie wondered about what Betsie had said earlier about a camp and a house. "We are to have this camp in Germany? Instead of the big house in Holland?"

"Oh no. You know we have the house first."

Betsie began to cough, and Corrie noticed blood on the bed. "We'll be together, Betsie? We're doing all this together?"

"Always together, Corrie. You and I . . . always together."

..

THE FOLLOWING MORNING Corrie again tried to take Betsie to the hospital, but a guard turned her back.

How could they be so cruel? Corrie thought. She returned Betsie to bed and then appeared for roll call. When she returned to the barrack, two orderlies were setting a stretcher by Betsie's bed. The guard who had turned Corrie back minutes earlier supervised.

"Prisoner is ready for transfer."

As Corrie followed the procession to the door, a Polish friend of theirs saw Betsie and kneeled, making the sign of the cross. Outside, sleet rained down and as they walked, Corrie tried to form a shield to keep it from hitting her sister. Inside the hospital the orderlies set the stretcher on the floor and Corrie bent down to hear something Betsie was trying to say.

". . . must tell people what we have learned here. We must tell them that there is no pit so deep that He is not deeper still. They will listen to us, Corrie, because we have been here."

They will listen to us. The words echoed in Corrie's mind.

Nurses came and moved Betsie to a cot by a window. Corrie knew she couldn't follow so she rushed outside and ran around the building until she found the window to Betsie's room. They exchanged silent smiles and then a guard shouted at Corrie to return to the barrack.

She did, but kept thinking about what Betsie had said.

They will listen to us.

THE FOLLOWING AFTERNOON Corrie requested a pass to visit Betsie and, surprisingly, the guard gave it. At the hospital, though, the nurse in charge wouldn't let Corrie in, pass notwithstanding. So back to Betsie's window she went. She tapped on the glass until her sister caught her eyes.

"Are you all right?" Corrie mouthed silently.

Betsie nodded but didn't try to speak. Her lips were blue.

"You must get a good rest."

Betsie began to murmur something and Corrie bent forward.

". . . so much work to do . . ."

Corrie returned to the barrack and tried to get another pass in the late afternoon and evening, but each time the guard refused. The next morning, she didn't ask; after roll call she raced back to Betsie's window. Cupping her hands to the glass, she peered in but a nurse blocked the patient's face. A moment later another nurse stepped to the foot of the bed and it dawned on Corrie that a nude body lay between them. Or, not so much a body— more like an ivory carving with protruding ribs.

As the nurses lifted the corpse by the sheets, Corrie saw the face.

Betsie.

Chapter 23

THE LIST

ON THE DAY BETSIE DIED, December 16, 1944, Hitler commenced his most audacious and desperate attack of the war. At five-thirty in the morning, along an eighty-mile western front in the Ardennes region of Belgium and Luxembourg, three German armies—SS general Sepp Dietrich's Sixth Panzer Army, General Hasso von Manteuffel's Fifth Panzer Army, and General Erich Brandenberger's Seventh Army—began the assault. Two days later General Manteuffel sieged the Allied position at Bastogne, eventually surrounding the American Tenth Armored Division and 101st Airborne Division.

Though the Germans drove far into the Allied line—creating a wedge sixty miles deep and fifty miles wide (hence the later moniker, "Battle of the Bulge")—the advance was eventually thwarted when General George S. Patton's Third Army arrived.

For the Third Reich, this was the beginning of the end.

Prisoners at Ravensbrück were unaware of the success of the Allied defense and counter, but the prior bombing of the Siemens factory, together with the recurring sight of American planes overhead, gave them hope.

Whether Corrie and so many others at Ravensbrück could hold out was another story. In the barrack next to Corrie's, typhus* broke out and hundreds of women had to be quarantined. Lice—swarming in every barrack—carried the disease and multiplied by the hour.

At morning lineups women collapsed and died where they fell.

Two days after Betsie passed a problem arose at roll call: Barrack 28 was off by one number. The guards dismissed women from the other barracks, but those from Barrack 28 remained until they located the missing prisoner. For hours they stood, long after the sun came up, until Corrie's ankles and legs had swollen—evidence of edema.† By noon she had no feeling in either leg, but she refused to fall. Late in the afternoon the women of Barrack 28 finally were dismissed. The missing prisoner, they learned, had been found dead on an upper platform.

Amidst the grief of losing Betsie and the ongoing hardships of Ravensbrück, Corrie maintained her spiritual endurance through prayer and writing, penning this poem:

Teach me, Lord, to bear the burden,
In this dark and weary day.
Let me not complain to others
Of a hard and lonely way.

Every storm to Thee is subject,
Storms of earth, or mind and heart.

---

* Typhus was not unique to Ravensbrück; it affected all camps. About the situation at Auschwitz, Viktor Frankl wrote: "In the winter and spring of 1945 there was an outbreak of typhus which infected nearly all the prisoners. The mortality was great among the weak, who had to keep up with their hard work as long as they possibly could. The quarters for the sick were most inadequate, there were practically no medicines or attendants."

† Edema is common in cases of starvation because the sufferer has insufficient protein. Since protein plays an important part in the body's water balance, the lack of it causes areas such as the abdomen and legs to accumulate and retain water.

Only to Thy will submitting
Can to me Thy peace impart.

So to suffer, so keep silence,
So be yielded to Thy will.
So in weakness learn Thy power—
Teach me, Father, teach me still.

In the bowels of Ravensbrück administration, though, darkness spread. Commandant Fritz Sühren and one of the camp physicians, Dr. Richard Trommer, had been meeting daily to address Himmler's order that all women who were sick or incapable of marching were to be killed. Each day they made a list of those headed to the gas chamber.

To keep the intended victims docile, Sühren created a subterfuge. Prisoners on the list would be told that they were being transferred to "Mittwerda"—a fictitious camp—then in the evening they would be loaded onto a truck and driven to a facility for delousing, not an unwelcome activity for women who for months had been swarmed by lice and fleas. After the women undressed and had been moved inside, the door would be locked behind them. Poison gas would then be dropped in from the roof and the wailing would begin.

There were so many prisoners to be executed, though, Sühren and Trommer had to spread the killing schedule over several weeks. The sick and weak were to be disposed of first, and after that, all women over fifty.

Corrie's group.

AROUND CHRISTMASTIME A newcomer arrived in Barrack 28, a Russian named Marusha. The barrack was full, though, leaving Marusha without a bed. When night fell Corrie saw her wandering aimlessly between the rows, looking for a place to sleep. If she found none, she would have to sleep on the floor—without mattress, blanket, or pillow. Russians were not received well by other prisoners, however, and everywhere Marusha went women shook their heads.

Corrie considered the woman's plight. How dreadful it would be as a concentration camp prisoner not to have a place to sleep, she thought. Catching Marusha's desperate and haunted eyes, Corrie motioned her over. Turning back the cover, Corrie pointed to the spot Betsie had occupied. Beaming, Marusha slipped in.

As the Russian reclined and put her head on the pillow, Corrie wondered if there was a way to communicate with this person just inches away. She didn't know Russian, and Marusha apparently knew nothing else. Surely there had to be a way to bridge the languages.

"*Jesoes Christoes?*" Corrie finally uttered.

"Oh!" Marusha's eyes sparkled and she made a sign of the cross, then threw her arms around Corrie and kissed her.

Corrie later wrote: "She who had been my sister for fifty-two years, with whom I had shared so much of weal and woe, had left me. A Russian woman now claimed my love; and there would be others too who would be my sisters and brothers in Christ. I wondered if the Lord would provide further opportunities for me to give others the love and care that Father and Betsie no longer needed."

Corrie, though, needed love and care herself. After that day when she and all of Barrack 28 had been compelled to stand in the biting cold for more than twelve hours, five women—including Corrie—fell deathly ill. Whether it was typhus or something else, no one knew.

Within ten days the other four women were dead.

ONE FRIGID MORNING in late December a guard shouted: "Prisoner 66730!"

"That is my number," Corrie answered.

"Ten Boom, Cornelia."

"That is my name."

"Come forward."

Corrie stepped out of rank, her mind racing. *Is this it?* The gas chamber or perhaps another concentration camp? Or maybe just punishment for something?

The guard shouted again. "66730!"

Corrie took a few more steps forward and gave the appropriate response: "*Schutzhäftling ten Boom, Cornelia, meldet sich.*" ("Prisoner ten Boom, Cornelia, answers.")

The guard pointed to the far end of the lineup. "Stand on Number 1 on the roll call."

As Corrie shuffled toward the spot, frigid wind whipped through her dress. She stood there alone until a few minutes later a young girl was directed to the spot next to hers. Seeing Corrie shaking, the girl rubbed her back when the guards weren't looking.

As roll call continued Corrie turned to her. "Why must I stand here?"

The girl said it quietly and calmly.

"Death sentence."

Chapter 24

EDEMA

CORRIE MOUTHED A SHORT PRAYER.

"Perhaps I'll see you soon, face-to-face, like Betsie does now, Lord. Let it not be too cruel a killing. Not gas, Lord, nor hanging. I prefer shooting. It is so quick. You see something, you hear something, and it is finished."

Turning back to the girl, Corrie asked her name.

"Tiny."

"I am Corrie. How long have you been here?"

"Two years."

"Did you ever read the Bible?"

"No, I never did."

"Do you believe that God exists?"

"I do. I wish I knew more about Him. Do you know Him?"

Corrie said she did and for the next three hours—standing at attention with Tiny—she presented the Gospel.

"My sister died here," she told Tiny. "She suffered so much. I, too, have suffered. But Jesus is always with us. He did a miracle in taking away all my hatred and bitterness for my enemies."

Tiny appeared receptive and Corrie asked her to pray to the Lord, "a Friend who never leaves you alone."

The siren sounded to indicate the completion of roll call, and a guard shouted for everyone to get to work. Women scurried in every direction and Tiny, too, disappeared.

Corrie remained on spot Number 1 and waited. Would the Lord answer her prayer with a quick death?

"When you are dying," she later reflected, "when you stand at the gate of eternity—you see things from a different perspective than when you think you may live for a long time. I had been standing at that gate for many months, living in Barracks 28 in the shadow of the crematorium. Every time I saw the smoke pouring from the hideous smokestacks I knew it was the last remains of some poor woman. . . . Often I asked myself, 'When will it be my time to be killed or die?'"

Tiny in fact had been right about the death sentence; Corrie later discovered the girl had been executed shortly after leaving roll call. But what was Corrie's fate?

The guard who had called her out reappeared and told Corrie to follow her into the administration barrack. Corrie joined a short line of prisoners standing before a desk and watched as a clerk stamped a woman's papers and said, *"Entlassen!"*

Entlassen? Released? Could it be? Moments later the man announced: "Ten Boom, Cornelia."

Corrie approached and the man scribbled on a paper, stamped it, and handed it to her. She glanced down and saw one word in bold: *Entlassungsschein* (Certificate of Discharge).

Following the line to another desk, she received a railway pass for transportation to the Netherlands, and then a guard pointed down the corridor to another room. Inside, the women who had been ahead of Corrie in line undressed.

"Entlassen physical," a prison trustee told her.

Corrie nodded. One more humiliation. She removed the Bible from her neck, slipped her dress off, and tossed both into the pile of prisoner belongings.

As Corrie stepped closer, she was surprised at the doctor's youth—a freckled-faced boy who could have been one of her nephews. His demeanor, though, was all business. As each woman stood before him he asked them to bend, turn around, and spread their fingers.

Corrie stepped before him and the doctor's eyes fell immediately to her swollen legs and feet.

"Edema," he announced. "Hospital."

The trustee escorted her to the hospital and Corrie asked: "Then—we're not—aren't we to be released?"

"I imagine you will be, as soon as the swelling in your legs goes down. They only release you if you're in good condition."

It made sense. The SS didn't want to suffer bad press for mistreating prisoners, so anyone to be freed had to appear relatively healthy. She would have to wait.

The hospital was packed, though. A cluster of women waited in the sick call line, but dozens of new prisoners with terrible injuries had been brought in. A prisoner train making its way to Ravensbrück had been bombed, she learned, and the women were torn to shreds. To one side a patient lay on a table with a doctor and four nurses working around her. She screamed in pain and the shrill cries pierced Corrie's heart.

Just then a skeletal woman shuffled into the room. Her spindly legs were so feeble that she could hardly walk, and her eyes bulged with trauma. She called out for help, but one of the staff answered that she could walk just fine on her own.

Corrie sighed. Was there no end to the suffering of Ravensbrück?

She closed her eyes and tried to block everything out, but she couldn't; terror and cruelty reigned all around.

Finally, the trustee led her through a door and into a ward with double-stacked beds. Assigned a top bunk, Corrie pulled herself up and elevated her feet against the wall. That night sleep was impossible, though, because all through the wee hours patients cried out for bedpans. Corrie climbed down, edema notwithstanding, and went to comfort those most in pain.

Before sunrise three patients had fallen out of bed and died on the floor.

It was Christmas Day.

IN HAARLEM, PETER van Woerden reminisced about the ten Booms. As long as he could remember he had shared Christmas Day at the Beje with Opa and the rest of the family.

"The sweet ways of this old gentleman had made him beloved by all who knew him," Peter remembered, "especially his family. This year things would be different. His absence would be keenly felt."

But Christmas parties were the last thing on the minds of Hollanders. The German blockade of food had been on so long that hundreds died of starvation each day.* Beyond beets and tulips, there was nothing to eat. "Misery, starvation, and sickness were everywhere," Peter observed.

And death continued to touch those around him.

His longtime friend who was also his sister Aty's fiancé, Piet, fell victim next. Piet had been active in the underground and one day he left for a meeting at Resistance headquarters. The gathering, however, was a Gestapo trap, and he was taken to Amsterdam prison.

He was executed by firing squad.

***

_____
* During this winter 16,000 Hollanders died of starvation.

When Corrie finished her "ministry calls," she returned to her bunk. Opposite her, two Hungarians rested, one of whom had a severely gangrenous foot. Diagonally across was a young girl who looked about fifteen but had the mental development of an eight-year-old. She had a sweet face but her entire body was emaciated. When the girl turned, Corrie noticed a fresh scar, evidence that she had had some kind of back operation. Given the girl's mental condition, it had likely been a medical experiment.

Her name was Oelie and she often cried out for her mother. Corrie assumed the role of adopted mother and evangelist, explaining the Gospel to her in the most simple terms.

"Oelie, Mommy cannot come, but do you know who is willing to come to you? That is Jesus." Oelie seemed to understand.

"I will ask Jesus to make me brave when I have a pain," the girl said. "I will think of the pain that Jesus suffered to show Oelie the way to heaven."

Corrie then prayed with her, and it seemed clear why she needed to spend Christmas at Ravensbrück.

That night the temperature plummeted and Corrie noticed that the hospital windows were completely frosted. It was twenty below.

In the morning Corrie went for a reevaluation of her condition. "Edema of the feet and ankles," the doctor said again. Heading back to the sleeping ward, Corrie noticed a dead young woman lying in the snow. Her delicate hands were folded, as if in prayer, but her knees were pulled close, as if she had died in pain. She had a sweet face and her dark hair curled around her head as if a halo.

Corrie looked around and figured out what had happened. The woman had been forced to wait outside for entrance to the hospital, but the subzero air consumed her before she was allowed in.

Two days later, on December 28, Corrie passed the medical

Corrie's official discharge from Ravensbrück.

exam and the doctor stamped her release form. First, though, the processing. In a small hut near the camp's outer gate a guard issued her new clothes: underwear, a woolen skirt, a silk blouse, a hat, an overcoat, and almost-new shoes. She then received a package containing the clothes she had brought from Scheveningen, as well as some of Betsie's things. Here she also had to sign a form stating that she had never been ill at Ravensbrück, had never had an accident, and that the treatment had been good.

With a small group—two Hollanders and eight Germans— Corrie made her way to the gate. As if she needed one more reminder of life at Ravensbrück, the other Dutch lady mentioned that Mrs. Waard and Mrs. Jensen—two women whom Corrie and Betsie had prayed with—had died.

Outside the gate, another guard led them to a small office where Corrie received a day's bread ration and food coupons for three days. She also received back her money, watch, and her mother's gold ring.

An *Aufseherin* would escort them to the train station, the group was told, and Corrie retraced the path she had made entering the camp. They went up a small hill and she remembered the beautiful lake they had passed, only now it was completely frozen. On the other side the ancient castle and abbey highlighted picturesque Fürstenberg; in the distance the church steeple shined like a beacon of deliverance.

At the station the guard left and Corrie took stock of her belongings. Hunger pains gripped her so she reached in her coat for the bread. Curiously, it and the food ration coupons were gone. Had she lost them or did someone steal them?

Frantic, she jumped up and looked around the bench, then retraced her steps into the station. Nothing. After surviving on starvation rations at Ravensbrück, would she now die of hunger on a train home?

On the platform she waited with the other women until the late afternoon, when a mail train arrived. Two stops later, however, the entire group was told to disembark to make room for a food shipment.

Food.

Mere mention of the word heightened Corrie's hunger.

ANOTHER TRAIN FINALLY arrived and Corrie boarded with the others, but there was no food. Exhausted and faint, she fell asleep. Several trains and days later, she awoke one evening as they pulled into the Berlin terminal. It was after midnight, New Year's Day, 1945.

Corrie shuffled off the train in her new stiff shoes and wondered how she would find her connection. She had to go next to Uelzen, but there were no signs for it on the platform. An old man was raking up bomb rubble not far away, and she asked him for help. Kindly, he escorted her by the arm to the correct platform, but that train did not depart for several hours, Corrie found out. Nonetheless, she boarded. Dizzy with hunger, she knew that if she fainted she might miss the departure.

The train finally pulled out and at the first stop she disembarked and followed other passengers into the station café. She told the clerk that she had lost her food coupons, but that she could pay in Dutch guilders. Corrie opened her hand to show the money and the woman scoffed.

"That's an old story! Get out of here before I call the police!"

Back to the train Corrie trudged. Maybe she would see Betsie and her father sooner than expected. The train eventually pulled out, but for countless miles they inched along. The Allies had apparently bombed a number of tracks and stations, and Corrie had to disembark and board multiple trains. From each window she saw the devastation of what was once beautiful Germany. Everywhere, buildings and houses destroyed, and millions of German families without homes.

At one station Corrie asked an officer on the platform if there was any chance of getting food. Perhaps recognizing that she was on the verge of collapse, he called over a boy transferring baggage in a motorized cart. The next thing Corrie knew, she and the officer were riding on the vehicle to a small house nearby.

He said a few words to the woman living there, and moments later Corrie had bread, jam, and coffee before her. It was the kindest act she had witnessed since arriving in Germany.

No sooner had Corrie finished than an air-raid siren wailed and the officer said they needed to return to the station immediately. A day or so later, after what seemed like weeks of travel, Corrie arrived at the station in Bad Nieuweschans, a Dutch town half a mile from the German border.

She had returned, finally, to Holland. Seeing a number of German soldiers along the tracks, though, she reminded herself that this was still *occupied* Holland. A kind Dutchman saw Corrie's hobbled gait and helped her to yet another train. This one only went to Groningen, however—some thirty miles west of the border—since the railroad tracks beyond had been bombed.

When they arrived Corrie found out about a place called the Deaconess House—something of a hybrid between a hospital and convalescent home—a few blocks away. With her last strength, she dragged herself to it and asked a nurse if she could speak to the superintendent.

"Sister Tavenier cannot come at the moment," the woman said, "for she has to attend a religious service in one of the wards. I'm afraid you will have to wait."

"Could I perhaps attend it also?"

The nurse said she could.

"Have you anything for me to drink?"

The nurse brought out tea and dry toast, telling her that it would be best in her condition. For a moment Corrie had forgotten that she was gaunt and emaciated—a scarecrow—and here was a woman who actually cared for her.

After a few minutes the worship service began and an elderly minister led them in singing hymns. In the back of Corrie's mind, she kept replaying their singing in the filthy, lice-infested Barrack 28. When the service ended the nurse returned.

"Now, what must be done with you?"

Corrie shrugged. For more than a year she had not been allowed to make a decision, only to follow orders. "I don't know, Sister."

"I know what." The woman rang a bell and a young nurse came in.

"Sister," the older woman said, "take this lady to the nurses' dining room and give her a warm dinner."

The girl took Corrie's arm and led her down the corridor.

"Where are you going? Where is your home?"

"I am going to Haarlem."

"Oh, Haarlem. Do you know Corrie ten Boom there?"

Corrie looked at the girl a moment and it came to her. This was one of the YWCA leaders she had worked with before the war.

"Truus Benes!"

"Why, yes, that is my name. But I don't believe I know you."

"I am Corrie ten Boom."

Truus stopped walking and searched Corrie's face. "Oh, no, that's impossible. I know Corrie ten Boom very well. I have been in girls' camp with her several times. She is much younger than you."

And that was it—further proof that Corrie had been at Ravensbrück. Aged and emaciated beyond recognition. She considered what the girl saw: a sickly woman with hollow eyes, gray hair, and a thin, pale face.

"But really, I am Corrie ten Boom."

Truus looked again and reached for Corrie's hand. "Yes . . . yes . . . it is you. It *is*!"

They went to the dining room and Truus brought out plate after plate with meat and gravy, potatoes, Brussels sprouts, an apple, and pudding with currant juice. With every bite Corrie could feel her body responding with energy and healing.

At a table nearby, another nurse whispered to her companion: "I have never seen anyone eat so intensely."

After dinner, Truus escorted Corrie down the hall to a large room where she could take a hot bath. Steam rose from a sparkling white tub and Corrie sank down to her chin, the clean warm water soothing her lice-bitten, scab-crusted skin.

Truus returned later and knocked on the door.

"Just five minutes more!" Corrie begged.

Truus let her be but each time she returned Corrie asked for another five minutes. She had ten months of living in filth to wash away, after all, and when she would have another opportunity for this luxury was unclear. Finally, Corrie relented and got out and Truus handed her a nightgown. They went down the hall to a cozy bedroom assigned to a nurse who was on leave.

Corrie paused at the entrance. Color. All she had seen for almost a year was gray and here was a bright display of coordinated colors. She glanced at the bed, its thick woolen blankets turned back to reveal crisp white sheets. She let her hands slide over the soft cotton, back and forth. Truus invited her to recline on the bed, put a pillow under her feet, and then left her to rest.

Looking around the room, Corrie continued to absorb and enjoy her newfound haven. Across from the bed was a shelf filled with all sorts of books, and outside she could hear the familiar sounds of Holland: the whistle of a boat on a canal, children playing and calling to one another in the street, and, in the distance, a choir singing with the chimes of a carillon.

Home.

Chapter 25

DÉJÀ VU

LATE THAT AFTERNOON A NURSE stopped by and took Corrie to another room where she would stay a few days. Somewhere nearby, a radio was playing a Bach composition. It was the first music Corrie had heard in ten months.

Overcome, she sank to the floor and sobbed. God had indeed restored her life. She had been a prisoner and the Lord had ransomed her and set her free. There had to be purpose in all of this, she felt, and from here on—like Saul of Tarsus after his conversion—she would have a new mission. Ravensbrück was her Road to Damascus.

First, though, she had to notify Willem and Nollie of her release, and then get to Haarlem. A travel ban prevented going home, however, and telephone service was limited. For ten days she recuperated at the Deaconess House, and finally someone arranged for her to hitch a ride on an illegal food truck. It was being diverted from a shipment to Germany, so they would have to travel at night, without lights.

For hours the truck bounced through the dark, and when they reached Hilversum, Corrie directed the driver to Willem's house. Moments later Willem, Tine, and two of their daughters were in Corrie's arms.

Corrie explained Betsie's illness and death, and Willem's

countenance fell. "Almost I could wish to have this same news of Kik. It would be good for him to be with Betsie and Father." They had not heard from their son, he told Corrie, since Kik had been deported to Germany.

Corrie stayed with them two weeks—partly to adjust to normal life again, but mostly to enjoy time with her brother and his family. Willem had suffered greatly in his own confinement, she saw, and walked with a cane and limp. He was also dying. He had contracted tuberculosis in prison, and the ill effects were evident in his emaciated body.

First Father, then Betsie, probably Kik, and soon Willem. But her brother paid no attention to his ailments. They had fifty patients in the nursing home he ran, and Willem cared for and comforted all of them.

After several days Corrie noticed something else. Willem had employed scores of young women to help administer the home, some as nurses' aides, some as kitchen workers, others as secretaries. However, these were not girls at all, but young men dressing as women to escape the German forced-labor camps. While his capacity was limited, Willem continued to assist the Resistance.

Corrie longed to see Nollie and her beloved Beje, though, and Willem secured transportation. It would be another illegal trip, but he found a car that could drive the thirty miles from Haarlem to pick her up. The German authorities had allowed Willem to use his nursing home car as far as the city limits, so they arranged the transfer at a secret spot in Hilversum.

When they arrived Corrie saw a long black limousine waiting in the snow beside the road. It had government plates, and curtains covered the back windows. She kissed Willem goodbye and slipped into the strange car.

"Herman!"

"My dear Cornelia," Pickwick said, "God permits me to see you again."

The last time Corrie had seen him was on the bus to The Hague, bruised and bleeding. Now he seemed normal, as if nothing had happened to him, except for his missing teeth.

As always, Pickwick provided the latest news. The underground remained active, he said, but many of the young men were in hiding. Corrie asked about the Jews whom she had left in the Angels' Den and he said that all were safe except for Mary van Itallie, who had been arrested and sent to Poland.

The limousine passed over the Spaarne bridge leading into central Haarlem and Corrie was swept up by the sight of the Grote of St. Bavokerk.* This majestic Gothic church—built between 1245 and 1520—boasted a 246-foot spire and housed the renowned Christian Müller[†] organ. When built in 1738 it was the largest organ in the world. Covering the entire western wall of the church, it rises almost one hundred feet and is adorned with twenty-five statues, all carved by Jan van Logteren, an Amsterdam sculptor. At the pinnacle sit two gilded lions holding the Haarlem coat of arms.

Hearing of this organ, George Frideric Handel came to play it in 1740 and 1750. Sixteen years later, in 1766, a ten-year-old prodigy was at the pedals.

Wolfgang Amadeus Mozart.

Because the church was so close to her home, Corrie considered it as much of a friend as the ten Boom watch shop. But first was the Beje. When the limo turned onto the Barteljoris-straat, Pickwick warned her that the house was not quite the same. After removal of the police guard, he said, the authorities

---

* The church is often referred to as the Grote Kerk, meaning "Big Church," or simply St. Bavo Church.
† Ironically, Müller was a German.

housed several homeless families there. It was vacant now, he thought, although one of their loyal colleagues, Mr. Toos, had reopened the shop.

Corrie couldn't make it to the side door fast enough, and a moment later she fell into Nollie's embrace; her sister had come early that morning with her girls to clean the place for Corrie's arrival. They toured the entire house and Corrie noticed that a number of things had been stolen: four Oriental rugs, her typewriter, some books, and all of the watches and clocks that had been left for repair. Three of the most beloved possessions, however—Corrie's piano, the portrait of Father, and his favorite chair—remained.

In the kitchen they reminisced about how meticulously Betsie would set out cups, and in the living room how Martha would scold Eusi for leaving out his pipe. When they went into Opa's room Corrie slumped against his bed, fighting tears. She now would be alone in a house that for as long as she could remember had been filled with the gaiety of family, friends, and guests.

The next day Corrie went to the Grote Kerk, the ancient church that brought forth cherished memories of playing in the majestic cathedral as a child. Each old door, spiral staircase, or hidden closet provided an adventure for hide-and-seek. She also remembered the many times her uncle Arnold had gone with the family to hear the giant Müller organ.

At the door an elderly usher asked if he could show her around. "If it is alright," Corrie said, "I would like to be alone."

As she walked over the gravestones that formed the church floor, the scraping of her shoes brought an echo in the empty sanctuary. She found a seat and recalled the time as a child when she had played with a friend in that very spot. As the afternoon had waned that day, the cathedral darkened. Little light leaked through the stained-glass windows and the gas lamps on the side walls cast mysterious, flickering shadows. Her friend became scared, but Corrie felt peaceful. There was a Presence amidst them, she thought—the Light of the World.

Now, forty-five years later, she pondered the foreshadowing.

Light in the midst of darkness.

AS DAYS PASSED Corrie grew restless. She began accompanying Mr. Toos in the shop, but there was no longer joy in the work. Sometimes she would catch herself, realizing that she had been staring into space for an hour. Even the Beje provided little warmth. In an attempt to rekindle the homey felicity that Betsie had brought, Corrie bought plants for every windowsill.

She forgot to water them, though, and they died.

Something was missing. *Activity*. Work that mattered. The war was still on, after all, and she missed the underground.

She didn't have to wait long. In early February someone came by the Beje with an all too familiar request. "Miss ten Boom, I have a friend in prison," the man said. "You know the director of the prison, he is a good Dutchman and on our side. Will you go with me, introduce me to the director, and ask him to set my friend free?"

Corrie agreed and when they arrived at the prison and the director came out, Corrie's heart began to race. She had never seen this man before. Was this another quisling* trap? Would

---

* Vidkun Quisling, the Norwegian cofounder of the Nordisk Folkereisning (Nordic Folk Awakening) in 1931, a group that embraced Nazi ideology, was head of the Nazi-controlled puppet government ruling Norway from 1942 to 1945. In 1939 he had invited the Nazis to occupy his country, and later met the invading force in April 1940. Quisling inspired the London *Times* to use his name as a euphemism for all traitors and collaborators.

they return her to Ravensbrück? Or perhaps to save the trouble they would simply shoot her.

Blood drained from her face as she stumbled through the request for the prisoner.

"Wait a moment," the director said. "I'll phone the Gestapo to see if this request can be approved."

Chapter 26

THE FACTORY

THE GESTAPO? *PLEASE, GOD, NO.*

The director called them into his office, closed the door, and glared at Corrie.

"Are you an underground worker?"

Corrie said nothing. This was a repeating nightmare.

"What stupid work you do," the man went on. "You put us all in danger. If I should do what you ask I'd have to hide myself and my helpers immediately."

Corrie remained silent and the director said: "I'll give you advice on how to get this young man out, but don't come here again."

Never had an admonishment felt so good.

IN MARCH THE Gestapo began another round of house raids in Haarlem, once again targeting those who had connections to the underground. On the fifteenth they raided the Poley house, and in the nick of time Hans scrambled into a hidden space beneath the living room floor. The Gestapo was not after him, though. They interrogated and beat his father, but Mr. Poley played the part of a weak, innocent old man and the Germans bought it. They moved on to other houses, arresting, interrogating, and later shooting many of the Poley neighbors.

Hans emerging (with a banned radio) from the hiding place beneath the living room floor in his house.

When Hans emerged from the hiding place, he knew it was imperative to lie low. He had heard that Corrie had returned to the Beje, though, and he desperately wanted to talk to her. One evening when the Germans were not around, he and Mies went to visit her. Corrie had much to say—especially about the horrors of Ravensbrück—and told them she still awoke at roll call time: four-thirty a.m.

The most pressing problem now, they agreed, was Holland's lack of food. Countless thousands had already starved to death, and in late April the Allies began Operation Manna: a massive daily airdrop of food.

AS WEEKS PASSED Corrie reflected on what Betsie had said at Ravensbrück: "We must tell people, Corrie. We must tell them what we learned." She remembered, too, what Betsie had said about a place where people shattered and heartbroken from the war could come and put their lives back together. Betsie had imagined a beautiful home, with polished wood and ample gardens so the residents could plant flowers.

It was time, Corrie felt, to start the ministry. She began speaking at churches, clubs, and private homes, telling everyone who would listen what she, Betsie, and her father had been through, and what they had learned about faith and forgiveness. Finally, she told them about Betsie's vision of the convalescent home for the emotionally destroyed.

After one speaking engagement an elegantly dressed lady approached her. Corrie recognized the woman—Mrs. Bierens de Haan—as her home in Bloemendaal was considered one of the finest in Holland. Mrs. de Haan asked if Corrie still lived in the old house on the Barteljorisstraat and Corrie said she did. Little did Corrie know that Mrs. de Haan's mother had often visited the Beje to meet with Tante Jans, Corrie's aunt, for charity work.

"I am a widow," Mrs. de Haan said, "but I have five sons in the Resistance. Four are still alive and well. The fifth we have not heard from since he was taken to Germany." She went on to say that she wanted to open her home for Betsie's vision, and she invited Corrie to take a look.

The estate, a fifty-six-room mansion surrounded by giant oaks and gardens, was even more impressive than Corrie imagined.

"We've let the gardens go," Mrs. de Haan said. "But I thought we might put them back in shape. Don't you think released prisoners might find therapy in growing things?"

Corrie was speechless.

She gazed up at the giant windows and collected herself. "Are there inlaid wood floors inside, and a broad gallery around a central hall?"

"You've been here then!"

"No. I heard about it from—" Corrie stopped, unsure of what to say about Betsie's vision.

"From someone who's been here."

"Yes. From someone who's been here."

Inside, Mrs. de Haan ran her hand along the rich paneling. "Have you observed how beautiful the woodwork is?"

Corrie smiled, recalling what Betsie had said at Ravensbrück: "Our house is so elegant that the woodwork is equally beautiful. . . . And it should be, too, because the people we are going to help will need such an attractive environment that they will forget this dreary camp."

This was the place.

✳✳✳

On Saturday, May 5, in the village of Wageningen, German general Johannes Blaskowitz surrendered the forces occupying Holland to British-Canadian general Charles Foulkes. The First Canadian Army was expected in Haarlem any day now, and Dutch flags appeared all over the Grote Markt.

On Sunday morning Corrie went to the Grote Kerk and the pews were packed. It was the first service in liberated Holland, and as the Müller organ played, the congregation sang:

> *If God had not stood with us,*
> *And strengthened us to stand,*
> *How soon we would have fallen*
> *And perished from the land.*

After the closing prayer the organ boomed out the "Wilhelmus," the national anthem and tune that had led to Peter's arrest. Many were singing but others, like Corrie, were choked up.

She joined the sea of people exiting the church and when she was outside, she heard shots. A moment later she saw several cars flying down the Koningstraat. Inside them, German soldiers were shooting into the crowd. Corrie and others ran for cover into the adjacent Smedestraat. The German army had surrendered, but the danger remained.

Two days later, though, on May 8, the Canadians liberated Amsterdam and Haarlem. Hans and Mies stopped by the Beje again to visit Corrie, who was arranging a memorial to Opa in the shop window. They admired the display: beneath the painting of her father Corrie had arranged several photos, mementos, and a Bible open to Psalm 91. It was a fitting tribute to a great man.

After hugs and reminiscing, Hans, Mies, and Corrie decided to join the celebrating crowds in the Grote Markt. Thousands cheered and sang while red, white, and blue flags fluttered from almost every window.

The war was over. The Netherlands, like most of Europe, lay devastated. More than 200,000 Netherlanders had lost their lives in the war, including countless Jews and 16,000 Hollanders who had starved to death. Thousands of Dutch boys who had been sent to work in German factories—like Kik ten Boom— were unaccounted for. By any account, rebuilding lives and cities would take years.

Queen Wilhelmina, however, remained confident. "He who led us through the dark valley of anxiety and oppression," she told her people in May, "to the freedom and space in which we can be ourselves again is able to realize the vision of a better future. . . . It is no wishful thinking when we persist in our confidence in that finer, better nation that seemed round the corner at the liberation; we are not led by something we would like to be true, but by a profound experience of God's Guidance of people and nations."

..

CORRIE BEGAN HER new life. She moved into the de Haan home in Bloemendaal, and soon countless other survivors followed.

"Because I had lived so close to death," Corrie remembered, "looking it in the face day after day, I often felt like a stranger among my own people—many of whom looked upon money, honor of men, and success as the important issues of life. Standing in front of a crematorium, knowing that any day could be your day, gives one a different perspective."

The words of an old German saying came to her mind again and again:

"What I spent, I had; what I saved, I lost; what I gave, I have."

A summary of her experience as a prisoner, it also served as a motto for her new ministry. And she, too, needed healing. Six months removed from the suffering of Ravensbrück, Corrie decided to seal her forgiveness of enemies. *All* enemies. She had already forgiven the Germans, but there was another who was most difficult: the Dutchman who had betrayed her to the Gestapo—Jan Vogel—"Mr. Six Hundred Guilders."

On June 19, 1945, she wrote to him:

Dear Sir,

Today I heard that most probably you are the one who betrayed me. I went through 10 months of concentration camp. My father died after 9 days of imprisonment. My sister died in prison, too.

The harm you planned was turned into good for me by God. I came nearer to Him. A severe punishment is awaiting you. I have prayed for you, that the Lord may accept you if you will repent. . . .

I have forgiven you everything. God will also forgive you everything, if you ask Him. . . . If it is difficult for you to pray, then ask if God will give you His Spirit, who works the faith in your heart. . . .

I hope that the path which you will now take may work for your eternal salvation.

Corrie ten Boom

BY THE END of June the Bloemendaal house had accepted more than a hundred residents, all of them damaged and scarred. Some had been in concentration camps, others had been hiding in attics and closets for years, and still others had lost their entire family in bombing raids.

In this haven each resident learned that countless others had suffered just as they had. All of them needed the same healing, too. "Each had a hurt he had to forgive," Corrie recalled, "the neighbor who had reported him, the brutal guard, the sadistic soldier. Strangely enough, it was not the Germans or the Japanese that people had most trouble forgiving; it was their fellow Dutchmen who had sided with the enemy."

These former collaborators were now pariahs throughout Holland. Many had their heads shaved and were paraded through the streets. Most had been turned out of their homes and apartments and couldn't find employment. All were jeered in public.

Corrie believed they needed healing, too, so she tried admitting some into the Bloemendaal house, but the anger boiling within those who had suffered fostered arguments and fights. Corrie pivoted, relocating the collaborators to the Beje. The home that had once been the center of underground resistance now worked to heal the very persons who had betrayed them.

Soon Corrie had doctors, psychiatrists, and nutritionists making free calls at the Bloemendaal house, and she installed morning and evening worship services. The residents could come and go as they pleased. Many of them healed by planting flowers and vegetables in the garden, just as Betsie had said. Others seemed to recover by taking long walks in the middle of the night.

The collaborators in the Beje, however, were a bit more difficult. No one visited them, and they received no mail. Eventually, though, the healing at Bloemendaal manifested itself with simple kind gestures to the outcasts. "Those people you spoke of," a resident said to Corrie one day, "I wonder if they'd care for some homegrown carrots."

Corrie's plans had come to fruition: Bloemendaal and the Beje became effective centers for healing and forgiveness.

ONE NIGHT CORRIE felt restless. She missed Haarlem and the Beje, but there was something else, something she couldn't quite put her finger on.

It was after midnight when she arrived on the Barteljorisstraat. The streetlights were dim, and the moon and stars provided a majestic canopy. When she came to the Beje, she let her hands glide across the front door of the shop. Watchmaking had been the only business she knew, and the bond between her work and her father was more than any child could ask for. But others lived in this house now, and that was the source of the discomfort: the Beje was part of her.

Father was gone. Betsie was gone. The Beje was gone. She went around the corner into the side alley—the very spot where she had admitted countless Jews and divers—and placed her hands on the cold stone. Stepping closer, resting her face against the wall, it came to her.

For more than fifty years the Beje had been her own hiding place, her refuge. But Ravensbrück had taught her that this magnificent home—with all of its memories—was but a shadow; her true hiding place was in Christ.

As she rested against the stone the chimes of the Grote Kerk began to play. It was timely and soothing, but it was nostalgic, too, because all her life she had heard this beautiful music day and night. She made her way to the Grote Markt and gazed up at the church's towering cathedral and spire. Looking into the stars, she said, "Thank you, Jesus, that I am alive."

Just then the chimes began to play Martin Luther's classic, "A Mighty Fortress Is Our God," and Corrie found herself singing it, not in Dutch, but in German. How ironic, it seemed, that God would remind her of his grace and care from a German hymn.

Over ensuing weeks and months, Corrie spoke all over Holland, and in other parts of Europe. Bloemendaal ran on donations, which were coming in, but she was eager to spread her message.

In the fall of 1945 Corrie felt the urge to continue her ministry in America. Passage to the United States was almost impossible, but one day she inquired about travel and learned that a freighter was leaving the following week. She made the journey, arriving in New York with fifty dollars.

She found boarding in a YWCA and began to network. She knew no one in America, but did have an address of a group of Jewish-Christians who met regularly in the city. She contacted them and they invited her to speak. When she arrived, she found that most of them were German immigrants, so she spoke to them in their native tongue.

About a week later she went to the YWCA office to pay her bill. To her surprise, the clerk said that a week was their limit for guests; Corrie would have to find other accommodations. With little money and no friends, she'd have to scramble.

As she turned to leave the clerk called her over, saying she had mail.

Mail? Corrie wondered. *No one knows where I live.*

She opened the envelope and read: "I heard you speak to the Jewish congregation," a woman wrote. "I am aware that it is almost impossible to get a room in New York City. My son happens to be in Europe, so you are welcome to use his room as long as you are in New York."

OVER THE NEXT few weeks Corrie met a number of ministers and Christian leaders. She visited a man named Irving Harris, editor of a magazine called *The Evangelist*. He suggested that she make an appointment to see Abraham Vereide, a prominent Christian leader, in Washington, D.C. Corrie had dinner with Vereide several days later, along with three professors he had invited, and they asked her questions throughout the evening. The next morning Vereide spun into action, arranging a speaking engagement for Corrie that afternoon. Afterward, one of the ladies in attendance handed her a check.

"Corrie, this is your message. Share it wherever you go."

Vereide continued to make introductory calls, and soon Corrie received invitations to speak all over the country. For several months she gave her testimony at churches, prisons, universities, schools, and clubs. As the year drew to a close, though, she felt called to return to Europe. Again and again her mind returned to what Betsie had said at Ravensbrück—that they would have to minister in Germany itself.

"Corrie, there is so much bitterness," Betsie had said. "This concentration camp here at Ravensbrück has been used to destroy many, many lives. There are many other such camps throughout Germany. After the war they will not have use for them anymore. I have prayed that the Lord will give us one in Germany. We will use it to build up lives."

Corrie had found the idea repulsive at the time. Never again did she want to step foot in Germany. But Betsie's words echoed in her mind: "The Germans are the most wounded of all the people in the world."

Corrie considered the state of Germany: the land lay in ruins and rubble, countless husbands, fathers, and brothers were gone, and some nine million people were homeless.

She would go.

SPEAKING OPPORTUNITIES CAME easily in Germany, and one day she received an invitation to speak to a hundred families living in an abandoned factory. Sheets and blankets had been hung to create makeshift rooms, but the cry of a baby or outburst of a resident resounded throughout the building. All around Corrie could see nothing but misery and desperation. How could she minister to these people? She had her own life now, traveling and speaking, but the needs here burdened her.

If she wanted to have a meaningful impact, she realized, there was only one way.

She would have to live with them.

Chapter 27

LOVING THE ENEMY

AND SO CORRIE MOVED INTO the factory, sharing the Germans' plight and bearing their burdens. For months she loved, comforted, and cared for them, asking nothing in return.

One day a director of a relief organization visited Corrie at the factory. He had heard about her work, he said, and perhaps there was yet another avenue for her special ministry. "We've located a place for the work. It was a former concentration camp that's just been released by the government."

Corrie was floored. Another piece of Betsie's vision come true. She went with the man to Darmstadt, a dilapidated former concentration camp, and walked between the barbed wire to the gray buildings. It was too familiar.

Inside a barrack Corrie decided it would all have to be transformed.

"Window boxes. We'll have them at every window. . . . Green paint. Bright yellow-green, the color of things coming up new in the spring."

In 1946, one year removed from her own incarceration in a camp like this, Corrie opened the Darmstadt facility to mirror what the Bloemendaal home had become in Holland. With the extra space, though, Darmstadt could house one hundred sixty residents. Soon the facility reached capacity and had a waiting

Left: *Darmstadt as a concentration camp*. Right: *Corrie's Darmstadt healing center. Notice the abundant flowers, including flower boxes at each window.*

list. The German Lutheran Church agreed to help with administration, and another group, the Lutheran Sisterhood of Mary, assisted with women and children residents. Corrie continued to speak to raise money for Darmstadt, and soon pastors and members of various churches began building homes around it. Corrie now had three havens of healing.

In December 1946, sad news arrived. Willem, who had continued to suffer from tuberculosis, died. Corrie continued on with her work, though, burdened that the ten Boom death toll from the war had now reached four: Father, Betsie, Willem, and most likely Kik.

IN EARLY 1947 Corrie spoke at a church in Munich, the town where Adolf Hitler had begun his political career with the ill-fated "Beer Hall Putsch."* When she finished, a man worked his way through the crowd to speak with her. Balding and heavyset, he wore an overcoat and carried a brown felt hat. As he stepped

---

* On November 8–9, 1923, Hitler and his Nazi Party followers attempted a coup d'état in Munich, hoping to seize control of the country. At a beer hall they were confronted by police and a shoot-out ensued; fourteen Nazis and four police officers were killed, and Hitler was arrested. Convicted of treason, he was sentenced to five years in prison. There he wrote his ideological treatise, *Mein Kampf*. He was released after serving only nine months.

closer, though, Corrie instead saw a blue uniform, cap with skull and crossbones, and a swinging leather crop.

Her stomach churned. It was him all right—the first SS guard she had seen in the Ravensbrück shower room. The undressing and nakedness, the pile of clothes, the leering and mocking men, Betsie's ashen face. Of all the sadistic camp guards, he was one of the most cruel.

"How grateful I am for your message, *Fraulein*," the man said. "To think that, as you say, He has washed my sins away!"

He held out his hand but Corrie didn't reciprocate. How could she touch this vermin?

"You mentioned Ravensbrück in your talk," he continued. "I was a guard there. But since that time I have become a Christian. I know that God has forgiven me for the cruel things I did there, but I would like to hear it from your lips as well."

He extended his hand again. "*Fraulein*, will you forgive me?"

Corrie wrestled with her bitterness. This man represented the worst of the place that had taken Betsie's life. Forgiveness seemed impossible.

At the same time, though, she remembered Jesus's admonition: "If you do not forgive men their trespasses, neither will your Father in heaven forgive your trespasses." She had preached the importance of forgiveness the last twelve months, and she had seen firsthand at Bloemendaal and Darmstadt the practical impact: those who were able to forgive their former enemies resumed their lives, while those who could not remained emotional invalids.

Corrie tried to smile, but she felt not the slightest spark of warmth or charity. Quickly, she said a silent prayer: "Jesus, help me! I can lift my hand. I can do that much. You supply the feeling."

Mechanically, she lifted her arm. As she gripped the man's hand, something remarkable happened: a current of energy passed between them, and a healing warmth flooded her body. More than forgiveness, Corrie suddenly felt a genuine love for this man.

Her eyes filled with tears. "I forgive you, brother! With all my heart."

For several moments she held his hand. "I had never known God's love so intensely as I did then," she later remembered. This lesson she would not soon forget: one often cannot forgive without the power and grace of God.

With a settled heart and peace, Corrie decided to tell her story to a wider audience, and later that year she published an autobiography—*A Prisoner and Yet.** It was a simple book, but it shared the most salient elements of her ordeal: hiding Jews and refugees in the Beje, the betrayal and arrest of her family, prison at Scheveningen, and concentration camp life at Vught and Ravensbrück.

※※※

In early 1951, almost seven years after his release from prison, Peter went to Bremen, Germany, as part of a group conducting evangelistic meetings. Officially, he was the interpreter for an American speaker, but he also provided most of the music for the events. One evening the topic was the "Second Coming of Christ," and the speaker asked the audience: "If Jesus were to come tonight, would *you* be ready?"

When the service was over a German worked his way to the front of the room. At first Peter didn't recognize the man, but then the face came to him: Hans Rahms. The lieutenant had aged considerably, and Peter could tell he was or had been ill.

---

* The book was published in Canada in 1947, but the American edition would not appear until 1970.

"Mr. Rahms, do you remember me? I was your prisoner seven years ago at Scheveningen prison."

The German nodded and Peter asked what had happened to him after the war. Rahms said he had been imprisoned several years, but now he was working as a window washer.

They spoke for a few minutes, and then Peter cut to the chase: "I remember asking you then if you would be ready if Christ came then. You didn't answer me. Tonight, I'd like to ask you the same question. If Jesus came tonight, would you be ready?"

"Yes, Peter. I think I'm ready."

SOME MONTHS LATER while Corrie toured Germany, she also ran into Lieutenant Rahms. Her thoughts replayed how he had freed Peter and many of her friends, and had thrown her incriminating papers into the furnace, saving her life.

"I shall never forget your sister's prayers," Rahms told her. Through the discussions and prayers with Betsie, her, and Peter, he explained, he had become a Christian.

This news, Corrie confided later, "was one of life's richest moments for me, for on that day I glimpsed a little of God's side of the pattern of my life."

Over the next several years Corrie's pace intensified. Throughout the decade she went from church to church, club to club, home to home, speaking in more than forty countries. In 1954, while on a short return to Haarlem, she slipped on wet pavement and took a nasty fall. Bystanders helped her to a taxi, and then a policeman appeared.

"What is your name?"

"Corrie ten Boom."

"Are you a member of the family of that name whom we arrested about ten years ago?"

"That is right."

Corrie with Hans Rahms in 1951.

Without asking, Corrie knew that this man was a loyal Dutch policeman, many of whom had worked for the specific purpose of helping political prisoners.

"I am so sorry about your accident, but I am glad to see you again. I will never forget that night in the police station. You were all sitting or lying on the floor of the station. Your old father was there with all his children and many of your friends. I have often told my colleagues that there was an atmosphere of peace and joy in our station that night, as if you were going to a feast instead of prison and death.

"Your father said before he tried to sleep, 'Let us pray together.' And then he read Psalm 91."

"You remember!"

Ten years after the event and this policeman recalled not only the happenings that night, but the exact psalm Opa had asked Willem to read. The improbable reunion confirmed to Corrie that she was doing the right thing.

Corrie continued to travel the world alone for three more years, often not knowing where she would stay, or where she would speak. She had been on a nonstop schedule for twelve years and, at age sixty-five, it was time to hire an aide and traveling companion. On a visit to England she met a young Dutch woman, Conny van Hoogstraten, who accepted her invitation to join in this most unusual ministry. With someone to handle logistics, Corrie now worked harder than ever.

In 1959 she joined a group going to Germany to honor the tens of thousands* of women—including Betsie—who had died at Ravensbrück. While visiting the camp Corrie learned something startling: her release had been due to a clerical error.

A week later all women over fifty were executed in the gas chambers.

FOR TEN YEARS Corrie and Conny were inseparable. Conny's likability and easygoing personality made transitions from home to home seamless, and Corrie became dependent on her. In early 1967, however, Conny told Corrie that she had met someone special, and that they planned to marry later in the year. The news crushed Corrie, who confided: "I loved her like a sister."

They prayed that God would provide a suitable replacement. Corrie went on to engagements in Vietnam and Indonesia, and then she and Conny convened in Amsterdam for their last months. There they met Ellen de Kroon, a tall, fair-haired Dutch nurse with an infectious smile. Conny married on September 1 but, because she lived not far from Corrie, she came over often to assist Ellen in the transition.

Shortly after the New Year, Corrie learned that the State of Israel had chosen her for induction into Righteous Among the

---

* The exact figure of the number of women who died at Ravensbrück is unknown, but the estimates range from 30,000 to 92,700.

Nations, an honorific honoring Gentiles who had risked their lives during the war to save Jews.*

Two months later a most unusual opportunity arose. In May, while speaking at a church in Germany, an American writing couple, John and Elizabeth Sherrill, approached her. They had read her autobiography, *A Prisoner and Yet*, and were fascinated by her experience. Believing that Corrie's story needed to be retold, they proposed to write a new book with her. Their credentials were sterling, as in 1963 they had helped David Wilkerson write his famous autobiography, *The Cross and the Switchblade*, and in 1967 they had helped Andrew van der Bijl ("Brother Andrew," as he was known to many) write his memoir, *God's Smuggler*. Not only that, but they planned to launch their own publishing company, Chosen Books, and Corrie's would be their first title. Thus with Corrie's story and the Sherrills' writing, Chosen Books published in 1971 the runaway bestseller, *The Hiding Place*, which sold three million copies over the next four years.

In her last leg of public speeches after the book came out, Corrie liked to end on a story she called "Black and Whites." In January 1969 an American friend of hers had stopped by to visit. The man knew her well and felt free to bring up a sensitive subject. Years before, Corrie had been taken advantage of by some fellow Christians, the man knew, and he inquired whether there had been resolution and reconciliation.

"It is nothing," Corrie said. "It is all forgiven."

"By you, yes. But what about them? Have they accepted your forgiveness?"

"They say there is nothing to forgive! They deny it ever happened. No matter what they say, though, I can prove they were wrong."

---

* The designation occurred in 1967, and the presentation was held in Jerusalem on February 28, 1968. As part of the ceremony, Corrie planted a memorial tree on the Avenue of the Righteous.

Corrie went to her desk, opened a drawer, and waved at some papers. "See, I have it in black and white! I saved all their letters and I can show you where—"

"Corrie!" Reaching under her arm, he gently closed the drawer. "Aren't you the one whose sins are at the bottom of the sea? Yet are the sins of your friends etched in black and white?"

Corrie paused, stunned. Her ministry for more than twenty years had been about forgiveness, and yet she had saved— *relished*—the "black and white" evidence she had against her colleagues. She remembered the passage again: "Forgive our trespasses," Jesus taught, "as we forgive those who trespass against us."

The American left but Corrie sat at her desk and stared at the papers. *Incriminating* papers. For several minutes she pondered forgiveness, and how to genuinely embrace it. Glancing at her fireplace, it came to her.

Lieutenant Rahms.

She gathered up the papers and fed them into the fire.

EPILOGUE

IN 1975, FOUR YEARS AFTER publication of *The Hiding Place*, World Wide Pictures released a film version of the book. While pre-showings for selected groups, theater owners, and media began in May, the movie premiered on September 29 at the Beverly Hills Theater. Jeannette Clift George portrayed Corrie, while Julie Harris played Betsie. Arthur O'Connell played the role of Casper, Robert Rietti played Willem, and Paul Henley portrayed Peter. For her starring role, George was nominated for a Golden Globe (Most Promising Newcomer–Female).

That fall Corrie and Ellen went to Tulsa, Oklahoma, for a special event at Oral Roberts University. The university chaplain, Robert Stamps, coordinated the presentations with Ellen and soon a deep friendship ensued, followed by romance. Seven months later, in May 1976, Bob and Ellen became engaged and Corrie had to say goodbye to her second aide. Before Ellen left, though, Corrie found Pamela Rosewell, an English woman who had been Brother Andrew's personal secretary for eight years. Pam accepted the new job and they began the transition.

In April 1976, just a week before Corrie's eighty-fourth birthday on April 15, she had a touching farewell with Ellen. Corrie and Pam were scheduled to fly to America again for another speaking engagement, and Ellen went with them to the Amsterdam airport. For nine years Corrie and Ellen had gone in and out of this airport traveling the world, and all that time seemed to coalesce where they stood. Ellen remembered vividly what Corrie had said the day they met: "I am so happy that God is going to give you to me."

Now it was a bittersweet parting, and neither Corrie nor Ellen knew exactly what to say. Corrie drew Ellen and Pam close and prayed, and then it was time for them to board. Instinctively, Ellen grabbed the handles of Corrie's wheelchair just as she had done hundreds of times, and then it dawned on her: it was now Pam's time. Ellen released the handles, stepped aside, and watched Corrie's new aide lead her down the ramp.

No sooner than Ellen had arrived back at Corrie's apartment, the phone rang. It was someone from the airport with a message from Corrie: "Look on the desk, Ellen," the caller said, "for a little note."

Ellen glanced at the desk, wondering when Corrie had left it, and rushed over to read it. The letter was vintage Corrie.

My dear, dear Ellen,
Thank you for everything you have done and for who you have been during these important years of my life.
    Continue to keep Jesus on the throne of your heart; then you will stay in the boundaries where God's love can reach you.
    If you have time, go and look behind the painting of the "Castle of Brederode." I have written something on the other side of the painting.
    God bless you and Bob very specially.
                                    Your thankful Tante Corrie

The *Castle of Brederode* painting, Ellen knew, was a precious ten Boom heirloom. It was a beautiful rendering of a scene near Haarlem by the Dutch painter A. Miolée. She removed the frame from the wall and looked on the back at Corrie's inscription:

To Ellen de Kroon from Tante Corrie:
As a little remembrance of the blessed years that we wandered together as fellow tramps for the Lord in many countries. It

is great to know that whatever we do in love for the Lord is never lost and never wasted.

1 Corinthians 15:58

Corrie ten Boom

That painting now hangs in Ellen and Bob's home, and each time Ellen reflects upon it, she says, "Thank You, Lord, that You gave Tante Corrie to *me*."

IN 1977, AT AGE EIGHTY-FIVE, Corrie finally retired and moved to Placentia, a small town in northern Orange County, California. Her health deteriorated quickly, though, and she had two strokes the next year and lost the ability to speak.

In 1979 Corrie enjoyed perhaps her last special blessing, courtesy of the United Kingdom. For five nights, October 9–13, *The Hiding Place* musical was performed before sold-out crowds at the Birmingham Hippodrome Theater.

THROUGH THE EARLY 1980s Corrie remained active with the two ministry organizations she founded—Christians, Incorporated and the Association of Christian Prison Workers—attending board meetings and chairing planning committees.

In 1983 she suffered a third stroke, and on April 15, her ninety-first birthday, she died at home in Placentia. Corrie likely would have said it was fitting, since Psalm 91 had served as her and her father's favorite passage.

She had visited more than sixty countries telling her story of love, forgiveness, and grace. Scarcely has anyone been such a tireless evangelist, and she ministered to everyone—students in Uganda, farmers in Cuba, factory workers in Uzbekistan, villagers in Siberia, prisoners in San Quentin, officials in the Pentagon—even to a leper colony on an African island.

The three convalescent centers she developed—the Beje,* Darmstadt, and Bloemendaal—were highly successful, helping countless thousands rebuild their lives. Corrie's biography, *The Hiding Place*, sold upwards of four million copies, spawning her magazine, also called *The Hiding Place*. She was knighted by Juliana, Queen of the Netherlands,† honored by the State of Israel, adopted as an Indian sister by the Native American Hopi tribe,‡ and received an honorary doctorate from Gordon College.§ Finally, in her hometown of Haarlem, a street was named after her (Corrie ten Boomstraat).

There wasn't much, in fact, that she *didn't* accomplish.

Like the steadfast chimes of a grandfather clock, Corrie ten Boom's legacy continues to sound out her message of faith, hope, love, and forgiveness.

---

* The Beje now operates as the Corrie ten Boom Museum.
† On September 4, 1947, Queen Wilhelmina abdicated the throne so that her daughter, Juliana, could begin her reign as queen.
‡ For her work with the Christian Hope Indian Eskimo Fellowship, Corrie was given the name "Lomasi," which means "beautiful flower" in Hopi.
§ Corrie received a Doctor of Humane Letters on April 23, 1976.

MANY INDIVIDUALS PLAYED A PROMINENT role in Corrie's story, and what became of them after the war is worth noting. History should also mark the fate or accomplishments of those not necessarily connected to the ten Booms, but central to the overall Dutch World War II story.

Dr. Arthur Seyss-Inquart

As Hitler's Reich commissioner of the Netherlands, Seyss-Inquart oversaw and ordered the deportation of some 140,000 Dutch Jews to concentration camps, 117,000 of whom were murdered or worked to death. He was responsible also for the deaths of another 2,000 to 3,000 non-Jewish Dutchmen executed in Holland, and more than 20,000 who died in concentration camps in the Netherlands or Germany. These figures do not include the deaths of Dutch soldiers or Dutchmen who died in German forced labor camps.

To the end he remained faithful to his Führer, and for this Hitler (shortly before his suicide) appointed him foreign minister in the new government under Admiral Karl Dönitz.

On October 16, 1946, Seyss-Inquart was executed in Nuremberg prison for war atrocities and crimes against humanity.

Hanns Albin Rauter

As the Higher SS and Police Leader and chief of all SS troops in occupied Netherlands, Rauter implemented a reign of terror seldom seen in history. He ordered the execution of hundreds of

Dutch Resistance members, and sent thousands to their deaths in concentration camps.

On March 6, 1945, near Apeldoorn, Resistance agents attacked the car in which he was traveling. Rauter was the lone survivor of the attack, but he was so wounded that he spent the remainder of the war in a hospital.* In May the British captured him in Germany and turned him over to the Dutch, who tried him in 1948.

Rauter was sentenced to death and was executed in February 1949.

Otto, Edith, Margot, and Anne Frank

After their arrest on August 4, 1944, the Frank family was sent to the Auschwitz concentration camp. In October Margot and Anne were transferred to another camp, Bergen-Belsen, near Hanover, Germany. On January 6, 1945, Edith (Anne's mother) died from starvation and exhaustion. That winter typhus broke out at Bergen-Belsen and Margot and Anne died from it roughly two months† after their mother's passing.

Miraculously, father Otto survived Auschwitz, which was liberated by the Russians, and arrived back in Amsterdam on June 3, 1945.

Audrey Hepburn

After the war, on April 25, 1946, Audrey Hepburn returned to Velp for a dance recital to raise money for the Red Cross.

---

*   In retaliation for the attack on Rauter, SS general Karl Schöngarth ordered the execution of more than 250 prisoners. After the war, Schöngarth was tried for war crimes by a British military court on February 11, 1946. He was found guilty and was hanged at Hamelin prison a month later.

†   The date of death for both girls is generally marked as late February or early March 1945.

Eight years later, just one year removed from her starring role in *Roman Holiday*, she returned with her husband, Mel Ferrer, to Oosterbeek, Netherlands, to lay a wreath at the memorial to the British 1st Airborne Division.

Three years later, in 1957, Audrey met Anne Frank's father, Otto. With the release of his daughter's diary, he told her, a film was going to be made of their story. He asked if Audrey would play the role of Anne, but she told him that, for a number of reasons, she couldn't.

Fritz Sühren

As commandant of Ravensbrück, Fritz Sühren was ultimately responsible for the tens of thousands of women who died in the camp, including Betsie ten Boom. In an attempt to save his skin at the eleventh hour, he took one of his prisoners, SOE agent Odette Sansom, and drove in a two-car convoy to surrender to the Americans. As part of her own story to save her life, Odette had told the Germans that she was married to fellow agent Peter Churchill, relative of Winston Churchill. While she and Peter had fallen in love, they were not married, and he was not a relative of the prime minister. The Germans believed all of it, though, and Sühren assumed that his deliverance of a Churchill spouse would put him in good stead with his captors.

When they reached an American outpost, Sühren was arrested and imprisoned with others at Neuengamme concentration camp, to be tried for war crimes. Startlingly, he escaped and went to ground, avoiding authorities for years. Finally, on March 24, 1949, he was recaptured by American troops at Deggendorf and turned over to the French for prosecution.

On March 10, 1950, he was tried for war crimes and crimes against humanity by a military court in Rastatt, Germany. Convicted and sentenced to death, Sühren was hanged on June 12 at Sandweier, Baden-Baden.

Casper ten Boom

Corrie's father was inducted into the State of Israel's Righteous Among the Nations in 2007, and a street was named after him (Casper ten Boomstraat) in Haarlem.

Elisabeth ten Boom

Betsie was inducted into the State of Israel's Righteous Among the Nations with her father in 2007.

Willem ten Boom

Before his death in December 1946 Willem published several books, the last a study of sacrifice in the Old Testament. In the forefront of his mind, though, was his son Kik, who had not been heard from since he was deported to a German concentration camp. Shortly before Willem's last breath, he told his wife, Tine: "It is well—it is very well—with *Kik*." It was a poignant moment as Willem was quoting from Horatio Spafford's famous hymn, "It Is Well with My Soul."*

---

* In the fall of 1873, Spafford, an American lawyer and Presbyterian elder, had planned a vacation in England with his wife, Anna, and their four daughters: Annie, twelve; Maggie, seven; Bessie, four; and an eighteen-month old

Kik, like Spafford's daughters, apparently had perished, but with Horatio, Willem could say: "It is well."

Years after Willem died, Peter van Woerden visited a synagogue in Tel Aviv. After the service a friend introduced him to a Dutch Jew who was in attendance.

"Do you happen to know the name ten Boom?" the man asked Peter.

Peter acknowledged that he was Nollie's son, and the man said that Willem had hidden him in his home during the Nazi occupation. "When the Gestapo came," he explained, "I hid under the floor of Dr. ten Boom's study. When the soldiers came in, he started to scold them for disturbing his sermon preparation. The soldiers were intimidated by his self-confident manner and left him alone. Your uncle saved my life."

The Ten Boom School in Maarssen, Netherlands, is named after Willem.

---

baby. Late business demands kept Horatio from departing with his family and he sent them on, promising to join them soon. On November 21 Anna and the girls left for England aboard the French iron steamship the *Ville du Havre*. In the middle of the night the *Ville du Havre* collided with the *Loch Earn*, a British iron clipper, and sank within twelve minutes. All of the Spafford children— along with 222 other passengers—perished.

A nearby American vessel, the *Tremountain*, rescued Anna and eighty-six others. Arriving in England, Anna sent a telegram to her husband beginning with two words: "Saved alone." Horatio left to join her on the next outbound ship, and he asked the captain if he knew where the *Ville du Havre* had sunk. The captain said he did, and Horatio asked to be notified when they had reached the exact spot. In the wee hours of the morning the captain awakened Horatio, telling him that they were at the location. It was then, by starlight, that Horatio wrote:

When peace like a river attendeth my way
When sorrows like sea billows roll,
Whatever my lot, Thou hast taught me to say,
It is well, it is well with my soul.

Kik ten Boom

For seven years after the war, no one knew what had happened to Kik. When the Red Army liberated the concentration camp where Kik was being held, rather than releasing him they sent him to a Russian labor camp. A boy who had escaped the camp in 1953 brought the news: Kik had died there from starvation and abuse.

In 2019 an Argentinian, Guillermo Font, published an historical novel about Kik, calling it *Kik ten Boom: The Clockmaker's Grandson*. For years he had been fascinated by the ten Boom story and was particularly drawn to Kik, about whom there was so little information. Font knew that Kik had had a serious girlfriend during the war, Hanneke Dekema, and he wondered if she was still alive and would be willing to share memories. In 2017 he found her under her married name, Hanneke Vinke-Dekema. At ninety-one, Hanneke's mind remained sharp and she shared her thoughts about Kik in two letters:

> Yesterday Marina took me to the place were Kik and I stayed several hours on August 18, 1944, in the middle of a Lage Vuursche, a forest close to Hilversum. . . . It was the last place where we stayed together. Once again, I shed tears even though it happened seventy-three years ago. . . .
>
> The eighteen year old girl is long gone. After the war, there was hope. Kik had such a strong mind. He was so resourceful. He would have found a way to survive. To make it back. I waited. I waited for a long time.
>
> Kik did not return. He wasn't going to. I don't know how long it took me to accept this reality. When eventually I had,

I did keep Kik firmly locked in my heart. For many years, I did not allow there to be space for anyone else. But at the same time, I knew that life was waiting for me. . . . I found love again. I married a wonderful man. Three children and four grandchildren have brought further happiness to my life.

Kik never left my heart. And his memory lived on in many others. A street in Hilversum was named after him. His name turned up in many books and studies on the Dutch resistance. I told my children and grandchildren about him. . . .

No one can produce the story of the love Kik and I felt for each other. . . . Most feelings and experiences of this period could not be expressed in words. The perplexing mix of falling in love, feeling fear, courage, pain. . . . Laughing. . . . Having hope, expectations, uncertainty, losses . . .

The street in Hilversum named after Kik is called Ten Boom-straat, and on it appears a bronze sculpture of Kik in bas-relief, created by the Jewish-Dutch artist Johannes Gustaaf (Jobs) Wertheim, himself a survivor of the concentration camp in Theresienstadt, Czechoslovakia.

Peter van Woerden

Like Corrie, Nollie's son Peter felt led to combine his gifts with travel. While Corrie began circling the globe with her speaking engagements, Peter, his wife, and their five children toured Europe and the Near East as a family singing group with a simple message: God's love. Later, beginning in 1958, Peter began editing and co-producing

Peter and family at the piano in Geneva, Switzerland, 1960.

Corrie's bimonthly newsletter, *It's Harvest-Time*, often providing his own articles. In the mid-1970s he assisted Corrie with her second book* about her father, *Father ten Boom: God's Man*, published in 1978.

Beneath a portrait of Casper, Corrie and Peter sift through old family letters and documents at her home in Overveen, Holland.

Hans Poley

After the war Hans was awarded the Dutch Resistance Memorial Cross for his underground work. He went on to complete his studies at Delft Technological Institute, earning a PhD in physics. In February 1949 he and Mies Wessels married, and over the next few years they had three children.

Eusi, Corrie, and Hans together again in the Beje, March 6, 1974.

On March 6, 1974, Hans, Mies, Eusi, Dora, and Corrie had a touching reunion at the Beje, and the two couples signed the guestbook.

Hans had a long career in research physics, working for the Dutch Defense Research Council, and for Royal Dutch Shell's International Exploration and Production Division. After a stint in Houston with Shell's American office, he retired in 1984.

---

* Her first book about Casper ten Boom, *In My Father's House*, was published in 1976.

Beje guestbook. Above Hans's signature he cited Psalm 66:10–14, and to the right he gives his time in the Beje: May '43 to February '44. Beneath his name is Mies's signature, along with Anneke Poley. On the top right is the signature of Eusi's wife, Dora, who signed just below Eusi's name.

Nine years later, in 1993, he published *Return to the Hiding Place*—a personal account of his nine months hiding in the Beje.

Leendert Kip

After the war Leendert taught mathematics at the Dreefschool, a Haarlem elementary school, and then taught Dutch and literature at a teachers' college in Bloemendaal.

Mary van Itallie

As noted in the main text, Mary was arrested shortly after moving to a new hiding place after her liberation from the Angels' Den. Against all training, she went out to the street and met a Gestapo agent who posed as

On the Beje rooftop, 1943. Left to right: *Henk Wiedijk, Thea, Hans, Mary, Eusi.*

an underground worker, asking, "Who should be warned?" The agent arrested those she mentioned and sent her to a women's concentration camp in Theresienstadt, where she died.

When Hans and Eusi visited the Beje in 1974, they wrote and signed a collective note in the guestbook: "Mary was arrested a few days later. May her memory be a blessing."

From the Beje guestbook, March 6, 1974, Hans's and Eusi's benediction for Mary.

Mirjam de Jong

Hans, Mies, and Henk Wiedijk met with Mirjam in the summer of 1945, and she told them that she was one of the few in her family to survive the war. A year or so later Mirjam left the Netherlands to become an early Jewish resident in pre-Israel Palestine.

Meta (Tante Martha) and Paula Monsanto

The Monsanto sisters moved to The Hague after the war, both taking government jobs. Since Hans and Mies moved near this area after marriage, they and Hans's parents remained close with both sisters.

"Their friendship greatly enriched our family life for many years," Hans later wrote.

Hansje Frankfort-Israels ("Thea")

It's unclear what happened to Thea after the war, although it was known that her husband did not survive.

Reynout Siertsema ("Arnold")

Reynout Siertsema survived the war, and on March 18, 1976, he revisited the Beje and signed the guestbook. Next to his signature he wrote: "'Arnold,' *een van hen die in de engelenbak* [illegible]."

Translated to English, it reads: "'Arnold,' one of them who is in the angel box."

Walter Süskind

During the eighteen months that Walter Süskind was in charge of the Hollandsche Schouwburg, he and the Resistance workers he enlisted were able to save almost one thousand infants and children. In September 1943 Süskind and his family were arrested, spending three nights in Scheveningen prison. Walter was released, but his wife and daughter were not, both being sent to Westerbork. When Walter heard on September 2, 1944, that they were being scheduled for deportation to the Theresienstadt concentration camp, he decided to join them. All were sent to Auschwitz-Birkenau, and Walter's wife and daughter were gassed upon arrival. Walter, too, would die at Auschwitz, although the details of his death are unknown.

Jan Overzet and Theo Ederveen

The Dutch police officers who saved the refugees trapped in the Angels' Den, both of whom survived the war, were Theo Ederveen (left) and Jan Overzet (right).

Meijer Mossel ("Eusi")

In April 1945 Eusi was arrested at his hiding place in Sneek, Friesland, some eighty miles north of Amsterdam. Since the Allies had penetrated deeply into Germany, however, Eusi could not be transported to a concentration camp and was liberated from his cell at the police station. Surprisingly, all of his family survived the war.

Eusi returned to his synagogue in Amsterdam, and later served as a cantor and teacher at The Hague.

At their Beje reunion on March 6, 1974, Hans and Eusi had to climb that staircase one more time—emotions and memories flooding. When they reached Corrie's room, Eusi said: "I'm going to fulfill my promise." Hans remembered that when they were in the Angels' Den after a Gestapo raid thirty years before, Eusi had said that if he survived he would return to this place to give thanks and praise God.  And so there, in Corrie's room, Eusi began to sing with the booming voice that Hans remembered, lifting up praises to the Almighty.

Hans, Eusi, and Corrie reminisced for some time, and that afternoon Corrie took everyone to the location where the production crew was filming *The Hiding Place*. When the actors heard who Hans and Eusi were, they peppered them with questions about their months hiding in the Beje.

On the Beje rooftop, March 6, 1974. Left to right: *Hans, Mies, Eusi, and Dora.*

Before they left, Hans, Mies, Eusi, and Dora signed the Beje guestbook.

"Today, 30 years after I was hiding here," Eusi wrote, "I was here again. At this Hiding Place I said a special doxology that I have never said before: 'Praise be to Thee, Eternal, our God, King of the world, Who has done to me a miracle in this place.'"

Hans and Mies remained close friends with Eusi until his death, when they helped lay him to rest at Wassenaar, a suburb of The Hague in southern Holland.

Eusi signing the Beje guestbook.

APPENDIX

Beje Refugees

BEJE REFUGEES CAN BE DIVIDED into two groups—short-term or permanent—and two subgroups: Jewish or Dutch diver. Short-term guests usually were on the run and stayed only a night or two, while "permanent" refugees typically stayed weeks or months.

Date of entrance	Name	Status
1942		
May 25*	Mrs. Kleermaker	Jew/short-term
May 27	elderly couple	Jews/short-term
May 28	couple	Jews/short-term
late May	several unidentified	Jews/short-term
June 1	mother and baby, other children	Jews/short-term
1943		
May 13	Hans Poley	Diver/permanent
May 14	Hansje Frankfort-Israels (Thea)	Jew/permanent
June 8	Mary van Itallie	Jew/permanent
mid-June	Henk Wessels	Diver/permanent
mid-June	Leendert Kip	Diver/permanent
June 28	Meijer Mossel (Eusi)	Jew/permanent
early July	several unidentified	Unclear/short-term
July 15–18	Jop (shop apprentice)	Diver/permanent
July 15–18	Henk Wiedijk	Diver/permanent
July 19	Mr. de Vries	Jew/permanent
early August	Kik ten Boom with two friends	Divers/short-term
September 29	Mirjam de Jong	Jew/permanent
mid-October	several unidentified	short-term
late October	Nel	Jew/permanent
late October	Ronnie Gazan	Jew/permanent
1944		
January	Meta ("Martha") and Paula Monsanto	Jews/permanent
February 28	Reynout ("Arnold") Siertsema	Diver/short-term
February 28	Hans van Messel	Diver/short-term

---

* In *The Hiding Place* (p. 76), Corrie notes that Mrs. Kleermaker showed up at the Beje two weeks after Peter had been sent to prison. Since he was incarcerated on May 11, 1942, this would put the date on or after May 25.

AUTHOR'S NOTE

WINSTON CHURCHILL SAID THAT "WRITING a book is an adventure: it begins as an amusement, then it becomes a mistress, then a master, and finally a tyrant."

Churchill was on to something. No sooner than the amusement of a new book begins, the daunting door of research appears. And investigation to produce a scholarly nonfiction book is expensive, arduous, and time-consuming. For ten to eighteen months, mountains of archives, files, articles, and books become your mistress.

Then when the research is finished, you realize that much of what you had intended to write is inaccurate or inadequate. This body of archives then becomes your master and rules over your writing, often as a tyrant.

As such, before sending my agent a book proposal I try to do as much legwork as possible to prevent chasing a dead-end project.

When I was researching *Code Name: Lise*—the story about SOE agent Odette Sansom—my friend Susannah Hurt kept telling me to read *The Hiding Place*. I was familiar with Corrie ten Boom and her book, but I had never read it. I had a vague recollection that the Nazis had imprisoned Corrie, and that her book had been wildly successful.

Until Susannah mentioned it, though, I had no idea that Corrie had been imprisoned at Ravensbrück—the notorious SS concentration camp for women—while Odette Sansom was there. And Susannah was right: *The Hiding Place* proved to be an invaluable primary source as Corrie's recollections about the camp complemented Odette's perspective (much of which was spent secluded in the camp's Bunker). More importantly, I found Corrie's story uplifting and compelling. How one could go through prisons and concentration camps and come out ready to forgive is compelling and exemplary.

In February 2020 I turned in my manuscript for *The Princess Spy* and began looking for another story. I wanted to stay within my narrow genre—narrative nonfiction World War II espionage thriller—but I was running out of countries and espionage outfits. My first book, *Into the Lion's Mouth*, had been about Dusko Popov, the Serbian MI5/MI6 double agent who primarily served in Portugal. Then came *Code Name: Lise*, with SOE agent Sansom serving in France, followed by *The Princess Spy*, with OSS agent Aline Griffith serving in Spain. So I had covered the four western Allied espionage outfits—MI5, MI6, SOE, and OSS—and had written extensively about locales in Portugal, France, and Spain.

For my fourth book I wanted a new country and agency. As I scoured potential World War II subjects, my mind kept returning to Corrie ten Boom. Her story would bring not only a new country (Netherlands), but a different espionage angle (the Dutch Resistance). Yet I hesitated because *The Hiding Place* has sold millions of copies and is almost sacred within Christian circles. So I had to answer the obvious question: "Does *The Hiding Place* tell the whole story, or is there much more?"

To my surprise, *The Hiding Place* seemed to contain less than ten percent of the overall story. In fact, Corrie's own recollections about her family and the war were splintered into no less than six books: *A Prisoner and Yet* (1947), *The Hiding Place* (1971), *Tramp for the Lord* (1974), *Prison Letters* (1975), *In My Father's House* (1976), and *Father ten Boom: God's Man* (1978). Of the six, only *The Hiding Place* had wide distribution, and it contains not a single photo, fails to include valuable information found in her other books, and lacks important characters in the story.

And since Corrie kept no war diary, her recollections are often vague and without dates. Fortunately, the first permanent refugee into the ten Boom household, Hans Poley, kept a daily diary and his 1993 release, *Return to the Hiding Place*, provides dates and details not mentioned in Corrie's books. In addition, Corrie's nephew Peter van Woerden—a key character in the story— published his own memoir, *The Secret Place*, in 1954.

What was more, I found out that Corrie's entire collection of letters, photos, passports, scrapbooks, notes, and ministry publications is contained in the Buswell Library Archives and Special Collections, part of the Billy Graham Center Archives at Wheaton College.

This "perfect storm" of scattered material was precisely what I was looking for, and with additional details from other World War II material—including German—I knew I had the potential for a seminal book. Equally important, what Corrie did *after* the war—the impact she had on countless millions across more than sixty countries—is more significant than the horrifying part of her story in concentration camps. One of those specially touched by Corrie was Reverend Billy Graham, who wrote about her in tribute:

"When I first met her in the 1960s, stories about her testimony of God's love in the midst of tremendous trials and the forgiveness He can give us for our enemies were beginning to follow her around the globe. . . . Her stamina astounded me. She could speak four or five times a day and counsel people in between sessions. She used every known mode of transportation, from elephants to rickshaws, to transport her with her gospel messages."

··

MY AIM WITH *The Watchmaker's Daughter,* as with all of my books, was to present an accurate work of scholarship in a pace-driven thriller structure. But writing about Corrie's message of faith, hope, love, and forgiveness was an empowering and spiritually moving experience for me, and I trust that reading it has been for you as well.

One could summarize Corrie's war experience and ministry afterward with the Reformation creed, *Post Tenebras Lux.*

After darkness, light.

I hope this biography of Corrie ten Boom—the watchmaker's daughter from Haarlem, Holland—has provided you with a meaningful glimpse of the light she cast amidst darkness for more than half a century.

Larry Loftis
January 1, 2022

ACKNOWLEDGMENTS

MY FIRST DEBT OF GRATITUDE is to my longtime friend and beta-reader, Susannah Hurt. While I was conducting research for *Code Name: Lise* in 2017, Susannah insisted that I read *The Hiding Place* because Corrie ten Boom was incarcerated in the Ravensbrück concentration camp at the same time as Odette Sansom. Had Susannah not mentioned that book, you'd not have this one in your hands today. In addition, she inspired the last line of *The Watchmaker's Daughter*, which encapsulates the entire story.

Many thanks also to Emily Banas of the Buswell Library Archives and Special Collections, located in the Billy Graham Center at Wheaton College (Wheaton, Illinois). If you have read any of my books, you know that intensive research is critical, and the most important source is often official archives. Little did I know when I started researching Corrie's story, all of her archives—personal letters from prison, passports, photographs, notebooks, ministry newsletters and magazines, annual reports, and the Beje guest books—are located in the Buswell collections. I spent four days in these archives pouring over countless boxes and Emily knew by heart the location and contents of each. Truly, she was my archives angel.

To my brilliant editor, Mauro DiPreta, who not only championed the book from proposal to finished product, but who provided countless improvements and overall direction along the way.

To my eagle-eyed copyeditor, Tom Pitoniak, who caught everything Mauro and I missed.

To Danielle Bartlett and Amelia Wood, my remarkable publicist and marketing director, respectively.

To Allie Johnston, who keeps the Morrow trains on time; to Lauren Harms, who gave us this spectacular cover; and to everyone behind the scenes at William Morrow and HarperCollins.

To my incomparable literary agent, Keith Urbahn, a dream maker and all-wise visionary; and to Matt Carlini, agent extraordinaire and Javelin's foreign rights director.

To my kindred brothers, John Bill and J. D. Lopez, for their everlasting encouragement.

To Dee DeLoy, who created the magnificent art associated with our preorders. Aside from his talent, Dee's enthusiasm to spread the word about *The Watchmaker's Daughter* has been a wondrous blessing.

To Rev. Jim Henry, an early and important role model in my life, for his steadfast encouragement and excitement about the book.

Finally, to Steve Price, to whom this book is dedicated. Steve inspired my transition from lawyer to author by handing me a Vince Flynn novel in 2012, and I have been writing nonfiction thrillers ever since. More importantly, he has been my spiritual mentor—my Casper ten Boom, if you will—for more than forty years. To him, my endless thanks.

NOTES

Prologue

page

1 *Handsome and broad-shouldered, Lieutenant Hans Rahms:* Peter van Woerden, *In the Secret Place*, 98; Corrie ten Boom, *A Prisoner and Yet*, 43; *The Hiding Place*, 147; *Prison Letters*, 89; "People We Meet: Hans Rahms," *It's Harvest-Time*, November–December 1964, 2–3. See also Corrie ten Boom Museum's brochure, "Welcome to The Hiding Place," located in Papers of Cornelia Arnolda Johanna ten Boom, 1902–1983, Collection 78, Box 1, Folder 8, Buswell Library Archives and Special Collections, Wheaton College, Wheaton, IL ("Buswell Library Collections").

1 her *papers:* Corrie ten Boom, "People We Meet: Hans Rahms," *It's Harvest-Time*, November–December 1964, 2–3. See also Corrie ten Boom Museum brochure, "Welcome to The Hiding Place," located in Collection 78, Box 1, Folder 8, Buswell Library Collections.

1 *"Can you explain":* Corrie ten Boom, *He Sets the Captive Free*, 22–23; "A Rare Recording of Corrie ten Boom," vol. 1, Listen and Live Audio, 2019; *Prison Letters*, 89.

Chapter 1: The Watchmakers

3 *Willem ten Boom's:* Corrie ten Boom, *In My Father's House*, 11; *Father ten Boom: God's Man*, 25; Corrie ten Boom House Foundation, "History of the ten Boom Family," www.corrietenboom.com ("Corrie ten Boom House Foundation").

3 *Geertruida van Gogh:* Corrie ten Boom, *Father ten Boom*, 25; Corrie ten Boom House Foundation; Stan Guthrie, *Victorious: Corrie ten Boom and the Hiding Place*, 32.

3 *"You know the Scriptures":* In My Father's House, 11; Corrie ten Boom House Foundation.

4 *Elisabeth Bell: Father ten Boom*, 25–26; Corrie ten Boom House Foundation; Guthrie, 32.

4 *"As long as I can remember": In My Father's House*, 14, 16; *Father ten Boom*, 29, 39, 44; Corrie ten Boom House Foundation.

4 *Cornelia ("Cor") Luitingh: Father ten Boom*, 40; Corrie ten Boom House Foundation.

4 *Arnolda:* Corrie ten Boom House Foundation.

4 *premature, sickly: In My Father's House*, 17; Corrie ten Boom House Foundation.

4 *"The Lord gave us": Father ten Boom*, 53.

4 *when grandfather Willem died: In My Father's House*, 18. There is a slight

discrepancy about the year Willem died, as the Corrie ten Boom House
Foundation has Willem dying in 1891, the year before Corrie was born. Since
Corrie is a primary source, her date (Willem dying six months after her birth)
is likely more reliable.

5 *in 1897, Elisabeth:* *In My Father's House*, 18; Corrie ten Boom House
Foundation.

5 *apprenticing under Hoü:* *Father ten Boom*, 158; *In My Father's House*, 14.

5 *People's Trades:* *Father ten Boom*, 85.

6 *University of Leiden:* Ibid., 92.

6 *began to apprentice:* Ibid., 37.

7 *"I was captivated":* Ibid., 102–3.

7 *"Girl, I trust that":* Ibid., 123, 126.

8 *"I would like to have":* Ibid., 129–30.

9 *October 17, 1921, Corrie's mother:* *In My Father's House*, 107–8; Corrie ten
Boom House Foundation.

9 *"This is the saddest":* *In My Father's House*, 107.

9 *first licensed female watchmaker:* Corrie ten Boom House Foundation;
Corrie ten Boom, *Clippings from My Notebook*, vii (Foreword by Pamela
Rosewell); Corrie ten Boom, "A Rare Recording of Corrie ten Boom," vol. 1,
Listen and Live Audio, 2019.

9 *Dutch Society for Israel:* *Father ten Boom*, 103, 105.

9 *Institutum Judaicum:* Ibid., 106–7; Corrie ten Boom House Foundation;
In My Father's House, 90–91 (here, however, Corrie has him studying in
Dresden at the Delitcheanum).

10 *"I expect that":* *Father ten Boom*, 107–8.

10 *On January 30, 1933:* I. C. B. Dear and M. R. D. Foot, eds., *The
Oxford Companion to World War II*, 1321; Marcel Baudot et al., eds., *The
Historical Encyclopedia of World War II*, 527; John Thompson, *Spirit over
Steel: A Chronology of the Second World War*, 13.

11 *"Old President Hindenburg":* H. R. H. Wilhelmina, Princess of the
Netherlands, *Lonely but Not Alone*, 146.

11 *one-day boycott:* Martin Gilbert, *Kristallnacht: Prelude to Destruction*, 120;
Mitchell G. Bard, *48 Hours of Kristallnacht*, 1; Baudot et al., 16. For the most
comprehensive look at the Holocaust in general, see the four-volume work of
Israel Gutman, ed., *Encyclopedia of the Holocaust*.

11 *SA:* For background on the SA, see Gutman, vol. 4, 1319–21; Heinz
Höhne, *The Order of the Death's Head*, 17, 19, 57, 94; and Dear and Foot,
Oxford Companion to World War II, 974.

11 *Julie Bonhoeffer:* Gilbert, 120.

11 *no intention whatsoever:* William Shirer, *The Rise and Fall of the Third Reich*,
4. Von Hindenburg's slur, which the chancellor originally had coined in the
early 1930s as "Bohemian corporal," was due to a mix-up of towns. When
told that Hitler's hometown was Braunau, Hindenburg mistakenly assumed

it was not Braunau, Austria, but a town with the identical name in Bohemia. After learning that Hitler was Austrian, Hindenburg began to refer to him as "that Austrian corporal" (mocking Hitler's low military rank). Over time, though, Hindenburg went back to "Bohemian corporal" since Bohemians were considered gypsies and regarded as far less cultured and refined than Austrians. Peter Margaritis, *Countdown to D-Day: The German Perspective*, xiii, xv. The pejorative and disrespectful nickname for Hitler would later be used by several of his top army officers, including Field Marshals Gerd von Rundstedt, Erich von Manstein, and Friedrich Paulus. Margaritis, *Countdown to D-Day*, xv.

12 *practicing law or medicine:* Baudot et al., 16. This crackdown was especially significant for medical care because Jews comprised 20 percent of Germany's doctors. In 1932–33, Germany had approximately 50,000 licensed physicians, 10,000 of whom were Jewish. Bernt Engelmann, *In Hitler's Germany: Everyday Life in the Third Reich*, 13.

12 *nineteen more laws:* Gilbert, 120, 122.

12 *Nuremberg Laws:* Ibid.; Bard, *48 Hours*, 1; Baudot et al., 16; Gutman, vol. 3, 1076–77; Shirer, *The Rise and Fall of the Third Reich*, 233.

12 *prohibited from staying in hotels:* Bard, *48 Hours*, 2.

12 *they went after Christians:* Eric A. Johnson, *Nazi Terror: The Gestapo, Jews, and Ordinary Germans*, 195–250. For the Nazi persecution of Christians and the German Confessing Church, see generally John S. Conway, *The Nazi Persecution of the Churches*; Dietrich Bonhoeffer, *Letters and Papers from Prison;* E. C. Helmreich, *The German Churches under Hitler: Background, Struggle, and Epilogue.* See also Theodore S. Hamerow, *On the Road to the Wolf's Lair: German Resistance to Hitler*, 146–62, 205–7; and Bernt Engelmann, *In Hitler's Germany: Everyday Life in the Third Reich*, 24 (regarding an organization called Catholic Action).

An early example of the persecution of Christians was the case of Jesuit priest Josef Spieker. In a sermon titled "True and False Führers" on October 28, 1934, Spieker declared to his Cologne congregation: "Germany has only one Führer. That is Christ!" In the pews, however, was a lower-level Nazi functionary who delivered his notes on Spieker's sermon to the Gestapo. Spieker was immediately arrested and sent to a concentration camp. Johnson, *Nazi Terror*, 195.

12 *Martin Niemöller:* Gutman, ed., *Encyclopedia of the Holocaust*, vol. 3, 1061. For the full Niemöller story, see J. Bradley, *Martin Niemöller*; and C. S. Davidson, *God's Man: The Story of Pastor Niemöller.* See also Robert S. Wistrich, *Who's Who in Nazi Germany*, 180–82; Augustino von Hassell and Sigrid MacRae, *Alliance of Enemies: The Untold Story of the Secret American and German Collaboration to End World War II*, 51; Louis L. Snyder, *Encyclopedia of the Third Reich*, 248–49; Dear and Foot, *Oxford Companion to World War II*, 801.

12 *"First they came":* Gutman, ed., *Encyclopedia of the Holocaust*, vol. 3, 1061.

13 *Crown Princess Juliana:* Werner Warmbrunn, *The Dutch Under German Occupation, 1940–1945,* 4.

13 *hundred-year anniversary: In My Father's House,* 11; *The Hiding Place,* 9, 57.

13 *183,000 Austrian Jews:* Bard, *48 Hours,* 2.

13 *September 29, British prime minister Neville Chamberlain:* Gutman, ed., *Encyclopedia of the Holocaust,* vol. 3, 1001–6; Bard, *48 Hours,* 2–3; Dear and Foot, 535; Baudot et al., 527; Höhne, *The Order of the Death's Head,* xi.

13 *"The main question was":* H. R. H. Wilhelmina, Princess of the Netherlands, *Lonely but Not Alone,* 147.

14 *eighteen thousand German Jews:* Bard, *48 Hours,* 3; Gilbert, *Kristallnacht,* 23 (putting the number arrested and deported at 12,000).

14 *Grynszpan family:* Bard, *48 Hours,* 3; Gilbert, 23.

14 *Herschel:* Bard, *48 Hours,* 4; Gilbert, 24; Shirer, *The Rise and Fall of the Third Reich,* 430.

14 *"You are a* sale boche*":* Bard, 4; Gilbert, 24; Shirer, 430.

15 *"All German newspapers":* Bard, *48 Hours,* 7, citing Wolfgang Benz, "The Relapse into Barbarism," in *November 1938: From Kristallnacht to Genocide,* 1–43; Gilbert, 28–29.

15 *"Actions against Jews":* Bard, *48 Hours,* 9.

15 *Cologne:* Ibid., 10.

15 *two thousand synagogues:* Ibid., jacket cover. Martin Gilbert estimated similar numbers: more than a thousand synagogues burned, tens of thousands of Jewish businesses ransacked, 91 Jews killed, another 30,000 Jewish men arrested and sent to concentration camps. Gilbert, 13. See also Shirer, *The Rise and Fall of the Third Reich,* 431.

15 *some protested:* Hans Poley, *Return to the Hiding Place,* 10.

16 *donated 400,000 guilders:* Louis de Jong and Joseph W. F. Stoppelman, *The Lion Rampant: The Story of Holland's Resistance to the Nazis,* 172.

16 *Mr. Ineke:* Poley, 27–28.

16 *Henny van Dantzig:* Ibid.

16 *"Address Unknown": The Hiding Place,* 58.

Chapter 2: Hitler Youth

17 *Casper ten Boom, Holland's best:* Corrie ten Boom, *Father ten Boom: God's Man,* 158; *In My Father's House,* 114.

17 *annexed Austria and the Czech Sudetenland:* I. C. B. Dear and M. R. D. Foot, eds., *The Oxford Companion to World War II,* 279–80, 1091, 1308–9, 1322; Richard J. Evans, *The Third Reich in Power,* 666–710; Shirer, *The Rise and Fall of the Third Reich,* 358 *et seq.*; John Thompson, *Spirit over Steel: A Chronology of the Second World War,* 24; Heinz Höhne, *The Order of the Death's Head,* xi. For an excellent map showing dates and territories of Hitler's annexations, see Evans, *The Third Reich in Power,* 710.

17 *hell-bent on acquiring more:* Hitler had decided in May 1939 to attack
Belgium and the Netherlands. Werner Warmbrunn, *The Dutch Under
German Occupation,* 6; Chester Wilmot, *The Struggle for Europe,* 21. On
May 23, 1939, Hitler told his generals: "If Holland and Belgium are
successfully occupied and if France is also defeated, the fundamental
conditions for a successful war against England will have been secured."
Wilmot, *The Struggle for Europe,* 21.

17 *Casper's reputation: Father ten Boom,* 158.

17 *Otto Altschuler:* Corrie ten Boom, "Not Lost, but Gone Before," *The
Hiding Place,* memorial edition, 5; Collection 78, Papers of Cornelia Arnolda
Johanna ten Boom, 1902–1983, Box 2, Folder 2, Buswell Library Archives
and Special Collections, Wheaton College, Wheaton, IL ("Buswell Library
Collections"); *The Hiding Place,* 58–59. Note that Corrie's article "Not Lost,
but Gone Before" is the only place Otto's last name is given.

17 *Otto proudly announced: The Hiding Place,* 58.

18 *"slim and slender":* Dear and Foot, *Oxford Companion to World War II,*
540–41. For more details on the Hitler Youth, see also Israel Gutman, ed.,
Encyclopedia of the Holocaust, vol. 2, 677–79; Peter Fritzsche, *Life and Death in
the Third Reich,* 99–100; and Eric A. Johnson, *Nazi Terror: The Gestapo, Jews,
and Ordinary Germans,* 262–76.

18 *"All of the German youth":* Shirer, *The Rise and Fall of the Third Reich,* 253.

18 *"In the presence of":* Ibid.

18 *Jungmaedel:* Ibid., 254.

19 *numbered almost eight million:* Ibid., 254–55. See also Fritzsche, *Life and
Death in the Third Reich,* 100 (stating that in 1939, seven million girls and boys
participated in a national sports competition sponsored by the Hitler Youth).
The effectiveness in outlawing all other German youth organizations can be
seen in light of the Catholic youth organizations. When Hitler came to power
in 1933, Catholic youth groups, with 1.4 million members, were more than
twenty times as large as the Hitler Youth. Johnson, *Nazi Terror,* 268.

19 *"The world will see": The Hiding Place,* 58.

20 *"The boy is probably":* Ibid. Hitler Youth commonly carried weapons for
street terror, including brass knuckles and blackjacks (a leather device in the
shape of a thin flashlight that contained in the striking end a lead or steel ball).
Bernt Engelmann, *In Hitler's Germany: Everyday Life in the Third Reich,* 21.

20 *toward Mr. Christoffels:* Corrie ten Boom, *The Hiding Place,* 90. Corrie
doesn't mention the exact date of Christoffels's death, but she places the event
before spring, and Holland's coldest month is February.

20 *"It's very deliberate":* Ibid., 59.

21 *most ominous look:* Ibid., 59–60.

Chapter 3: Persecution

22 *Generals' Plot:* Fabian von Schlabrendorff, *The Secret War Against Hitler,* 99–119, 149–204, 220–92; Peter Hoffmann, *The History of the German Resistance, 1933–1945,* 38–96; Klemens von Klemperer, *German Resistance Against Hitler,* 105–9; Louis L. Snyder, *Encyclopedia of the Third Reich,* 135–36, 182–83, 192–93, 230–31, 256, 294–95; B. H. Liddell Hart, *The German Generals Talk,* 33; Larry Loftis, *The Princess Spy,* 87–92. See generally, Hans Bernd Gisevius, *To the Bitter End: An Insider's Account of the Plot to Kill Hitler 1933–1944*; and Anton Gill, *An Honourable Defeat: A History of German Resistance to Hitler, 1933–1945.*

22 *determined to shoot the Führer himself:* Hoffmann, *History of the German Resistance,* 129. See also entries for Halder and "Halder Plot" in Louis L. Snyder, *Encyclopedia of the Third Reich,* 135–36; and Liddell Hart, *The German Generals Talk,* 33.

23 *Colonel Hans Oster:* Klemperer, *German Resistance Against Hitler,* 194.

23 *The idea had originated:* Ibid.

23 *Major Gijsbertus Jacobus Sas:* Ibid., 194–95. For the relationship and considerable meetings between Oster and Sas, and Sas's warnings to Goethals, see also Harold C. Deutsch, *The Conspiracy Against Hitler in the Twilight War,* 91–101.

23 *April 3, 1940, Oster advised:* Klemperer, 195. For background on Müller, his relationship with the Vatican, and his warnings to Pope Pius XII, see Deutsch, *The Conspiracy Against Hitler in the Twilight War,* 112–48, 319, 335–52.

23 *"the pig":* Klemperer, 194.

23 *set-back theory:* Ibid.

24 *"My dear friend":* Ibid., 195; Walter B. Maass, *The Netherlands at War: 1940–1945,* 28; Deutsch, *The Conspiracy Against Hitler in the Twilight War,* 328.

24 *"Tomorrow at dawn":* Werner Warmbrunn, *The Dutch Under German Occupation, 1940–1945,* 7; Maass, *The Netherlands at War,* 29.

24 *Georges Goethals:* Klemperer, 194–95; Deutsch, 91–101.

24 twenty-nine *times:* Agostino von Hassell and Sigrid MacRae, *Alliance of Enemies,* 79; I. C. B. Dear and M. R. D. Foot, eds., *The Oxford Companion to World War II,* 785.

24 *"pitiful":* von Hassell and MacRae, 79; Dear and Foot, 785.

24 *three a.m. on May 10:* Warmbrunn, *Dutch Under German Occupation,* 7; Dear and Foot, 784; William Shirer, *The Rise and Fall of the Third Reich,* 721; Maass, *Netherlands at War,* 30 *et seq.*; John Thompson, *Spirit over Steel: A Chronology of the Second World War,* 72–74; Richard J. Evans, *The Third Reich at War,* 123.

24 *only seventy-two:* Dear and Foot, 785. See also Maass, *Netherlands at War,* 16 (putting the numbers at 116 and 23, respectively).

24 *Hitler's plan:* Shirer, *The Rise and Fall of the Third Reich,* 721.

25 *"Lord, make us strong":* Corrie ten Boom, *In My Father's House,* 179.

25 *queen Wilhelmina went to the radio:* H. R. H. Wilhelmina, Princess of the Netherlands, *Lonely but Not Alone,* 151.

25 *morning of May 12:* Shirer, 721–22.

26 *Hook of Holland:* Wilhelmina, 153. For a general summary of the invasion timeline, see Marcel Baudot et al., eds., *The Historical Encyclopedia of World War II,* 529.

26 *"The power of resistance":* Shirer, 722.

26 *fate of Warsaw:* James S. Corum, "The Luftwaffe's Campaigns in Poland and the West, 1939–1940," *Security and Defence Quarterly,* 173.

26 *death toll was twenty-one hundred:* Shirer, 721–22; Maass, *Netherlands at War,* 38–42; Richard J. Evans, *The Third Reich at War,* 123; Thompson, *Spirit over Steel,* 74; de Jong and Stoppelman, *The Lion Rampant,* 1–12; Dear and Foot, 785. For an eyewitness account of the initial days of the war, see also Diet Eman, *Things We Couldn't Say: A Dramatic Account of Christian Resistance in Holland During World War II,* 27–36.

26 *"The darkest time":* Corrie ten Boom, *In My Father's House,* 180.

27 *Dr. Arthur Seyss-Inquart:* Shirer, 332; Dear and Foot, 783, 998; Baudot et al., 11, 30; Robert S. Wistrich, *Who's Who in Nazi Germany,* 233–34; Snyder, *Encyclopedia of the Third Reich,* 320–21; Israel Gutman, ed., *Encyclopedia of the Holocaust,* vol. 4, 1344–46. See also generally, Jacob Presser, *Ashes in the Wind: The Destruction of Dutch Jewry.*

28 *Hanns Albin Rauter:* Warmbrunn, *The Dutch Under German Occupation,* 30–32; Dear, 783; Nikolaus Wachsmann, *KL: A History of the Nazi Concentration Camps,* 305, 369; Gutman, ed., *Encyclopedia of the Holocaust,* vol. 3, 1046. For details on Rauter's entire SS career, see Presser, *Ashes in the Wind.*

28 *fellow Aryans:* Warmbrunn, 23, 83. For a summary of the National Socialist Movement of the Netherlands (NSB), see Gutman, vol. 3, 1026, 1032–33; de Jong and Stoppelman, *The Lion Rampant,* 129–30, 160–63, 248–51, 258; Presser, *Ashes in the Wind,* 232–33, 356, 369; and Maass, *Netherlands at War,* 52–54, 57, 79, 132, 141.

28 *Hermann Goering promised:* Warmbrunn, 69.

28 *shops experienced a tremendous boon:* Robert Matzen, *Dutch Girl: Audrey Hepburn and World War II,* 52.

28 *"Soldiers frequently visited":* Corrie ten Boom, *The Hiding Place,* 65

29 *"The Germans tried to be":* Matzen, 27, 50.

29 *"A nation which has vitality":* Wilhelmina, 171.

29 *Jewish civil servants and professors:* Hans Poley, *Return to the Hiding Place,* 11; Dear and Foot, 782; Gutman, ed., *Encyclopedia of the Holocaust,* vol. 3, 1047; oral history interview with Louis de Groot, U.S. Holocaust Memorial Museum, Accession Number: 1999.A.0122.805 | RG Number: RG-50.477.0805.

29 *Delft Technological University:* Hans Poley, *Return to the Hiding Place,*

11; Warmbrunn, 105. For background on the Nazi persecution of Dutch universities, particularly Delft and the University of Leiden, as well as the student and faculty backlash, see de Jong and Stoppelman, *The Lion Rampant*, 252–61; and Presser, *Ashes in the Wind*, 28–29, 58–89.

29 *University of Leiden:* Oral history interview with Louis de Groot; Dear and Foot, 782; Warmbrunn, 105.

29 *Students began boycotting:* Poley, 11; Gutman, vol. 3, 1047; de Jong and Stoppelman, 252, 256–58.

29 *Delft and Leiden temporarily closed:* Poley, 11; Dear and Foot, 782; Gutman, vol. 3, 1047; de Jong and Stoppelman, 253–55.

29 *nationwide university raids:* Poley, 11.

29 *doctors, lawyers, and architects:* Dear and Foot, 782.

29 *identity cards:* Poley, 9–10; Presser, 39; Anne Frank, *The Diary of a Young Girl*, 8.

29 *reported in line to receive a Star of David:* Corrie ten Boom, *Father ten Boom*, 67.

30 *rationing of food:* Warmbrunn, *The Dutch Under German Occupation*, 11.

30 *Dutch had a large export:* Dear and Foot, 782.

30 *redirected all of those exports:* Ibid.; Baudot et al., 349.

30 *"Long glowing reports":* *The Hiding Place*, 65.

31 *"Is this the only radio":* Ibid., 66.

31 *On July 28 Radio Oranje:* Matzen, *Dutch Girl*, 53.

32 *"Measure for the Protection":* Ibid., 53–54.

32 JEWS WILL NOT BE SERVED: *The Hiding Place*, 67.

33 *"Father":* Ibid., 68.

33 *Founded in 1940, the SOE:* For the founding and background of the SOE, see Loftis, *Code Name: Lise*, 6–7. See also, generally, M. R. D. Foot, *S.O.E.: The Special Operations Executive, 1940–46*; M. R. D. Foot, *SOE in France*, xx; and William Mackenzie, *The Secret History of SOE: The Special Operations Executive 1940–1945* (regarding Holland, 302–8).

34 *"set Europe ablaze":* Hugh Dalton, *The Fateful Years: Memoirs, 1931–1945*, 366.

34 *"terrorists":* Foot, *S.O.E.*, 69; Philippe de Vomécourt, *An Army of Amateurs*, 66.

34 *Thys Taconis, a sabotage expert, and H. M. G. Lauwers:* Hermann Giskes, *London Calling North Pole*, 68–80; Foot, *S.O.E.*, 179; Mackenzie, *The Secret History of SOE*, 305.

34 *February 1942, the other was lost at sea:* Mackenzie, 305.

34 *it wasn't Lauwers:* Giskes, *London Calling North Pole*, 68–80; Mackenzie, 305; Foot, *S.O.E.*, 179–80.

Chapter 4: Razzias

35 *Major Hermann Giskes:* Giskes, 39, 44–45, 51; Foot, *S.O.E.*, 179.

35 *Ridderhof:* Giskes, 39, 44–45, 51; Foot, *S.O.E.*, 179.

35 *On March 6, Lauwers:* Giskes, 64–80; Foot, 179.

36 *Corrie, Betsie, and Opa went to a service:* Corrie ten Boom, *The Hiding Place*, 74; Peter van Woerden, *In the Secret Place*, 16–17.

36 *"My patriotic spirit":* van Woerden, 17.

36 *dispatched fifty-six agents*: William Mackenzie, *The Secret History of SOE*, 304; Pieter Dourlein, *Inside North Pole: A Secret Agent's Story*, 170.

37 *Many wept: The Hiding Place*, 75; van Woerden, 17.

37 *"We sang at the top": The Hiding Place*, 75.

38 *Nazi mayor of Velsen:* van Woerden, 21.

38 *"Peter! Wake up":* Ibid., 20–21.

38 *"Peter":* Ibid., 21, 31.

39 *"O surround us":* Ibid., 23–24.

39 *"Smart Mels":* Ibid.

40 *"Opa! Tante Corrie": The Hiding Place*, 76.

40 *"My name is Kleermaker":* Ibid.

40 *"In this household":* Ibid., 77.

41 *"It's getting harder":* Ibid., 77–78.

41 *"Is there any way":* Ibid., 79.

42 *"Prison under a Nazi":* van Woerden, 28–30.

43 *"It seemed suddenly":* Ibid., 33–34.

43 *"My friend took": The Hiding Place*, 79.

44 *"Get your bicycle":* Ibid., 81.

44 *Herman Sluring:* Ibid., 10, 17; van Woerden, 69.

45 *"the head of an operation": The Hiding Place*, 82.

45 *"Our freedom was":* Anne Frank, *The Diary of a Young Girl*, 1–8. For the most comprehensive look at the Holocaust in general, see the four-volume work of Israel Gutman, ed., *Encyclopedia of the Holocaust*.

46 *On June 15:* van Woerden, 37–38. June 15 is an approximate date; Peter was incarcerated on May 12 and writes that he was in prison "a little more than a month."

46 *Tulip bulbs:* Ibid., 49–50.

46 *"Save it":* Ibid., 51–52.

Chapter 5: Diving Under

48 *"Sir, just a moment":* van Woerden, 52.

49 *"recruiting agents":* Ibid., 56.

49 Onderduikers: Ibid., 69; Marcel Baudot et al., eds., *The Historical Encyclopedia of World War II*, 350; Werner Warmbrunn, *The Dutch Under German Occupation 1940–1945*, 187–88.

49 *deportation to Germany:* For a summary of the deportation of Dutch Jews, see Israel Gutman, ed., *Encyclopedia of the Holocaust*, vol. 3, 1051–55.

49 *the* Zentralstelle*:* Warmbrunn, 166–67.

49 *"Mother called me":* Frank, 21.

50 *263 Prinsengracht:* Ibid., 25.

50 *"Not being able to":* Ibid., 28.

50 *"Secret Annex":* Ibid., 23.

51 *"I'd go to the station":* Robert Matzen, *Dutch Girl: Audrey Hepburn and World War II*, 128–29.

51 *Hans Poley:* Hans Poley, *Return to the Hiding Place*, 11.

51 *"Our many Jewish friends":* Frank, 54–55.

52 *"With great attention":* H. R. H. Wilhelmina, Princess of the Netherlands, *Lonely but Not Alone*, 188.

52 *"Night after night":* Frank, 72–73.

53 *"due to a shortage":* Poley, 11–12.

53 *deport orphans, the elderly:* Warmbrunn, 169.

53 *"Terrible things are":* Frank, 82–83.

54 *save sugar beets:* Ibid., 57.

54 *"The battle against":* Poley, 12–13.

55 *their small radio:* Carole C. Carlson, *Corrie ten Boom: Her Life, Her Faith*, 82.

55 *"I want to raise a fiery":* Wilhelmina, 188.

55 *end of the month:* Poley, 12.

55 *"He can stay with us":* Ibid., 13.

55 *Mrs. Helena T. Kuipers-Rietberg:* Warmbrunn, 188.

56 *Landelijke Organisatie:* Ibid., 187–88.

56 *Uncle Herman:* van Woerden, 69.

56 *sent to a German concentration camp:* Warmbrunn, 188.

Chapter 6: The Angels' Den

57 *Hans Poley made his way:* Hans Poley, *Return to the Hiding Place*, 15. Strangely, Hans Poley is omitted altogether in *The Hiding Place* (published in 1971). On pages 99–102, for example, the permanent refugees are listed as Eusi, Henk, Leendert, Thea Dacosta (whose actual name was Hansje Frankfort-Israels), Meta Monsanto, Mary van Itallie, and Jop (an assistant in the shop). This is particularly odd for several reasons. To begin with, Hans was the first permanent refugee admitted to the Beje, and he stayed there longer than anyone else—nine months. In his note when signing the Beje guestbook on March 6, 1974, Hans provides his length of stay next to his signature: "Beje Mei '43–Feb. '44"). Collection 78, Papers of Cornelia Arnolda Johanna ten Boom, 1902–1983, Box 1, Folder 8, Buswell Library Archives and Special Collections, Wheaton College, Wheaton, IL ("Buswell Library Collections"); Poley, 202–3.

Second, in Corrie's 1947 autobiography, *A Prisoner and Yet*, she mentions

Hans five times as being one of the six permanent guests (pages 15, 18, 19, 20), the others being Eusi, Mary, Martha (Meta Monsanto), Peter (her nephew, although he wasn't a permanent resident, simply a regular visitor), and Leonard (presumably the Anglicized version of Leendert) (19). She also mentions a "Jim" as one of the refugees (18), writing, "He could . . . give an evening's program of magic." Since the Beje never had a refugee named Jim, this person apparently refers to Henk Wessels, to whom Hans Poley attributed the magic tricks. Poley, 65. See my Appendix for dates when each refugee arrived at the Beje.

Third, of the extant photos showing refugees in the Beje, Hans appears in the most (nine). He includes six photos in *Return to the Hiding Place*, along with two reunion photos with him, Corrie, and Eusi at the Beje in 1974. Emily S. Smith, who wrote *More Than a Hiding Place: The Life-Changing Experiences of Corrie ten Boom* on behalf of the Corrie ten Boom House Foundation, includes six photos (31, 33, 34, 36, and 81) of Hans at the Beje (three of which do not appear in Poley's *Return to the Hiding Place*). Corrie's archives in the Buswell Library Collections (Collection 78, Box 1) contain originals of two photos of Hans (both of which appear in Smith, one of which appears in Poley).

Note also that the first edition of *The Hiding Place* contained no photos, and *A Prisoner and Yet* contained only one photo—of Beje visitors during the war, the reverse side of which contains a caption stating that Hans Poley may have taken the picture. The original photo is located in Collection 78, Box 1, Buswell Library Collections.

Finally, in the Corrie ten Boom House Foundation's video tour of the Beje, Hans Poley is quoted at length about his stay with the ten Booms (visit virtualtour.corrietenboom.com).

Hans's absence from *The Hiding Place* appears to have occurred because the book was written not by Corrie, but by John and Elizabeth Sherrill (see the "*they wanted to write*" endnote in Chapter 26, which provides the places where Corrie acknowledged that the book was written entirely by the Sherrills), who seem to have missed Corrie's five references to him in *A Prisoner and Yet*, and the nine photos of Hans with the ten Booms and other refugees during the war.

57 "*Welcome! Come in, quickly*": Poley, 16.
58 "*We cannot offer*": Ibid., 16–17.
59 "*Stay away from the windows*": Ibid., 19–20.
59 *Henny van Dantzig*: Ibid., 27–28.
60 "*The Germans took*": Ibid., 28–29.
60 "*There is more to it*": Ibid., 30–31.
61 "*Last night the guns*": Anne Frank, *The Diary of a Young Girl*, 104–5.
61 "*Now look at this*": Poley, 23–24.
62 "*I think, my boy*": Ibid., 35–36.

63 *"A farewell address":* Ibid., 37–39.

64 *Mary van Itallie:* Ibid., 40. In *The Hiding Place* (102) the Sherrills list Mary's age as seventy-six. Extant photos of Mary at the Beje, however, reveal that she was decades younger, confirming Hans's recollection that she was forty-two. Two original photos of Mary with other Beje refugees can be found in Collection 78, Box 1, Buswell Library Collections. Photos of Mary also appear in Emily S. Smith's *More Than a Hiding Place* (31, 33, 34, 37, and 81) and Hans Poley's *Return to the Hiding Place* (unpaginated photo section). Note also that Hans knew Mary better than anyone as she stayed with him at his parents' home whenever the refugees had to flee the Beje.

64 *Henk Wessels and Leendert Kip:* Poley, 41; *The Hiding Place*, 99, 101. While *The Hiding Place* states that Meijer Mossel ("Eusi") was the first permanent refugee at the Beje, Hans's diary indicates that Eusi arrived *sixth*, on June 28, after Hans, Thea, Mary, Henk, and Leendert were in residence. See Poley, 40–41, 47. Carole C. Carlson, who published a short biography of Corrie in 1983, also noted that Hans was the first permanent refugee in the Beje. Carlson, *Corrie ten Boom: Her Life, Her Faith*, 77–78. The Corrie ten Boom House Foundation, which published Emily S. Smith's *More Than a Hiding Place* in 2010, also confirms (104) the accuracy of Hans's timeline.

64 *"I'll ask Pickwick":* Poley, 42; *The Hiding Place*, 83–84. In Corrie's retelling of this part of the story (or the Sherrills' recollection of what Corrie may have told them), she writes of meeting the architect who would design the hiding place at the Resistance gathering she went to with Kik (chapter 5)—perhaps as early as May 1942, and before Hans, Thea, Mary, Henk, or Leendert had arrived. Hans kept a detailed diary during this time, however, and he has the hiding place design and buildout commencing in mid-June 1943, after he and the first four refugees were in residence. Poley, 40–43.

64 *"Mr. Smit":* *The Hiding Place*, 83.

65 *mirror outside:* Peter van Woerden, *In the Secret Place*, 73.

65 *"Miss ten Boom":* *The Hiding Place*, 84.

65 *"One layer of bricks":* Poley, 42.

66 *A counterweight and wheel:* Ibid., 43.

66 *"Keep a water jug":* *The Hiding Place*, 85.

67 *"The Gestapo could search":* Ibid.

67 *"Angels' Den":* Poley, 43. In *A Prisoner and Yet* Corrie refers to the hiding place as the "Angelcrib" (19), while in *The Hiding Place* the Sherrills refer to it as the "secret room" (117, 119).

67 *alarm system:* Poley, 42; *The Hiding Place*, 99; van Woerden, 73.

68 *Three minutes, twenty-eight seconds:* Poley, 44.

68 *"Let's run through":* Ibid., 45.

68 *"You'll have to take down":* Ibid.

69 *On Flip's birthday:* *The Hiding Place*, 86.

69 *"Peter, hurry!":* van Woerden, 59. The Sherrill version is slightly different,

with Peter racing in from outside with his brother Bob, and both hiding in the cellar. *The Hiding Place*, 87.

69   *"Are there any boys":* van Woerden, 60. Corrie's remembrance of the dialogue exchange is slightly different from Peter's, but the end result was the same. *The Hiding Place*, 87–88.

Chapter 7: The Babies

70   *pounded so loudly:* Peter van Woerden, 59.

70   *"Don't take us":* Corrie ten Boom, *The Hiding Place*, 88.

70   *"Keep moving":* Hans Poley, *Return to the Hiding Place*, 46.

71   *"We don't have any food":* Ibid.

71   *"All right, you can":* Ibid.

71   *one hundred babies:* Corrie ten Boom, "A Rare Recording of Corrie ten Boom," vol. 1, Listen and Live Audio, 2019; Emily S. Smith, *More Than a Hiding Place: The Life-Changing Experiences of Corrie ten Boom*, 74. Note that Corrie mentions it as an orphanage, but this was a nursery for Jewish babies and small children run by Henriëtte Henriques Pimentel in central Amsterdam. Many of the babies and children were or became orphans, however, as their parents were killed or sent to concentration camps.

71   *Creche:* Mark Klempner, *The Heart Has Reasons: Dutch Rescuers of Jewish Children During the Holocaust*, 131.

72   *Hollandsche Schouwburg:* Ibid., 130–32; Warmbrunn, *The Dutch Under German Occupation* 170; Chris Webb, "The Story of Walter Suskind."

72   *Walter Süskind:* Ibid.

72   *Felix Halverstad:* Ibid.

72   *Henriëtte Henriques Pimentel:* "Henriëtte Pimentel: Whoever Saves One Person, Saves a Whole World," *Joodsamsterdam*, translated, https://www.joodsamsterdam.nl/henriette-pimentel-wie-een-mens-redt-redt-een-hele-wereld/; Roland Hughes, "Obituary: Johan van Hulst, the Teacher Who Saved Hundreds of Jewish Children," *BBC News*, March 30, 2018.

72   *"We will save them":* Corrie ten Boom, "A Rare Recording," vol. 1, Listen and Live Audio; Smith, *More Than a Hiding Place*, 74 (a transcript of the speech Corrie gave in "A Rare Recording"). In her recollection about the event, Corrie doesn't mention a date, although her reference to dialogue with "her boys" suggests that Hans, Henk, and Leendert were in the Beje, and that the remark came from one of them. In her speech Corrie stated: "After some time [in the underground] I had a gang of 80 people; 30 teenager boys, 20 teenager girls, 20 men and 10 women." Smith, *More Than a Hiding Place*, 74. Since only about twenty-five refugees—boys and girls, men and women—actually stayed in the Beje (see Appendix), Corrie's reference to her "gang" evidently referred to everyone in the Haarlem underground who had connections to the ten Booms (that is, Piet Hartog—Aty's boyfriend, Kik's friends in the underground, Peter, etc.), or who visited the Beje as couriers

(that is, Nils, who is referenced as an underground courier in *The Hiding Place*, 108). Given the danger of large meetings, Corrie would not have had more than three or four underground workers at the Beje at one time. Accordingly, Corrie's dialogue seems to have been with her three Dutch boys—Hans, Henk, and Leendert—putting the date of the event about this time in late June 1943.

72 *"We don't like":* Corrie ten Boom, "A Rare Recording," vol. 1, Listen and Live Audio; Smith, *More Than a Hiding Place*, 74.

73 *Betty Goudsmit-Oudkerk:* Hanneloes Pen, "Betty Goudsmit-Oudkerk (1924–2020) Saved Hundreds of Jewish Children from Deportation," *AD* (translated), June 15, 2020.

73 *Johan van Hulst:* Hughes, "Obituary: Johan van Hulst, the Teacher Who Saved Hundreds of Jewish Children," *BBC News*, March 30, 2018.

73 *one hundred babies were saved:* Corrie ten Boom, "A Rare Recording of Corrie ten Boom," vol. 1, Listen and Live Audio; Emily S. Smith, *More Than a Hiding Place*, 74. Corrie doesn't provide details of *how* the Dutch boys (dressed as German soldiers) actually assisted in the rescue, but the escort apparently was coordinated with the Pimentel-Süskind-Halverstad escape route.

73 *six hundred to one thousand:* Werner Warmbrunn, *The Dutch Under German Occupation 1940–1945*, 170 (estimating one thousand).

74 *"The strengthening words":* Poley, 47–48.

74 *"We have a man's watch":* The Hiding Place, 96.

74 *"The very first thing":* Ibid. Note that in this account, Corrie uses the similar phonetic "Mayer" for his first name. "Meijer," which is pronounced the same, appears to be the correct spelling. See Poley, 48, 50.

75 *"Is that your father?":* Poley, 48.

75 *"But now":* Ibid.

75 *"for obvious reasons":* The Hiding Place, 97.

75 *"You ask why":* Poley, 49.

75 *"Should I rather":* Ibid., 50.

76 *"Sir, we shall call you Eusi":* Ibid., 50–51. In *The Hiding Place* (98) the Sherrills have Corrie coming up with Eusi's name ("I think we'll call you Eusebius"). Given Hans's meticulous record keeping, along with the fact that it was his birthday—a memorable event—his account is more reliable.

A second discrepancy is the spelling of his nickname. Just as with Meijer Mossel's first name, there are two phonetic options for his nickname: Eusi or Eusie. In her books, Corrie always spelled his nickname as "Eusie," but Mossel himself spelled it "Eusi" (the spelling also used by Hans Poley). See Mossel's handwritten note found in the Beje guestbook on March 6, 1974, and his signature: "Eusi." Collection 78, Papers of Cornelia Arnolda Johanna ten Boom, 1902–1983, Box 2, Folder 2, Buswell Library Archives and Special Collections, Wheaton College, Wheaton, IL. See also Poley, *Return to the*

Hiding Place 202–3 (Hans signed at the same time and provides the date, which is not on the guestbook page), giving an English translation of the comments.

76 *"Of course, there's a provision":* The Hiding Place, 98.

77 *Ninth Commandment not to give:* See Deuteronomy 5:20.

77 *"Tell me I did not":* Poley, 52–53.

77 *"But, here we are":* Ibid., 54–55.

77 *"Many Dutch Christians":* Ibid., 55.

79 *"All young men":* van Woerden, 64–66.

79 *"Where is that man":* Ibid., 67.

79 *"How many Jews":* Poley, 55.

Chapter 8: Terror

80 *"Peter?":* van Woerden, 67.

81 *"Let me take care":* Poley, 54–55.

81 seventy *seconds:* Corrie ten Boom, *A Prisoner and Yet*, 20; *The Hiding Place*, 101.

81 *"Alarm! Germans around!":* Poley, 57–58.

82 *"Invasion in Italy!":* Ibid., 60.

82 *Henk Wiedijk:* Ibid., 64. Henk Wiedijk is not mentioned in *The Hiding Place*, but he was clearly a Beje resident. Aside from Hans's account, Henk appears in several photos with the ten Booms and other refugees, his towering height making his identification clear. See, for example, the July 1943 formal photo of him, Leendert, Eusi, Henk Wessels, Hans, Mary, Betsie, Opa, Corrie, and Thea in Poley, *Return to the Hiding Place* (unpaginated photo section), and the rooftop photo of him, Thea, Hans, Mary, and Eusi in Emily S. Smith, *More Than a Hiding Place: The Life-Changing Experiences of Corrie ten Boom*, 81.

82 *Jop:* Corrie ten Boom, *The Hiding Place*, 99, 115. The exact date of Henk Wiedijk's and Jop's entrance into the Beje is not specified in any account, but both appear to have arrived after July 14 and before the arrival of Mr. de Vries on July 19. After a reference to July 14, Hans Poley wrote that "[f]or the next few days . . . [s]everal new guests arrived. . . . Henk Wiedijk arrived. . . ." Hans doesn't mention Jop, but apparently he was one of the "several new guests." Poley, 64.

83 *constructed to hide eight: A Prisoner and Yet*, 19; van Woerden, 72–73.

83 *Hans taught astronomy:* Poley, 65–66.

83 *"Most of you know":* Ibid., 66.

83 *Peter would visit:* Poley, 67–68; van Woerden, 70–71.

84 *scraping sound:* Poley, 67.

84 *"Do not turn around":* The Hiding Place, 108. *The Hiding Place* has the window-washing event occurring in September, but Hans Poley's diary reveals that it happened in mid-July, before Nollie's arrest.

85 *Beje "permanent" refugees:* Poley, unpaginated photo section. A similar photo taken about this time is located in Collection 78, Papers of Cornelia Arnolda Johanna ten Boom, 1902–1983, Box 1, Buswell Library Archives and Special Collections, Wheaton College, Wheaton, IL ("Buswell Library Collections").

85 *"Just go on":* Poley, 67; *The Hiding Place*, 108.

85 *"What are you doing?":* *The Hiding Place*, 108.

86 *"Often I went":* Poley, 68–69.

86 *"Two searchlight beams:* Ibid., 70.

87 *"I don't know where":* Ibid., 71–72.

88 *Corrie assured everyone that angels:* Ibid., 73. Corrie's assumption that the Beje was being protected by angels likely stemmed from her father's (and perhaps her) favorite Bible passage—Psalm 91—which he asked to be read at the police station when the family was arrested (see Chapter 14). It was this psalm that Corrie set out in the memorial display for her father on May 8, 1945 (see Chapter 27), and from this psalm that she titled her 1971 release, *The Hiding Place*.

   The King James Version of Psalm 91 provides in pertinent part:

   "[1] He that dwelleth in the secret place of the Most High shall abide under the shadow of the Almighty. . . . [5] Thou shalt not be afraid for the terror by night; nor for the arrow that flieth by day . . . [7] A thousand may fall at thy side, and ten thousand at thy right hand; but it shall not come nigh thee. . . . [11] For he shall give his angels charge over thee, to keep thee in all thy ways."

   After the family's arrest on February 28, 1944—seeing that Corrie was shaken that angels had not protected them—Betsie corrected her sister's misunderstanding of God's promises. Without mentioning the executions of John the Baptist, Paul, or most of the twelve disciples, Betsie told Corrie that God's protection is of their *souls*, not of their lives or physical well-being. See Poley, 148.

88 *"North Amsterdam was":* Anne Frank, *The Diary of a Young Girl*, 115.

89 *seven hundred Allied bombers:* John Thompson, *Spirit over Steel: A Chronology of the Second World War*, 352. See also William Shirer, *The Rise and Fall of the Third Reich*, 996.

89 *RAF firebombed Hamburg:* Thompson, 354. The raid on Hamburg was a series of raids, with the RAF bombing it the nights of July 24, 27 (with incendiary bombs causing firestorms), 29, and August 2, while American bombers conducted daylight raids on July 25 and 26. I. C. B. Dear and M. R. D. Foot, eds., *The Oxford Companion to World War II*, 523.

89 *Bomber Command dropped 16,000 tons:* Thompson, 346.

90 *Nazis were sending Jews:* Poley, *Return to the Hiding Place*, 79.

90 *August 14 they arrested Nollie:* Ibid.; van Woerden, 63; Corrie ten Boom, *The Hiding Place*, 105; *Father ten Boom: God's Man*, 140; Carole C. Carlson, *Corrie ten Boom: Her Life, Her Faith*, 83.

Chapter 9: Resistance

91   *"Katrien!"*: *The Hiding Place*, 104–5; Hans Poley, *Return to the Hiding Place*, 79–80 (Hans remembering the maid's name as Marja).

92   *the other Jew they were hiding*: Peter van Woerden, *In the Secret Place*, 63; *Father ten Boom: God's Man*, 140; Carlson, 83, 85.

92   *escaped through the roof*: Carlson, 83.

92   *"Keep away"*: Poley, 80.

92   *"Jesus is Victor!"*: *Father ten Boom*, 141.

92   *"However can you"*: Ibid.

93   *Hans sneaked Mary*: Poley, 81.

93   *the de Leeuws*: Ibid., 82.

93   *Nollie was transferred*: *The Hiding Place*, 106.

94   *Gestapo would offer freedom*: Poley, 82.

94   *police officers, soldiers*: Carlson, 84–85.

94   *"People don't realize"*: *The Hiding Place*, 107.

95   *"How are your dogs?"*: Carlson, 85.

95   *Italy surrendered*: John Thompson *Spirit over Steel: A Chronology of the Second World War*, 364; I. C. B. Dear and M. R. D. Foot, eds., *The Oxford Companion to World War II*, 1332; Marcel Baudot et al., eds., *The Historical Encyclopedia of World War II*, 537.

95   *Nollie was released*: van Woerden, 63; Poley, 83. Note that Corrie was slightly off in her remembrance about Nollie's release, thinking that her sister had been incarcerated for seven weeks, and that she was released the second week of October. *The Hiding Place*, 112.

95   *Hans, Mary, Eusi, and Henk*: Poley, 85–86.

95   *eighteen-year-old Mirjam de Jong*: Ibid., 86.

95   *"Well, well"*: Ibid.

96   *Henk Wessels's father*: Ibid., 87.

97   *"And he does not yet know"*: Ibid., 89–90.

98   *"That's the answer"*: Ibid., 90–91.

98   *Nazis executed nineteen*: Ibid., 92.

Chapter 10: The Chief

99   *Hans, Mary, and Eusi returned*: Poley, 92, 96.

99   *twenty-four-year-old assistant minister*: Ibid., 95–96, 101.

100 *"The Exchange"*: Ibid., 102.

100 *"Who's there?"*: Corrie ten Boom, *The Hiding Place*, 110; "Not Lost, but Gone Before," *The Hiding Place* magazine, memorial edition, 5; Collection 78, Papers of Cornelia Arnolda Johanna ten Boom, 1902–1983, Box 2, Folder 2, Buswell Library Archives and Special Collections, Wheaton College, Wheaton, IL ("Buswell Library Collections").

101 *"What was that?"*: *The Hiding Place*, 111–12; "Not Lost, but Gone Before,"

The Hiding Place magazine, memorial edition, 7; Collection 78, Box 2, Folder 2, Buswell Library Collections.

102 *Nel . . . and Ronnie Gazan:* Poley, 97. Note that Emily S. Smith records Ronnie's last name as da Costa Silva. *More Than a Hiding Place*, 82.

102 *Gentile alias:* *More Than a Hiding Place*, 105.

103 *"That's wonderful!":* Ibid., 103.

103 *"Dear Mies":* Ibid., 104–5.

103 *"Here, my boy":* Ibid., 103.

103 Herinneringen van een Oude Horlogemaker: Collection 78, Box 1, Buswell Library Collections.

104 *Landelijke Organisatie:* Poley, 101. For another perspective of Christian resistance, see also Diet Eman, *Things We Couldn't Say: A Dramatic Account of Christian Resistance in Holland During World War II.* For the Resistance movement in general, see Louis de Jong and Joseph W. F. Stoppelman, *The Lion Rampant: The Story of Holland's Resistance to the Nazis.*

105 *317,000 new cards:* Poley, 100.

105 *she sometimes lost her notes:* Ibid., 101.

105 *dressed as a girl:* Ibid., 106.

106 *Brouwershofje:* Ibid., 107.

107 *they gave him a gun:* Ibid., 109.

107 *Henny van Dantzig:* Ibid., 110–11.

107 *"My greatly beloved grandson":* Corrie ten Boom, *Father ten Boom: God's Man*, 147–48.

108 *"We've heard so much":* Poley, 114–15.

109 *The Beje, Christmas 1943:* Ibid., unpaginated photo section. In the photo, Hans identifies the third person from the left as Meta Monsanto. By his own calendar, however, the Monsanto sisters did not arrive at the Beje until January 1944. Poley, 118. The resolution is likely that Meta visited the Beje for the Christmas gathering, but didn't move in with her sister until after the New Year.

109 *Corrie read Tolstoy's story:* Ibid., 115.

110 *"Then quickly, boy":* Corrie ten Boom, *The Hiding Place*, 115–16.

110 *"You will come":* Ibid., 113.

110 *"Miss ten Boom":* Ibid., 114.

111 *"Kill him":* Ibid. See also Carole C. Carlson, *Corrie ten Boom: Her Life, Her Faith*, 87.

Chapter 11: The Mission

112 *"Liquidation":* Werner Warmbrunn, *The Dutch Under German Occupation, 1940–1945*, 206–7.

112 *liquidation of General Hendrik Seyffardt:* Ibid., 206. For background on the NSB and its leader, Anton A. Mussert, see also Warmbrunn 83–89; Israel Gutman, ed., *Encyclopedia of the Holocaust*, vol. 3, 1026, 1032–33; Louis de Jong and Joseph W. F. Stoppelman, *The Lion Rampant: The Story of Holland's*

Resistance to the Nazis, 129–30, 160–63, 248–51, 258; Jacob Presser, *Ashes in the Wind: The Destruction of Dutch Jewry*, 232–33, 356, 369; and Walter B. Maass, *The Netherlands at War: 1940–1945*, 52–54, 57, 79, 132, 141.

112 *Hermannus Reydon:* Warmbrunn, 206.

112 *F. E. Postuma:* Ibid., 207.

112 *some forty National Socialist leaders:* Ibid.

113 *torture to wring confessions:* The torture methods of the Gestapo were nothing short of medieval. For those with strong stomachs, see what the Gestapo did to anti-Nazi Fabian von Schlabrendorff in his memoir, *The Secret War Against Hitler*, 312–13. In short, the Gestapo tortured him in four stages. The day after his stage 1 torture, where he had passed out due to excruciating pain, he had a heart attack (even though he had been in excellent health before). When he recuperated, stage 2 was initiated, followed by stage 3. During stage 4 the pain was such that he again passed out.

When they were prisoners together, Schlabrendorff gave British SOE agent Peter Churchill a detailed description of what the Gestapo did to him. See Larry Loftis, *Code Name: Lise*, 225–26, n. 49. Countless other tortures included driving pointed sticks under fingernails (Bernt Engelmann, *In Hitler's Germany: Everyday Life in the Third Reich*, 32) and ripping out toenails (Loftis, *Code Name: Lise*, 147–52).

113 *"Sir, I have always":* Corrie ten Boom, *The Hiding Place*, 114–15. See also Carole C. Carlson, *Corrie ten Boom: Her Life, Her Faith*, 87.

113 *Jop had been arrested: The Hiding Place*, 116.

113 *"Why are you afraid?":* Carlson, 88. For an explanation of why Corrie assumed that angels would protect the ten Booms from arrest or harm, see the *Corrie assured everyone that angels* endnote in Chapter 8.

114 *Meta and Paula Monsanto:* Hans Poley, *Return to the Hiding Place*, 118–19.

114 *"Our now widely known shelter":* Ibid., 119.

115 *Conversation in the Beje parlor:* This photo, which has the identities of the refugees on the reverse, is located in Collection 78, Papers of Cornelia Arnolda Johanna ten Boom, 1902–1983, Box 1, Buswell Library Archives and Special Collections, Wheaton College, Wheaton, IL.

116 *"Get your things":* Poley, *Return to the Hiding Place*, 121.

116 *Dora, had given birth:* Ibid., 122–23.

117 *"Hans, Hans, wake up!":* Ibid., 125.

117 *"Who are you?":* Ibid., 126.

118 *Vredehofstraat 23, Soest:* Ibid., unpaginated photo section.

119 *"Moreover":* Ibid., 127.

119 *"Ah, there's our preacher!":* Ibid., 129.

121 *"You do realize":* Ibid., 131.

122 *"The peace that came":* Ibid., 132.

122 *"Well, you probably know":* Ibid., 133.

Chapter 12: Six Hundred Guilders

123 *"God, be with me"*: Hans Poley, *Return to the Hiding Place*, 133.

123 *"What your parents admitted"*: Ibid., 134.

124 *"Hans, greetings from Tante Kees"*: Ibid., 135.

125 *"Tell them not to worry"*: Ibid., 135–36.

125 *Kik was arrested*: Carole C. Carlson, *Corrie ten Boom: Her Life, Her Faith*, 88–89.

125 *German military leaders had plotted*: For a brief summary of the German military's repeated attempts to kill or oust Adolf Hitler, see Larry Loftis, *The Princess Spy*, 87–91. See also Hans Bernd Gisevius, *To the Bitter End: An Insider's Account of the Plot to Kill Hitler, 1933–44*; Ulrich von Hassell, *The Von Hassell Diaries, 1938–1944: The Story of the Forces Against Hitler Inside Germany*; Fabian von Schlabrendorff, *The Secret War Against Hitler*; Peter Hoffmann, *The History of the German Resistance, 1933–1945*; Klemens von Klemperer, *German Resistance Against Hitler*; Ger van Roon, *German Resistance to Hitler: Count von Moltke and the Kreisau Circle*; Agostino von Hassell and Sigrid MacRae, *Alliance of Enemies: The Untold Story of the Secret American and German Collaboration to End World War II* (esp. pages 253–58 regarding the Canaris diaries); Charles Burdick and Hans-Adolf Jacobsen, *The Halder War Diary, 1939–42*; Michael Balfour, *Withstanding Hitler*; Harold C. Deutsch, *The Conspiracy Against Hitler in the Twilight War*; Anton Gill, *An Honourable Defeat: A History of German Resistance to Hitler, 1933–1945*; Constantine FitzGibbon, *20 July*; Theodore S. Hamerow, *On the Road to the Wolf's Lair: German Resistance to Hitler*; André Brissaud, *Canaris: The Biography of Admiral Canaris, Chief of German Military Intelligence*; Michael Mueller, *Nazi Spymaster: The Life and Death of Admiral Wilhelm Canaris*; and William Shirer, *The Rise and Fall of the Third Reich*. See also entries for Beck, Canaris, Halder, Oster, and the *Schwarze Kapelle* in I. C. B. Dear and M. R. D. Foot, eds., *The Oxford Companion to World War II*; Marcel Baudot et al, eds., *The Historical Encyclopedia of World War II*; and Louis L. Snyder, *Encyclopedia of the Third Reich*.

125 *Hitler twice, and another six times*: Shirer, 1024, 1026.

125 *Pastor Dietrich Bonhoeffer*: Ibid., 1024. For excellent biographies of Bonhoeffer, see Eberhard Bethge, *Dietrich Bonhoeffer*, trans. by Eric Mosbacher et al.; and Eric Metaxas, *Bonhoeffer: Pastor, Martyr, Prophet, Spy*. For short summaries of Bonhoeffer's life and work, see also entries for him at Snyder, 34–35; Dear and Foot, 152; and Robert S. Wistrich, *Who's Who in Nazi Germany*, 16–17.

125 *Hans von Dohnanyi, and diplomat Dr. Josef Müller*: Shirer, 1024.

126 *General Hans Oster*: Ibid.

126 *most popular man in Germany*: Recognizing his country's craving for a popular military hero, Hitler decided in 1941 to give them two: "one in the sun and one in the snow," Rommel being the former and General

Eduard Dietl (who operated in Norway and Finland) being the latter. When newsreels of Rommel's early successes leading the Afrika Korps reached the public, he was an instant celebrity—not only in Germany, but in Britain as well, where he was widely regarded as a hero.

After Rommel's victory in Tobruk, Egypt, in June 1942, Hitler promoted him to field marshal—the youngest in the Wehrmacht. Perhaps Rommel's greatest compliment, ironically, came from his enemy. The British Eighth Army—whom he fought in Africa—came to respect and admire him more than their own commanders. So much did they consider Rommel a hero that they coined a phrase—"a Rommel"—to reference any good performance. B. H. Liddell Hart, *The German Generals Talk*, 45–49; Richard J. Evans, *The Third Reich at War*, 150.

126 *movement to oust Hitler:* Shirer, 1030.
127 *"You are the only one":* Ibid., 1031.
127 *Hepburn and her family:* Robert Matzen, *Dutch Girl: Audrey Hepburn and World War II*, 131–32.
127 *Operation Argument:* Dear and Foot, 130–31. For day-by-day tallies, see John Thompson, *Spirit over Steel: A Chronology of the Second World War*, 412–14.
128 *two hundred civilians:* Thompson, 413.
128 *20,000 tons of bombs:* Dear and Foot, 131.
128 *All of the doctors:* Matzen, 137.
128 *private dance performances:* Ibid., 146.
129 *"Listen, we've run out":* Poley, 140.
129 *five hundred guilders:* Ibid., 141.
129 *February 28:* Corrie ten Boom, *A Prisoner and Yet*, 20; *The Hiding Place*, 117; Poley, 141.
129 *Betsie appeared:* *The Hiding Place*, 117. In Hans Poley's version of the story, it was not Betsie who told Corrie about the stranger downstairs, but Henny, the shop salesgirl. Poley, 141.
130 *"I'm sorry to wake":* *The Hiding Place*, 117.
130 *"Miss ten Boom!":* Ibid.
130 *"my wife was arrested in Alkmaar":* Carlson, *Corrie ten Boom*, 90; Poley, 141.
130 *"I'm a poor man":* *The Hiding Place*, 118.
130 *if he could provide references:* Poley, 141.
130 *"When I first showed up":* Diet Eman, *Things We Couldn't Say: A Dramatic Account of Christian Resistance in Holland During World War II*, 116–17.
131 *come back in half an hour:* *The Hiding Place*, 118. In Hans Poley's version of the story, Corrie told the man to come back late in the afternoon, he returned around five, and Corrie personally gave him the money. Poley, 141–42.
131 *sent a courier to the bank:* *The Hiding Place*, 118. In Poley's version of the story, Corrie had available funds in the Beje and neither a courier nor a bank was involved. Poley, 141–42. See also Carlson, *Corrie ten Boom*, 90–91 (a third

version of the story, where Corrie gathered all of the young people and told them: "Listen, within one hour I must have four hundred guilders. Do your best.").

Chapter 13: Trapped

132 *"Hurry! Hurry!":* Corrie ten Boom, *The Hiding Place*, 119.

132 *Martha and Ronnie:* Carole C. Carlson, *Corrie ten Boom: Her Life, Her Faith*, 93; Poley, 142. There are three recollections of this story: Corrie's, Hans's, and Arnold's (Reynout Siertsema). Since Arnold was one of the six trapped in the Angels' Den, his version (recorded in Carlson) carries the most credibility. In addition, Arnold's version is consistent with Hans's. According to Arnold, the five other refugees in the hiding place were Mary, Martha, Eusi, Ronnie, and Hans van Messel. Carlson, *Corrie ten Boom*, 93; Emily S. Smith, *More Than a Hiding Place: The Life-Changing Experiences of Corrie ten Boom* (published in 2010 by the Corrie ten Boom House Foundation), 105. According to Hans Poley, the den included "the four regulars" (presumably Mary, Martha, Eusi, and Ronnie, whom Hans mentions later as one of the six), plus "Arnold and Hans, two of the resistance workers." Poley, 142. Corrie's six (apparently recounted to John and Elizabeth Sherrill), on the other hand, are: Thea, Meta (Martha), Henk, Eusi, Mary, and an unnamed Resistance worker. In Corrie's recollection, Henk was likely Hans, and the unnamed Resistance worker was likely Arnold. That would leave only one discrepancy—Thea—who was actually Ronnie Gazan. Given the consistency of Arnold's and Hans's recollection, together with Emily Smith's official Corrie ten Boom House Foundation record, the trapped six were most certainly Mary, Martha, Eusi, Arnold Siertsema, Ronnie Gazan, and Hans van Messel. Note that Smith records Ronnie's last name as "da Costa Silva." *More Than a Hiding Place*, 82. Note also that when Arnold signed the Beje guestbook on March 18, 1976, he added to his signature: "'Arnold,' one of them who is in the angel box."

132 *"What's your name?":* *The Hiding Place*, 120; Poley, 143.

133 *"Never mind":* Poley, 143; Carlson, 91.

133 *Opa, Betsie, Willem:* Poley, 143. Both Corrie (*The Hiding Place*, 124) and Hans mistakenly include Peter van Woerden, Nollie's son and Corrie's nephew, as being one of those arrested at this time. In his own work, Peter explained that he was not yet at the Beje, and would not arrive until the evening, after it was "sufficiently dark." Peter van Woerden, *In the Secret Place*, 75. Corrie and the others had been taken to jail in the morning.

133 *"It was a signal":* Poley, 143; *The Hiding Place*, 121. In *The Hiding Place*, the Sherrills have the sequence of events reversed: the Alpina sign and signal discussion occurs after Corrie's beating.

134 *"My information says":* *The Hiding Place*, 121.

134 *take off her glasses:* Corrie ten Boom, *A Prisoner and Yet,* 21; Poley, 144; Carlson, 92.

134 *"Where are the Jews?":* *The Hiding Place,* 121.

134 *"Lord Jesus, protect me!":* *A Prisoner and Yet,* 21; Poley, 144.

135 *"Have you heard?":* *The Hiding Place,* 122.

135 *"Were you beaten?":* *A Prisoner and Yet,* 21; Poley, 144.

135 *"Prisoners will remain":* *The Hiding Place,* 122.

135 *"Fear God":* *A Prisoner and Yet,* 23; Poley, 145; *The Hiding Place,* 123.

136 *"This is the ten Boom":* *The Hiding Place,* 123; *A Prisoner and Yet,* 22.

136 *"there's a secret room":* *The Hiding Place,* 124.

136 *police station in the Smedestraat:* *A Prisoner and Yet,* 24; *The Hiding Place,* 125; Poley, 146.

137 *"Who's here?":* Poley, 155; Carlson, 93.

137 *Martha, Mary, Eusi, Ronnie:* Poley, 155; Smith, *More Than a Hiding Place,* 82, 105. For a detailed discussion of the six trapped in the Angels' Den, see the *Martha and Ronnie* endnote above in this chapter.

137 *three short rings:* van Woerden, *In the Secret Place,* 75. Hans Poley remembered the code as three short rings, one long. Poley, 157.

138 *"We have very sad news":* van Woerden, 76.

138 *"I'm sorry, sir":* Ibid., 77–78.

138 *"I think you'd better":* Ibid., 78.

138 *some thirty other friends:* Ibid., 78–79; *A Prisoner and Yet,* 24; *The Hiding Place,* 125 (Corrie remembering a total of thirty-five, including the ten Booms).

139 *"Let's have it quiet":* *The Hiding Place,* 125.

139 *"Give it to me":* Poley, 149–51.

139 *Peter was next up:* Ibid., 151.

139 *Psalm 91:* *A Prisoner and Yet,* 24; van Woerden, 80; Poley, 147.

140 *"He that dwelleth":* van Woerden, 80. Presumably, Willem would have been reading Psalm 91 from the Dutch translation of the King James Version of the Bible.

140 *where were the protecting angels?:* Poley, 148. For background on Corrie's assumption that angels would protect the ten Booms from arrest or harm, see the *Corrie assured everyone that angels* endnote in Chapter 8.

140 *St. Bavo Church chime:* Carlson, 93 (quoting Arnold's account).

140 *Splintering wood:* Poley, 158; Carlson, 94.

Chapter 14: Privileged

141 *"I will trust in Adonai":* Hans Poley, *Return to the Hiding Place,* 158.

142 *"Grand Old Man":* Corrie ten Boom, *The Hiding Place,* 126; Peter van Woerden, *In the Secret Place,* 81.

143 *"Peter, I've suffered":* van Woerden, 81–82.

143 *urinating on bedsheets:* Poley, 158; Carole C. Carlson, *Corrie ten Boom: Her Life, Her Faith*, 94 (quoting Arnold's later account).

143 *"If you trust":* Poley, 158.

144 *"Alle Nasen gegen":* van Woerden, 82; Corrie ten Boom, *A Prisoner and Yet*, 27; *The Hiding Place*, 128. Corrie is inconsistent where the Gestapo headquarters was located. In *A Prisoner and Yet* she writes that it was located in Scheveningen, but in *The Hiding Place* she has it at The Hague. Since Peter van Woerden remembered that it was at The Hague, I have used that location.

144 *"That old man!":* *The Hiding Place*, 128.

145 *Scheveningen prison: A Prisoner and Yet*, 28; *The Hiding Place*, 130; *Father ten Boom: God's Man*, 10; Poley, 153.

145 *"The Lord be with you": A Prisoner and Yet*, 28; Corrie ten Boom, *He Sets the Captive Free*, 16.

145 *"If you persist":* Corrie ten Boom, *Prison Letters*, 20; *A Prisoner and Yet*, 45; Poley, 153.

145 *Betsie to 314, Corrie to 397, Opa to 401:* Corrie ten Boom, *Prison Letters*, 20; *A Prisoner and Yet*, 45; Poley, 153.

145 *"Women prisoners follow me!":* *The Hiding Place*, 130.

146 *"Ten Boom, Cornelia":* Ibid., 132; *He Sets the Captive Free*, 11–12.

146 *"I'm sorry that":* *A Prisoner and Yet*, 30.

146 *"O Lord, may they":* van Woerden, 85.

147 *first twelve chapters:* Ibid., 86.

147 *"going home":* Ibid.

148 *eight-foot jump:* Carlson, 94 (Arnold's account giving a leap distance of 2.5 meters, or 8.2 feet); Poley, 159 (citing only a three-foot jump).

148 *"Siertsema":* Poley, 160 (Siertsema being Arnold's real last name); Carlson, 94 (stating that the voice said, "Arnold, answer!"). Given Poley's personal knowledge about, and association with, Arnold, Hans, and the other refugees, his dialogue is more reliable.

Chapter 15: Prison

149 *"It's okay":* Hans Poley, *Return to the Hiding Place*, 160; Carole C. Carlson, *Corrie ten Boom: Her Life, Her Faith*, 94.

149 *Jan Overzet:* Poley, 159; Emily S. Smith, *More Than a Hiding Place: The Life-Changing Experiences of Corrie ten Boom*, 82, 105.

149 *Theo Ederveen:* Smith, *More Than a Hiding Place*, 82.

150 *"Sh, Eusi":* Poley, 160.

150 *the policemen returned:* Carlson, 95; Poley, 160–61.

150 *watery porridge:* Corrie ten Boom, *The Hiding Place*, 132–33.

151 *twelve-by-twelve cell:* Corrie ten Boom, *A Prisoner and Yet*, 31 (describing the cell as "six paces up, six paces back). In *The Hiding Place* (132), however, the Sherrills describe the cell as "deep and narrow, scarcely wider than the door." Since *A Prisoner and Yet* was published in 1947, just two years after

the war (*The Hiding Place* coming in 1971), it should be regarded as the more reliable of the two accounts.

151 *Scheveningen prison for two years: A Prisoner and Yet*, 30. In *The Hiding Place* (133), however, the Sherrills describe the woman as having been in prison for three years.

151 *an Austrian woman: A Prisoner and Yet*, 30; *The Hiding Place*, 133.

151 *prisons and concentration camps:* See generally, Nikolaus Wachsmann, *KL: A History of the Nazi Concentration Camps*; and Tom Segev, *Soldiers of Evil*. For an excellent map showing all camps (concentration and extermination) and locations, see Louis L. Snyder, *Encyclopedia of the Third Reich*, 57.

151 *despised by the professional military:* For details of the animosity between the Nazis and the Wehrmacht (particularly between SS troops and the Wehrmacht), and between the Nazi Gestapo and anti-Nazi Abwehr, see Larry Loftis, *The Princess Spy*, 87–92; *Code Name: Lise*, 155, 224–26; and *Into the Lion's Mouth*, 180, 187, 189, 227. See also, generally, Peter Hoffmann, *The History of the German Resistance, 1933–1945*; Klemens von Klemperer, *German Resistance Against Hitler*; and Ger van Roon, *German Resistance to Hitler*.

   For background on the SS itself, see generally Heinz Höhne, *The Order of the Death's Head: The Story of Hitler's SS*; and Richard Grunberger, *Hitler's SS*. See also Edward Crankshaw, *Gestapo: Instrument of Terror*, 19–32.

152 *"In the quietness of my cell":* Peter van Woerden, *In the Secret Place*, 90.

152 *"When Christ calls":* Dietrich Bonhoeffer, *The Cost of Discipleship*, 89.

152 *"Lord, whatever you want":* van Woerden, 91.

152 *Amstelveenseweg prison:* Poley, 165–67.

153 *"The packages were the highlights":* Ibid., 167.

153 *her first hearing:* Corrie ten Boom, *Prison Letters*, 19.

153 *Ramar clinic:* Poley, 154.

153 *died on March 9, 1944: A Prisoner and Yet*, 28; *The Hiding Place*, 145, 153; Corrie ten Boom, *Father ten Boom*, 155 (showing the date as March 10); Poley, 154.

153 *in Loosduinen cemetery:* Poley, 154.

153 *"consultation bureau": A Prisoner and Yet*, 32.

154 *"Quick, is there any way": A Prisoner and Yet*, 33; *The Hiding Place*, 135; *Prison Letters*, 32.

154 *pleurisy with effusion: A Prisoner and Yet*, 33; *The Hiding Place*, 135; *He Sets the Captive Free*, 17.

154 *"I hope that I am doing": A Prisoner and Yet*, 33; *The Hiding Place*, 135–36.

154 *two bars of soap and copies:* What Corrie asked the nurse for differs in her two accounts. In *A Prisoner and Yet* (33), she asks for a Bible, pencil, toothbrush, and safety pins. In *The Hiding Place* (135–36), she asks for a Bible, needle and thread, toothbrush, and soap. In both accounts she is given copies of the four Gospels.

154 *"Ten Boom, Cornelia": A Prisoner and Yet*, 33; *The Hiding Place*, 136.

154 *Number 384: A Prisoner and Yet*, 37; *Prison Letters*, 18.

154 *Solitary confinement: The Hiding Place*, 140; *He Sets the Captive Free*, 17.

154 *four cold, gray stone walls: Prison Letters*, 17; *A Prisoner and Yet*, 34; *The Hiding Place*, 137.

155 *Someone had vomited: The Hiding Place*, 137.

155 *"Is my father still living?": A Prisoner and Yet*, 35; *The Hiding Place*, 138 (with slightly different dialogue).

156 Kalte-kost: *A Prisoner and Yet*, 35–37.

156 *pattern of God's activity:* Ibid., 41; *The Hiding Place*, 139.

156 *"We are all at school":* Charles Spurgeon, *Spurgeon's Gold*, 130.

156 *twelfth chapter of Hebrews:* van Woerden, 93.

156 *"Therefore, since we":* Hebrews 12:1–3 (NIV).

157 "Zo God voor": van Woerden, 92.

157 *An eyeball:* Ibid.

Chapter 16: Lieutenant Rahms

158 *"In this manner":* Peter van Woerden, *In the Secret Place*, 93.

158 *Amersfoort:* Hans Poley, *Return to the Hiding Place*, 168.

159 *"Johannes Poley!":* Ibid., 169.

159 *"Nollie and all friends":* Corrie's original (in Dutch) letter to Nollie, as well as the English translation, is located in Collection 78, Papers of Cornelia Arnolda Johanna ten Boom, 1902–1983, Box 1, Buswell Library Archives and Special Collections, Wheaton College, Wheaton, IL ("Buswell Library Collections"). See also Corrie's English translation of this correspondence in *Prison Letters*, 18–19.

159 *SOE spy Odette Sansom:* Larry Loftis, *Code Name: Lise*, 203–7, 211.

160 *"The rush of great waters":* Betsie's original (in Dutch) letter to Cocky is located in Box 1, Buswell Library Collections. The English translation of this letter can be found in Corrie's *Prison Letters*, 20–22.

165 *"Quiet in there":* Corrie ten Boom, *The Hiding Place*, 140.

165 *"The shower . . . was glorious":* Corrie ten Boom, *A Prisoner and Yet*, 35; *The Hiding Place*, 140–41.

165 *had been nine weeks:* See Corrie's original (in Dutch) and English translation of "Airing in Scheveningen" in Collection 78, Box 1, Wartime Correspondence folder, Buswell Library Collections. See also *A Prisoner and Yet*, 39; *Prison Letters*, 38–39.

165 *freshly dug grave: A Prisoner and Yet*, 39; *Prison Letters*, 38–39.

166 *"And Enoch walked with God": A Prisoner and Yet*, 39; *Prison Letters*, 38–39.

166 *the prison's* Sachbearbeiter: van Woerden, 98; *A Prisoner and Yet*, 43; *The Hiding Place*, 147; *Prison Letters*, 89; Corrie ten Boom, "People We Meet: Hans Rahms," *It's Harvest-Time*, November–December 1964, 2–3. See also Corrie ten Boom Museum's brochure, "Welcome to The Hiding Place," located in Papers of Cornelia Arnolda Johanna ten Boom, 1902–1983,

Collection 78, Box 1, Folder 8, Buswell Library Collections ("Corrie ten Boom Museum brochure, Buswell Collections").

166 *"He might have been"*: van Woerden, 97–98.

167 *"Are you a Christian, too?"*: Ibid., 98–99.

167 *"We do not expect"*: Ibid., 99–100.

168 *"My time for an interview"*: Ibid., 101.

168 *For two months she had dreaded: A Prisoner and Yet*, 43. In *The Hiding Place* (146), however, the waiting time to see Lieutenant Rahms was three months.

169 *"I am Lieutenant Rahms"*: *The Hiding Place*, 147; *A Prisoner and Yet*, 43–44. (Note that the dialogue is slightly different in the two accounts.) See also "People We Meet: Hans Rahms," 2–3; Corrie ten Boom Museum brochure, Buswell Collections.

169 *Corrie prayed:* Corrie's words of this prayer are slightly different in her two accounts: *A Prisoner and Yet*, 43; *The Hiding Place*, 147.

169 *"Tell me, now"*: *A Prisoner and Yet*, 44 (with slightly different dialogue in *The Hiding Place*, 147).

170 *"Your other activities"*: *The Hiding Place*, 148; *A Prisoner and Yet*, 45; "A Rare Recording of Corrie ten Boom," vol. 1, Listen and Live Audio, 2019.

170 *"Isn't that a waste"*: *A Prisoner and Yet*, 45. With slightly different dialogue in each, see also *The Hiding Place*, 148; *He Sets the Captive Free*, 21; and "A Rare Recording of Corrie ten Boom," vol. 1.

170 *"The Lord Jesus"*: *A Prisoner and Yet*, 45. With slightly different dialogue, see also *The Hiding Place*, 148; *He Sets the Captive Free*, 21; and "A Rare Recording of Corrie ten Boom," vol. 1.

170 *"You get far too little"*: *A Prisoner and Yet*, 46–47. With slightly different dialogue, see also *The Hiding Place*, 148–49; *He Sets the Captive Free*, 21; and "A Rare Recording of Corrie ten Boom," vol. 1.

171 *"What can you know of darkness"*: *The Hiding Place*, 149.

171 *"God never makes"*: *A Prisoner and Yet*, 47.

171 *"Prisoner's condition contagious"*: *The Hiding Place*, 149.

172 *"Walk slowly"*: Ibid., 150.

Chapter 17: Bones

173 *"Mr. Rahms, it is important"*: Corrie ten Boom, *Prison Letters*, 89; *A Prisoner and Yet*, 47 (with slightly different dialogue).

174 her *papers:* Corrie ten Boom, "People We Meet: Hans Rahms," *It's Harvest-Time*, November–December 1964, 2–3. See also Corrie ten Boom Museum brochure, "Welcome to The Hiding Place," located in Collection 78, Box 1, Folder 8, Buswell Library Archives and Special Collections, Wheaton College, Wheaton, IL ("Corrie ten Boom Museum brochure, Buswell Library Collections").

174 *"Can you explain these pages"*: Corrie ten Boom, *He Sets the Captive Free*, 22–23; "A Rare Recording of Corrie ten Boom," vol. 1; *Prison Letters*, 89.

174 *tossed them into the fire:* Ibid.; "People We Meet: Hans Rahms," 2 ("He knew better than we did, how dangerous these papers were. Suddenly he opened the door of the stove and threw all the papers into the fire."); Corrie ten Boom Museum brochure, Buswell Library Collections ("Hans Rahms, the Sachbearbeiter Judge who threw dangerous papers into the stove to try to save our lives.").

174 *"Blotting out the handwriting": Prison Letters*, 89; *He Sets the Captive Free*, 23; "People We Meet: Hans Rahms," 2 ("When I saw how the flames burned the dangerous papers, it was as if for the first time I understood the meaning of Col. 2:14."); Corrie ten Boom Museum brochure, Buswell Library Collections ("As I watched the flames destroy the horrible papers, it was as if I understood for the first time the meaning of Colossians 2:14.").

174 *On May 3 Corrie received: Prison Letters*, 22–23, 25–26. Nollie's letter is dated April 21, 1944, so she had to be released sometime between April 11 and 21. Given Nollie's longing to communicate with her sisters, it is likely she wrote them the day after being released. *A Prisoner and Yet*, 48, 50. Corrie's version of this letter in *A Prisoner and Yet*, written in 1947, is slightly different than the transcribed letter included in *Prison Letters* (25–27), published in 1975, which appears more reliable.

175 *"Please stay with me": A Prisoner and Yet*, 48–49.

175 *"His death has left": A Prisoner and Yet*, 50; *Prison Letters*, 30–32.

176 *"Everything is fine with me": Prison Letters*, 28–29.

177 "Häftlinge, Die Augen": Hans Poley, *Return to the Hiding Place*, 171.

177 *"Angel of Amersfoort":* Ibid., 174–75.

177 *"You will come":* Corrie ten Boom, *The Hiding Place*, 152.

178 *"And now?":* Ibid., 153.

179 *"Lord Jesus":* Ibid., 154.

179 *"Now I really know": Prison Letters*, 32.

179 *"the General": A Prisoner and Yet*, 53–54.

180 *"Whether there was":* Ibid.

180 *"Get your things": A Prisoner and Yet*, 55; *The Hiding Place*, 155; *Prison Letters*, 43; *He Sets the Captive Free*, 12.

180 *It was June 6: Prison Letters*, 45; Carole C. Carlson, *Corrie ten Boom: Her Life, Her Faith*, 102.

180 *"Everybody out!": A Prisoner and Yet*, 55; *The Hiding Place*, 156.

181 *held hands and wept: A Prisoner and Yet*, 56; *The Hiding Place*, 157.

181 *stopped in Vught: A Prisoner and Yet*, 56; *The Hiding Place*, 157; *Prison Letters*, 43; *He Sets the Captive Free*, 12–13. For background on the Vught concentration camp and later transfer of prisoners to Ravensbrück, see Nikolaus Wachsmann, *KL: A History of the Nazi Concentration Camps*, 305, 546. For a summary of the camp and the associated Philips factory, see Israel Gutman, ed., *Encyclopedia of the Holocaust*, vol. 4, 1584–86.

181 *"Ahead of us is a forest":* Prison Letters, 44.

182 *"Oh Lord, not that":* A Prisoner and Yet, 56.

182 *"Can you comfort me?":* Ibid., 57; Prison Letters, 44.

182 *Barrack 4:* Prison Letters, 44–45.

182 *The General:* The Hiding Place, 159.

183 *After nine days:* Prison Letters, 45 (quoting from Betsie's diary that they had gone into the camp on June 15); The Hiding Place, 159 ("almost two weeks").

183 *"You're free":* The Hiding Place, 159–60; A Prisoner and Yet, 60–61.

183 *one large room with tables:* The Hiding Place, 161; A Prisoner and Yet, 57.

183 *"Betsie, how long":* The Hiding Place, 161.

184 *"We now had association with":* A Prisoner and Yet, 57.

184 *"Whoever wishes to become":* Ibid., 59.

184 *"You have tuberculosis":* Ibid. See also Prison Letters, 36 (where Nollie asks in a letter to her: "Did the doctor tell you that you have TB?"). At the time of Nollie's letter, however, Corrie was in Scheveningen prison, rather than Vught.

184 *ticket to the gas chambers:* See Larry Loftis, Code Name: Lise, 209.

Chapter 18: Mrs. Hendriks

185 *"You are going to work":* Corrie ten Boom, A Prisoner and Yet, 59.

185 *"After we were together":* Corrie ten Boom, Prison Letters, 46–47.

186 *"You wrote once":* Ibid., 46.

186 *"As I prayed":* A Prisoner and Yet, 63.

186 *"Yesterday, many blessings":* Prison Letters, 51.

187 *"Bep and I are well":* Ibid., 55–56.

187 *"We sometimes hear":* A Prisoner and Yet, 74–75.

188 *"It's hot and the blankets":* Prison Letters, 58.

188 *Schreibstube:* Hans Poley, Return to the Hiding Place, 179.

188 *Poley, number 9238:* Ibid., 180.

188 *"Report to sick parade":* Ibid.

189 *high-ranking general or field marshal:* Fabian von Schlabrendorff, The Secret War Against Hitler, 276–92; Hans Bernd Gisevius, To the Bitter End: An Insider's Account of the Plot to Kill Hitler, 1933–1944, 490–575; Ulrich von Hassell, The Von Hassell Diaries, 1938–1944: The Story of the Forces Against Hitler Inside Germany, 256–58; Anton Gill, An Honourable Defeat: A History of German Resistance to Hitler, 1933–1945, 235–50; Constantine FitzGibbon, 20 July (see in particular the official putsch documents, including a post-Hitler address to be made by Field Marshal Erwin von Witzleben, on 279–307); I. C. B. Dear and M. R. D. Foot, eds., The Oxford Companion to World War II, 982–83.

189 *Among the conspirators . . . field marshals:* Larry Loftis, The Princess Spy,

91–92. See also Schlabrendorff, *The Secret War Against Hitler*, 293–302; von Hassell, *The Von Hassell Diaries*, 359–363; Gill, *An Honourable Defeat*, 251–63; Peter Hoffmann, *The History of the German Resistance*, 412–60; William Shirer, *The Rise and Fall of the Third Reich*, 1033–69; Klemens von Klemperer, *German Resistance Against Hitler*, 375–85; Dear and Foot, 982–83; and the entries for Beck, Canaris, Halder, "Halder Plot," "July Plot," Oster, Rommel, von Rundstedt, von Stuelpnagel, Tresckow, and von Witzleben in Louis L. Snyder, *Encyclopedia of the Third Reich*, 19–20, 49–50, 135, 135–36, 184–87, 263, 298–99, 303, 338–39, 350–51, and 382, respectively.

190 *"We are ordered to appear"*: *Prison Letters*, 60–61; *A Prisoner and Yet*, 66.

190 *"We were practically"*: Viktor Frankl, *Man's Search for Meaning*, 7.

191 *"In the washroom of Barrack 42"*: *Prison Letters*, 63. See also Corrie's summary of this in *A Prisoner and Yet* (87), wherein she referred to the woman as "Mrs. Diederiks."

191 *"Last night Mr. Hendriks was shot"*: Ibid.

Chapter 19: Summary Justice

192 *"We are continually protected"*: Corrie ten Boom, *Prison Letters*, 63–64.

192 *sent to the Philips factory*: Ibid., 69, 71.

193 *measured small glass rods*: Corrie ten Boom, *The Hiding Place*, 162.

193 *On August 4 a large sedan*: Anne Frank, *The Diary of a Young Girl*, 338–39.

193 *"There is so much bitterness"*: *Prison Letters*, 70–71.

194 *"Pretty but nondescript"*: Ibid.; Corrie ten Boom, *A Prisoner and Yet*, 81–82.

194 *he walked out of the camp*: Hans Poley, *Return to the Hiding Place*, 180.

194 *"You're the first woman worker"*: *The Hiding Place*, 163.

195 *"Sweet summer smells came"*: Ibid., 164–65.

196 *"Don't you feel"*: Ibid., 165.

197 *Wake-up time at five*: *A Prisoner and Yet*, 71.

197 *"In the camp"*: *Prison Letters*, 73, 77.

197 *"Thick clouds"*: *A Prisoner and Yet*, 82, 85; *The Hiding Place*, 167; *Prison Letters*, 69.

197 *"If anybody passes on news"*: *Prison Letters*, 73.

197 *Princess Irene Brigade*: *A Prisoner and Yet*, 85–86.

197 *thousands of planes overhead*: *Prison Letters*, 72–73.

198 *kept their mouths open*: *A Prisoner and Yet*, 87; *The Hiding Place*, 169.

198 *bullets and shell fragments kicked up*: *Prison Letters*, 77. Corrie's sketch is undated, but appears between sketches dated August 22 and August 25. As such, the presumptive date of this sketch is August 23 or 24.

198 *General Dietrich von Choltitz*: Hans Spiedel, *Invasion 1944*, 133–35; Agostino von Hassell and Sigrid MacRae, *Alliance of Enemies*, xix; "Gen. Dietrich von Choltitz Dies; 'Savior of Paris' in '44 Was 71," *New York Times*,

November 6, 1966, 88. See also I. C. B. Dear and M. R. D. Foot, eds., *The Oxford Companion to World War II*, 865–66; Marcel Baudot et al., eds., *The Historical Encyclopedia of World War II*, 90.

198 *ordered mass executions:* Larry Loftis, *Code Name: Lise*, 210–11.

198 *"Corrie":* *The Hiding Place*, 169.

199 *"I can see my husband":* *A Prisoner and Yet*, 87.

199 *"transported to Germany":* *Prison Letters*, 79–80. In her recollection about this note, Corrie wrote that it said they were being transported to Ravensbrück concentration camp. However, while she knew the train was headed for Germany, she could not have known exactly where. In *A Prisoner and Yet* (92) and *The Hiding Place* (173), Corrie doesn't know that Ravensbrück is her destination until she arrives there. For Corrie's transport to Germany and Ravensbrück, see also Corrie ten Boom, *Tramp for the Lord*, 15–18.

199 *slaughtered one hundred and eighty Dutchmen:* *A Prisoner and Yet*, 87; Carole C. Carlson, *Corrie ten Boom: Her Life, Her Faith*, 106. In *The Hiding Place*, Corrie (through the writing of John and Elizabeth Sherrill) remembered that the number executed was more than seven hundred. Since Corrie wrote *A Prisoner and Yet* almost immediately after the war ended, publishing it in 1947, the figure she remembered there is more credible under the evidentiary rule of "closer in time" (*The Hiding Place* not being published until 1971, some twenty-four years after the event).

Chapter 20: Ravensbrück

200 *"Betsie, I cannot":* Corrie ten Boom, *A Prisoner and Yet*, 88.

200 *six the next morning:* Corrie ten Boom, *The Hiding Place*, 170.

201 *every few boxcars:* *A Prisoner and Yet*, 89; *The Hiding Place*, 170; Corrie ten Boom, *Prison Letters*, 79; Corrie ten Boom, *Tramp for the Lord*, 15–16.

201 *"Do you know what":* *The Hiding Place*, 171.

202 *"If you ever need my help":* *A Prisoner and Yet*, 90; *The Hiding Place*, 171; Carole C. Carlson, *Corrie ten Boom: Her Life, Her Faith*, 107.

202 *"It's bullets":* *A Prisoner and Yet*, 90; *The Hiding Place*, 171; Carlson, 107.

202 *"Adieu beloved":* *A Prisoner and Yet*, 91.

203 *being transported to Germany:* *Prison Letters*, 79–80. In her recollection about this note, Corrie wrote that it said they were being transported to Ravensbrück concentration camp.

203 *"Nurse, please give me":* *A Prisoner and Yet*, 92.

203 *Fürstenberg:* Ibid.; *The Hiding Place*, 172.

204 *"Ravensbrück":* *The Hiding Place*, 173; *Tramp for the Lord*, 16; Corrie ten Boom, *He Sets the Captive Free*, 13–14. For background on the Ravensbrück concentration camp, see generally, Jack Gaylord Morrison, *Ravensbrück: Everyday Life in a Women's Concentration Camp*; Nikolaus Wachsmann, *KL: A History of the Nazi Concentration Camps*; Tom Segev, *Soldiers of Evil*; and Israel Gutman, ed., *Encyclopedia of the Holocaust*, vol. 3, 1226–27.

205 *"We never let our courage"*: *A Prisoner and Yet*, 93; Carlson, *Corrie ten Boom*, 108.

205 *Fritz Sühren:* Corrie didn't know who the commandant was, and never had any interaction with him, but another Ravensbrück prisoner—SOE spy Odette Sansom—had numerous encounters with him. See Larry Loftis, *Code Name: Lise*, 201–12, 221–30.

205 *"I don't understand"*: *A Prisoner and Yet*, 93. Note that Corrie did not hear this comment personally, but wrote, "Even the commander was said to have remarked."

206 *as she cut Betsie's hair:* Ibid., 93–94; *The Hiding Place*, 173–74; *He Sets the Captive Free*, 26–27.

207 *ladle of turnip soup:* Viktor Frankl wrote after the war that the daily ration at the men's camp at Auschwitz was 10.5 ounces of bread (although sometimes they received less) and 1.75 pints of thin soup. Frankl, *Man's Search for Meaning*, 28.

207 *women were undressing: A Prisoner and Yet*, 97; *The Hiding Place*, 175; *Tramp for the Lord*, 117.

207 *"O Lord, save us": A Prisoner and Yet*, 98.

208 *"Use the drainholes": The Hiding Place*, 175; *Tramp for the Lord*, 117.

208 *"Lord, cause now": A Prisoner and Yet*, 99; *Tramp for the Lord*, 117.

209 *Barrack 8: A Prisoner and Yet*, 100–101; *The Hiding Place*, 176–77. In *Tramp for the Lord* (18), Corrie omits the first few days in the camp, as well as the time in the quarantine barrack (8), mentioning only the second barrack where she eventually stayed, Barrack 28.

209 *"Everybody out": The Hiding Place*, 177.

209 *Corrie's number was 66730: The Hiding Place*, 179; *Tramp for the Lord*, 19.

209 *punishment barrack next door: The Hiding Place*, 177.

209 *"A man counted only":* Frankl, *Man's Search for Meaning*, 7.

210 *step up to a rack:* Loftis, *Code Name: Lise*, 204–5. SOE agent Odette Sansom—who had been sentenced to death and was confined to a lightless cell in the Ravensbrück "Bunker"—heard this torture daily as her cell was next to a punishment room.

210 *told to undress: A Prisoner and Yet*, 103; *The Hiding Place*, 178. See also Loftis, *Code Name: Lise*, 200.

210 *Jesus had hung naked: The Hiding Place*, 178.

210 *forty-seven SOE agents:* Pieter Dourlein, *Inside North Pole*, 170. In *The Secret History of SOE* (304), William Mackenzie wrote in 2000 that only thirty-six agents were executed. Dourlein's account appears more accurate, however, as he was a Dutch SOE agent and published his report in 1953. For the entire German operation, see Hermann Giskes, *London Calling North Pole*, 39–136.

211 *Operation Market Garden:* I. C. B. Dear and M. R. D. Foot, eds., *The Oxford Companion to World War II,* 718–19, 783; Marcel Baudot et al., eds., *The Historical Encyclopedia of World War II,* 350. See also Dick Winters, *Beyond Band of Brothers,* 122–33.

211 *Hunger Winter:* John Toland, *The Last 100 Days,* 567; Hans Poley, *Return to the Hiding Place,* 184–85; Peter van Woerden, *In the Secret Place,* 105; Baudo et al., *Historical Encyclopedia of World War II,* 350. The effect of the German reprisal was devastating; by end of October the daily caloric intake of Hollanders fell to 450. Starvation deaths ensued the following month. Toland, *The Last 100 Days,* 567, footnote.

211 *second week in October: The Hiding Place,* 179; *He Sets the Captive Free,* 27.

212 *"Fleas!": The Hiding Place,* 179–80; *He Sets the Captive Free,* 27.

212 *"Encourage the timid":* New International Version translation.

212 *"We can start right now": The Hiding Place,* 180–81; *He Sets the Captive Free,* 27.

213 *the Siemens factory: A Prisoner and Yet,* 109–10; *The Hiding Place,* 182–83.

213 *seven hundred women died or were killed: He Sets the Captive Free,* 29.

214 *"But that's impossible": A Prisoner and Yet,* 113; *He Sets the Captive Free,* 42–43.

Chapter 21: Murder

215 *gathered in the Westergracht:* Hans Poley, *Return to the Hiding Place,* 185–86.

215 *held worship services:* Corrie ten Boom, *The Hiding Place,* 183.

216 *"Look what Madame Baroness":* Corrie ten Boom, *A Prisoner and Yet,* 131–32; *The Hiding Place,* 185–86. For a slightly different version of this story, see Corrie's *He Sets the Captive Free,* 36–37 (for example, different dialogue, Corrie being held back by other prisoners, blood all over Betsie's face).

217 *four-thirty morning roll call: A Prisoner and Yet,* 114; *The Hiding Place,* 186.

217 *Betsie's temperature: The Hiding Place,* 189, 192.

218 *talking about what their ministry: A Prisoner and Yet,* 117; *He Sets the Captive Free,* 51–52. Note that in *A Prisoner and Yet,* Betsie's vision was that the first project would be to renovate the Beje so that it could be their initial care center for Ravensbrück women who had no place to go after the war.

218 *"We have learned so much": He Sets the Captive Free,* 51–52.

218 *"It's such a beautiful": The Hiding Place,* 192–93.

218 *"It would be an error":* Viktor Frankl, *Man's Search for Meaning,* 89–91.

219 *"Must we stay": He Sets the Captive Free,* 52.

219 *beat a prisoner to death: A Prisoner and Yet,* 147.

219 *Betsie's pulse was weak:* Ibid., 116.

219 *second week of December: The Hiding Place*, 194.

220 Nacht-und-Nebelbarak: *A Prisoner and Yet*, 120.

220 Kanienchen: Ibid.

220 *"O Savior, full of mercy":* Ibid., 121.

220 *Mrs. Leness:* Ibid., 118–19.

222 *"Sick transport!":* *The Hiding Place*, 192–93; *A Prisoner and Yet*, 114–15.

222 *directly to the crematorium: The Hiding Place*, 192–93; *A Prisoner and Yet*, 114–15.

222 *heard more screams:* Larry Loftis, *Code Name: Lise*, 253; London *Times*, December 17, 1946; Imperial War Museum, Oral History, interview with Odette Marie Céline Sansom, produced October 31, 1986, catalog number 9478, Reel 2.

222 *"For the great majority":* Frankl, *Man's Search for Meaning*, 12.

Chapter 22: The Skeleton

223 *he met with commandant Fritz Sühren:* Larry Loftis, *Code Name: Lise*, 210–11; Imperial War Museum, Oral History, interview with Odette Marie Céline Sansom, produced October 31, 1986, catalog number 9478, Reel 2.

223 *"Distress teaches some":* Corrie ten Boom, *A Prisoner and Yet*, 136.

223 *"It was born":* Viktor Frankl, *Man's Search for Meaning*, 18, 33.

224 *"Oh, Corrie, this is hell":* *A Prisoner and Yet*, 137.

225 *"Your whole life":* Corrie ten Boom, *Tramp for the Lord*, 10–11.

225 *"It has certainly been":* *A Prisoner and Yet*, 138–39.

226 *"get to the hospital!":* Corrie ten Boom, *The Hiding Place*, 195; Corrie ten Boom, *He Sets the Captive Free*, 51–52 (Corrie setting the conversation a week or so earlier, before Betsie is on her deathbed).

226 *"We are to have":* *The Hiding Place*, 196; *He Sets the Captive Free*, 52. Note that the dialogue in the two accounts is slightly different, as is the date of occurrence. Corrie apparently had two conversations with Betsie about her vision—about a week before Betsie died, and then again a day or so before she died.

227 *"Prisoner is ready":* *The Hiding Place*, 196–97; *A Prisoner and Yet*, 158.

227 *"Are you all right?":* *The Hiding Place*, 197.

228 *Betsie began to murmur: A Prisoner and Yet*, 157–59; *The Hiding Place*, 198;

Chapter 23: The List

229 *day Betsie died:* The exact date of Betsie's death is uncertain. Hans Poley, who was most meticulous about dates, marks her passing as occurring on December 14 (*Return to the Hiding Place*, 198); the ten Boom family marks her death on December 16 (*In My Father's House*, 189); while Corrie gives a rough date of December 19 or later (*A Prisoner and Yet*, 157–59; *The Hiding Place*, 195–98). In these two accounts, Corrie writes that Betsie grew deathly ill "the week before Christmas" and died two days later. As such, the *earliest* that Betsie could have died would have been December 19. Of the three

possible dates—December 14, 16, or 19—the middle date, December 16, seems most reliable since the ten Boom family used the last page of *In My Father's House* to give the birth and death dates of the entire family, including Corrie's.

229 *three German armies:* Marcel Baudot et al., eds., *The Historical Encyclopedia of World War II*, 71–72.

229 *Patton's Third Army arrived:* For Patton's details on the drive to—and battle in—Bastogne, see chapter 4 of his memoir, *War as I Knew It*, 193–229.

230 *typhus broke out: A Prisoner and Yet*, 149.

230 *women collapsed and died:* Ibid., 149.

230 *Corrie's ankles and legs:* Ibid., 161; *The Hiding Place*, 200.

230 *"Teach me, Lord": A Prisoner and Yet*, 160.

230 *"In the winter and spring":* Viktor Frankl, *Man's Search for Meaning*, 34.

231 *Sühren and one of the camp physicians:* Larry Loftis, *Code Name: Lise*, 212–13; Jack Gaylord Morrison, *Ravensbrück*, 288–89.

231 *"Mittwerda":* Loftis, *Code Name: Lise*, 212–13; Morrison, 288–89.

231 *women over fifty:* Corrie ten Boom, *Prison Letters*, 80; Corrie ten Boom, *Tramp for the Lord*, 23.

231 *Marusha: A Prisoner and Yet*, 160; *Tramp for the Lord*, 41.

232 "Jesoes Christoes": *A Prisoner and Yet*, 160; *Tramp for the Lord*, 141.

232 *four women were dead: A Prisoner and Yet*, 161.

233 *"Prisoner 66730!": Tramp for the Lord*, 19.

233 *"Death sentence":* Ibid., 20.

Chapter 24: Edema

234 *"Perhaps I'll see you":* Corrie ten Boom, *Tramp for the Lord*, 20.

235 *"When you are dying":* Ibid., 23.

235 "Entlassen!": Corrie ten Boom, *A Prisoner and Yet*, 162–63; Corrie ten Boom, *The Hiding Place*, 201.

236 *"Edema": A Prisoner and Yet*, 163; *The Hiding Place*, 201–2.

236 *prisoners with terrible injuries: A Prisoner and Yet*, 165; *The Hiding Place*, 202.

237 *fallen out of bed and died: A Prisoner and Yet*, 164–65.

237 *It was Christmas Day: The Hiding Place*, 203.

237 *"The sweet ways of this old":* Peter van Woerden, *In the Secret Place*, 105.

237 *Piet:* Ibid., 106–8. Piet was the fiancé of Peter's sister, Aty van Woerden. Aty's public notice of Piet's death can be found at Collection 78, Papers of Cornelia Arnolda Johanna ten Boom, 1902–1983, Box 1, Buswell Library Archives and Special Collections, Wheaton College, Wheaton, IL.

237 *16,000 Hollanders died:* van Woerden, *In the Secret Place*, 105; I. C. B. Dear and M. R. D. Foot, eds., *The Oxford Companion to World War II*, 998; Marcel Baudot et al., eds, *The Historical Encyclopedia of World War II*, 350.

238 *two Hungarians: A Prisoner and Yet*, 166.

238 *Her name was Oelie:* Ibid., 166–67; Corrie ten Boom, *Corrie's Christmas Memories*, 56.

238 *"Oelie, Mommy cannot come":* *Corrie's Christmas Memories*, 56–57.

238 *It was twenty below:* A Prisoner and Yet, 167.

238 *"Edema of the feet":* The Hiding Place, 203.

238 *dead young woman lying:* A Prisoner and Yet, 168.

238 *on December 28:* Corrie ten Boom, *Prison Letters*, 80. That very day in Berlin, Lutheran pastor Dietrich Bonhoeffer was struggling with the same thoughts as Corrie's: *Will I survive? Will God save me?* From his cell at the Prinz-Albrecht-Strasse prison, he wondered if the Nazis had discovered his part in the conspiracy to rid Germany of Hitler. Reflecting on his captivity, his possible release, or perhaps an upcoming execution, he penned a prayer he called "Powers of Good" (*Letters and Papers from Prison*, 400–401):

> With every power for good to stay and guide me,
>   comforted and inspired beyond all fear,
> I'll live these days with you in thought beside me,
>   and pass, with you, into the coming year.
>
> The old year still torments our hearts, unhastening;
>   the long days of our sorrow still endure;
> Father, grant to the souls thou hast been chastening
>   that thou hast promised, the healing and the cure.
>
> Should it be ours to drain the cup of grieving
>   even to the dregs of pain, at thy command,
>   we will not falter, thankfully receiving
>   all that is given by thy loving hand.
>
> But should it be thy will once more to release us
>   to life's enjoyment and it's good sunshine,
> that which we've learned from sorrow shall increase us,
>   and all our life be dedicate as thine. . . .
>
> While all the powers of good aid and attend us,
>   boldly we'll face the future, come what may.
> At even and at morn God will befriend us,
>   and oh, most surely on each newborn day!

239 *issued her new clothes:* A Prisoner and Yet, 169; The Hiding Place, 204.

239 *Mrs. Waard and Mrs. Jensen:* A Prisoner and Yet, 169.

239 *money, watch, and her mother's gold ring:* Ibid., 169; The Hiding Place, 204.

240 *it and the food ration coupons: A Prisoner and Yet,* 170; *The Hiding Place,* 204.

240 *pulled into the Berlin terminal: A Prisoner and Yet,* 170–71; *The Hiding Place,* 205. Viktor Frankl observed after the war that the death rate at Auschwitz between Christmas Day 1944 and New Year's 1945 was abnormally high. The chief physician at the camp, he recalled, had suggested that it was not due to harder work or less food, but simply because the majority of prisoners had lived in the hope that they would be home by Christmas. The disappointment and despair caused by missing this date, the doctor held, significantly reduced prisoners' powers of resistance and will to live. Frankl saw this as confirmation of Nietzsche's axiom: "He who has a *why* to live for can bear with almost any *how.*" Frankl, *Man's Search for Meaning,* 76.

241 *"That's an old story!": The Hiding Place,* 205.

241 *any chance of getting food: A Prisoner and Yet,* 172.

241 *Bad Nieuweschans: The Hiding Place,* 206; *A Prisoner and Yet,* 175; *Tramp for the Lord,* 24.

242 *"Sister Tavenier cannot come": A Prisoner and Yet,* 175–76; *Tramp for the Lord,* 24–25; *The Hiding Place,* 206.

242 *"Where are you going?": A Prisoner and Yet,* 177; *Tramp for the Lord,* 26.

243 *"Truus Benes!": A Prisoner and Yet,* 177; *Tramp for the Lord,* 26.

243 *"I have never seen anyone": A Prisoner and Yet,* 178; *Tramp for the Lord,* 27.

243 *"Just five minutes more!": A Prisoner and Yet,* 178–79; *The Hiding Place,* 206–7; *Tramp for the Lord,* 27.

244 *the whistle of a boat: A Prisoner and Yet,* 179; *Tramp for the Lord,* 28.

Chapter 25: Déjà Vu

245 *playing a Bach composition:* Corrie ten Boom, *A Prisoner and Yet,* 179; Corrie ten Boom, *Tramp for the Lord,* 28.

246 *"Almost I could wish":* Corrie ten Boom, *The Hiding Place,* 207.

246 *"Herman!":* Ibid., 208–9.

247 *Grote of St. Bavokerk:* See the church's official website at https://www .bavo.nl/en/. See also https://www.bavo.nl/en/about-bavo-and-nieuwe-kerk /grote-of-st-bavo/organ/ and https://www.atlasobscura.com/places/grote-kerk.

247 *as much of a friend: Tramp for the Lord,* 28.

248 *fell into Nollie's embrace: The Hiding Place,* 209.

248 *things had been stolen: A Prisoner and Yet,* 180.

248 *Betsie would set out cups: The Hiding Place,* 209.

248 *slumped against his bed: A Prisoner and Yet,* 180.

248 *"If it is alright": Tramp for the Lord,* 28–29.

249 *Light of the World:* Ibid., 30.

249 *accompanying Mr. Toos: The Hiding Place,* 210.

249 *"Miss ten Boom": The Hiding Place,* 210; Corrie ten Boom, *Clippings from*

My Notebook, 30–31; Corrie ten Boom, "Outside His Boundaries," *The Hiding Place* magazine, July/August 1980, 4–5; Carole C. Carlson, *Corrie ten Boom: Her Life, Her Faith*, 123. Note that the version of this story in *The Hiding Place* differs slightly from Corrie's recollection in *Clippings from My Notebook* and "Outside His Boundaries," and from Carlson's account. The Sherrills wrote in *The Hiding Place* that the event occurred at the Haarlem jail (which includes dialogue with Rolf, a local policeman Corrie knew), while the *Clippings from My Notebook*, "Outside His Boundaries," and Carlson versions have it at the prison, and her conversation is not with Rolf, but with the governor of the prison. Second, in *The Hiding Place*, the Sherrills wrote that Corrie was to go alone carrying false papers, while *Clippings from My Notebook*, "Outside His Boundaries," and Carlson state that Corrie was to go with the man making the request to make an introduction. Given the consistency of Corrie's personal recollection, her version of the story seems more reliable than the Sherrill version.

249 *Vidkun Quisling:* Israel Gutman, ed., *Encyclopedia of the Holocaust*, vol. 3, 1203–4.

Chapter 26: The Factory

251 *"an underground worker?":* Corrie ten Boom, *Clippings from My Notebook*, 30–31; Carole C. Carlson, *Corrie ten Boom: Her Life, Her Faith*, 123.

251 *raided the Poley house:* Hans Poley, *Return to the Hiding Place*, 186–87.

252 *awoke at roll call time:* Ibid., 187.

252 *Operation Manna:* Ibid., 188. See also Walter B. Maass, *The Netherlands at War: 1940–1945*, 239–41; and John Toland, *The Last 100 Days*, 567. After a meeting between Walter Bedell Smith, who was General Dwight D. Eisenhower's chief of staff, and Seyss-Inquart in early April, an agreement was reached to allow an airdrop of food. On April 29, 1945, the airdrop began, with RAF Bomber Command delivering over 500,000 rations near Rotterdam and The Hague. The drop continued to surrounding areas until the end of the war, May 8, with the British and American planes supplying more than 11 million rations. Toland, *The Last 100 Days*, 567, footnote.

252 *"We must tell people":* Corrie ten Boom, *The Hiding Place*, 211.

253 *"I am a widow":* Ibid., 212.

253 *"You've been here then!":* Ibid., 212–13.

254 *"Our house is so elegant":* Corrie ten Boom, *A Prisoner and Yet*, 185.

254 *general Johannes Blaskowitz:* Marcel Baudot et al., eds., *The Historical Encyclopedia of World War II*, 58; Robert S. Wistrich, *Who's Who in Nazi Germany*, 14; Maass, *The Netherlands at War*, 243; Diet Eman, *Things We Couldn't Say: A Dramatic Account of Christian Resistance in Holland During World War II*, 306.

254 *"If God had not":* A Prisoner and Yet, 182–83.

255 *Canadians liberated Amsterdam:* See https://www.holland.com/global

/tourism/holland-stories/liberation-route/canada-and-the-liberation-of
-holland.htm. See also Eman, 302–4; Hugo Bleicher, *Colonel Henri's Story: The War Memoirs of Hugo Bleicher, Former German Secret Agent*, 168.

255   *Hans and Mies stopped by:* Poley, 188–89.

255   *"He who led us through the dark":* H. R. H. Wilhelmina, Princess of the Netherlands, Wilhelmina, *Lonely but Not Alone*, 221–22.

256   *"Because I had lived":* Corrie ten Boom, *Tramp for the Lord*, 31.

256   *"Dear Sir":* Corrie ten Boom, *Prison Letters*, 81.

257   *accepted more than a hundred residents:* The Hiding Place, 213.

257   *"Each had a hurt":* Ibid., 213.

258   *"Those people you spoke of":* Ibid., 214.

259   *"Thank you, Jesus":* Tramp for the Lord, 32–33.

259   *Corrie found herself singing:* Ibid., 33.

260   *"I heard you speak":* Ibid., 37–38.

260   *"Corrie, this is your message":* Ibid., 44–45.

260   *"Corrie, there is so much":* Ibid., 39–40.

261   *living in an abandoned factory:* The Hiding Place, 215.

261   *have to live with them:* Ibid., 215. Corrie's love for these Germans is echoed by what Viktor Frankl learned at Auschwitz: "Love is the only way," he wrote after the war, "to grasp another human being in the innermost core of his personality. No one can become fully aware of the very essence of another human being unless he loves him. By his love he is enabled to see the essential traits and features in the beloved person." Frankl, *Man's Search for Meaning*, 111.

Chapter 27: Loving the Enemy

262   *"We've located a place":* Corrie ten Boom, *The Hiding Place*, 216.

262   *one hundred sixty residents:* Corrie ten Boom, *Tramp for the Lord*, 47.

263   *German Lutheran Church:* The Hiding Place, 218; Tramp for the Lord, 47.

263   *December 1946, sad news:* The Hiding Place, 218.

263   *In early 1947 Corrie spoke:* Tramp for the Lord, 55; Corrie ten Boom, *Clippings from My Notebook*, 75.

263   *"Beer Hall Putsch":* William Shirer, *The Rise and Fall of the Third Reich*, 68–79; Louis L. Snyder, *Encyclopedia of the Third Reich*, 20–21.

264   *"How grateful I am":* Tramp for the Lord, 55–56; The Hiding Place, 215; Clippings from My Notebook, 75–76.

264   *"You mentioned Ravensbrück":* Tramp for the Lord, 56; Clippings from My Notebook, 76.

264   *felt not the slightest spark:* The Hiding Place, 215.

264   *"Jesus, help me!":* Clippings from My Notebook, 77.

265   *"I forgive you":* Tramp for the Lord, 57; Clippings from My Notebook, 78.

265   *"If Jesus were to come":* Peter van Woerden, *In the Secret Place*, 102.

266   *"Mr. Rahms, do you remember me?":* Ibid., 103.

266 *"Yes, Peter":* Ibid.

266 *"I shall never forget":* Corrie ten Boom, *Prison Letters*, 90.

266 *"What is your name?":* *Tramp for the Lord*, 60–61.

267 *Corrie with Hans Rahms:* This photo is located in Collection 78, Papers of Cornelia Arnolda Johanna ten Boom, 1902–1983, Box 1, Buswell Library Archives and Special Collections, Wheaton College, Wheaton, IL ("Buswell Library Collections").

268 *Conny van Hoogstraten:* *Tramp for the Lord*, 65.

268 *due to a clerical error:* *The Hiding Place*, 219.

268 *"I loved her like a sister":* *Tramp for the Lord*, 65.

268 *Ellen de Kroon:* Ibid., 67; Ellen de Kroon Stamps, *My Years with Corrie*, 22.

268 *Righteous Among the Nations:* Corrie ten Boom, *A Prisoner and Yet*, 187; Corrie ten Boom, *Father ten Boom*, 151–52. Corrie's induction into the Righteous Among the Nations in 1967 can be found at the official website, Yad Vashem: The World Holocaust Remembrance Center, https://www .yadvashem.org/yv/pdf-drupal/netherlands.pdf. For Corrie's photos and commentary on the event, see her untitled ministry letter to supporters in *It's Harvest-Time*, May–June 1968.

For a detailed background of the Righteous Among the Nations and Yad Vashem, see Israel Gutman, ed., *Encyclopedia of the Holocaust*, vol. 3, 1279–83, and vol. 4, 1681–86, respectively.

268 *30,000 to 92,700:* In *KL: A History of the Nazi Concentration Camps* (628), Nikolaus Wachsmann estimates the figure between 30,000 to 40,000, while *The Oxford Companion to World War II* (929) suggests the number could be as large as 92,700.

269 *John and Elizabeth Sherrill:* See Elizabeth's website, ElizabethSherrill.com, as well as John and Elizabeth's preface to *The Hiding Place*.

269 *They had read her autobiography:* Carole C. Carlson, *Corrie ten Boom: Her Life, Her Faith*, 199.

269 *they proposed to write:* While *The Hiding Place* is written in the first person, it is an authorized biography, as Corrie noted numerous times. In the December 1970 issue of *It's Harvest-Time* (12), just before *The Hiding Place* came out in 1971, Corrie acknowledged that the book was being written entirely by John and Elizabeth Sherrill, stating: "John and Tibby Sherrill are busy finishing my biography. This book is produced and carried by prayer. Some friends prayed day and night for John and Tibby when the enemy brought all kinds of difficulties along. Last week I was with them, and read the manuscript almost to the end. Now we need to pray for inspiration for Tibby who is working on the last chapters."

See also a similar statement in the July 1969 issue of *It's Harvest-Time* ("now being written by John and Tibby Sherrill"), 5. Later, after the book was released, Corrie wrote a letter to her American benefactor, stating: "I am so thankful. John Sherrill's book, *The Hiding Place*, is a good seller and has opened many doors and hearts for me." Carlson, *Corrie ten Boom*, 200.

269   *three million copies:* See the Billy Graham library at: https:// billygrahamlibrary.org/3-millionth-copy-of-the-hiding-place/.

269   *"It is nothing":* *Tramp for the Lord*, 182–83. In her opening article for the January 1969 issue of *It's Harvest-Time*, the bimonthly periodical she coproduced with Peter van Woerden (editor of the newsletter), Corrie relates this story in detail. The dialogue and actions in this 1969 piece differ slightly from the version appearing in *Tramp for the Lord*, released in 1974. See also Corrie's telling of the story before a live audience in Corrie ten Boom, "A Rare Recording of Corrie ten Boom," vol. 1, Listen and Live Audio, 2019.

Epilogue

271   *World Wide Pictures released:* See Walter G. Gastil's memorandum to the Board of Directors of Christians, Incorporated on July 24, 1975, and his "Repost of Status of 'The Hiding Place' Motion Picture," September 1, 1975, both located in Collection 78, Papers of Cornelia Arnolda Johanna ten Boom, 1902–1983, Box 1, Folder 3, Buswell Library Archives and Special Collections, Wheaton College, Wheaton, IL ("Buswell Library Collections").

In his letter to the board, he reported on the success of the early showings: "The response to 'The Hiding Place' overwhelmed World Wide Pictures. For example, in Minneapolis, they had booked 5 theaters, expanded to 9, and still could not handle the crowds. No picture has ever received such a flood of requests for advance paid tickets in film industry history."

See also Corrie's August 1975 announcement of the premiere to ministry friends, also located in Collection 78, Box 1, Buswell Library Collections.

For background on the film and production photos, see Robert Walker, "The Hiding Place Revisited," *Christian Life*, January 1975, 16–17. For photos from the film's production, the film's official poster, and photos from the premiere, see the Winter 1975 edition of *The Hiding Place* magazine, found in Collection 78, Box 3, Buswell Library Collections.

For Corrie's fond memories of interacting with the cast and crew, see "On the Set with Corrie and Bill Brown," *The Hiding Place* magazine, Spring 1974, 4–7, and "On the Set with Corrie and Bill Brown, *The Hiding Place* magazine, Winter 1974–1975, 6–7, both located in Collection 78, Box 3, Buswell Library Collections.

271   *Beverly Hills Theater:* Carole C. Carlson, *Corrie ten Boom: Her Life, Her Faith*, unpaginated photo section.

271   *"I am so happy that God":* Ellen de Kroon Stamps, *My Years with Corrie*, 24.

272   *"Look on the desk":* Ibid., 124.

272   *"My dear, dear Ellen":* Ibid.

272 *"To Ellen de Kroon"*: Ibid., 125.

273 *"Thank you, Lord"*: Ibid.

273 *In 1977, at age eighty-five:* See Corrie ten Boom, "New Beginnings," *The Hiding Place* magazine, January/February 1978, 10–11; Emily S. Smith, *More Than a Hiding Place*, 86. For photos of Corrie and Pamela Rosewell at the Placentia home, see the photo archive in Collection 78, Box 1, Buswell Library Collections; *The Hiding Place* magazine, Summer 1977, Collection 78, Box 3, Buswell Library Collections; and Smith, *More Than a Hiding Place*, 86–87.

273 *Birmingham Hippodrome:* Collection 78, Box 2, Folder 2, Buswell Library Collections. Note that this folder contains the musical's business plan, treatment, production budget and statistics, principal cast, scene sketches, official poster, reviews, and Nigel Swinford's (composer and musical director) complete script.

273 *Christians, Incorporated:* For the organization's certificate of incorporation, bylaws, list of original officers and directors, structure, annual meeting minutes, board of directors minutes, and financial statements, see Collection 78, Box 1, Folders 7 and 8, and Box 2, Folder 2, Buswell Library Collections. For names and photos of the board of directors in 1973, see *The Hiding Place* magazine, Summer 1973, 13, Collection 78, Box 3, Folder "Publications: The Hiding Place 1973–1982," Buswell Library Collections.

273 *Association of Christian Prison Workers:* See "The Association of Christian Prison Workers Launches Nationwide Training," *The Hiding Place* magazine, January–February 1979, 4–5; and June 30, 1979, correspondence from Duane Pederson, president of Christian Prison Volunteers, et al., to the board of directors, Association of Christian Prison Workers, Collection 78, Box 2, Folder 2, Buswell Library Collections.

273 *she died at home:* For Corrie's death certificate, see Collection 78, Box 5, Buswell Library Collections. See also the memorial edition of *The Hiding Place* magazine, April 1983, which includes special notes from Ruth Graham (wife of Billy Graham), William R. Barbour Jr. (chairman of Fleming H. Revell Company, Corrie's publisher), Jeannette Clift George (who portrayed Corrie in *The Hiding Place* film), and Pamela Rosewell, Corrie's aide, among others, found in Collection 78, Box 2, Folder 3, Buswell Library Collections. For photos from the funeral service, see Collection 78, Box 1, Folder "Corrie's Funeral Services 1983," Buswell Library Collections.

273 *sixty countries:* See Corrie's passports, 1948–72, Collection 78, Box 3, Folder 5, Buswell Library Collections. In January 1977, Corrie wrote that she visited her sixty-fourth country, Sweden. See *The Hiding Place* magazine, Spring 1977, 4, found in Collection 78, Box 3, Buswell Library Collections. See also Smith, *More than a Hiding Place*, 61, 72, 76, 78–79, 94–95; Carlson, *Corrie ten Boom*, 124, 166–78, 182–205.

273 *students in Uganda . . . factory workers:* Corrie ten Boom, *The Hiding Place*, 219; Smith, 88, 94–96, 107. Corrie spent considerable time in Uganda, as correspondence in her archives reveals. See, for example, Corrie's letter from Kampala, Uganda, to Beste Anne on December 15, 1965, located in Collection 78, Box 1, Folder 3, Buswell Library Collections; and correspondence on December 8, 1976, to Pamela Rosewell (Corrie's assistant) regarding the Church of Uganda, located in Collection 78, Box 1, Folder 7, Buswell Library Collections.

274 *villagers in Siberia:* Carlson, 191.

274 *prisoners in San Quentin:* Ibid., unpaginated photo section. Corrie spoke to the prisoners at San Quentin (near San Francisco) on September 25, 1977, when she was eighty-five, Smith, 107.

274 *officials in the Pentagon:* See correspondence from Corrie ten Boom to Brother Andrew on November 3, 1976, located in Collection 78, Box 1, Folder 7, Buswell Library Collections.

274 *leper colony:* Corrie ten Boom, "The Paddle of God's Love," *It's Harvest-Time*, September–October 1961, 4 *et seq.*; "Dear Friends," *It's Harvest-Time*, November–December 1961, 1. Both periodicals are located in Collection 78, Box 3, Buswell Library Collections.

274 *knighted by Juliana:* https://www.biography.com/activist/corrie-ten-boom.

274 *adopted as an Indian sister:* See Corrie's ministry letter to supporters dated August 8, 1977, found in Collection 78, Box 1, Folder 8, Buswell Library Collections; "Lomasi," *The Hiding Place* magazine, January/February 1980, 15, located in Collection 78, Box 3, Buswell Library Collections; and Pamela Rosewell's letter to Anne dated September 15, 1977 (with a photo of Corrie in the Indian headdress), Collection 78, Box 1, Buswell Library Collections.

274 *honorary doctorate:* Corrie's certificate, along with photos from the ceremony, can be seen in *The Hiding Place* magazine, Summer 1976, 4, found in Collection 78, Box 3, Buswell Library Collections.

274 *abdicated the throne:* H. R. H. Wilhelmina, Princess of the Netherlands, *Lonely but Not Alone*, 236–37. In 1959, once again as princess of the Netherlands, Wilhelmina published her memoir.

The Rest of the Story

275 *Dr. Arthur Seyss-Inquart:* I. C. B. Dear and M. R. D. Foot, eds., *The Oxford Companion to World War II*, 998; Israel Gutman, ed., *Encyclopedia of the Holocaust*, vol. 4, 1344–46; Werner Warmbrunn, *The Dutch Under German Occupation, 1940–1945*, 11, 30; William Shirer, *The Rise and Fall of the Third Reich*, 1143. For details on Seyss-Inquart's SS career, see, generally, Jacob Presser, *Ashes in the Wind*.

275 *Hanns Albin Rauter:* Warmbrunn, *The Dutch Under German Occupation*, 30–32.

276 *Otto, Edith, Margot, and Anne Frank:* Anne Frank, *The Diary of a Young Girl*, 339–40.

276 *typhus broke out:* Corrie ten Boom, *A Prisoner and Yet*, 149.

276 *Audrey Hepburn:* Robert Matzen, *Dutch Girl: Audrey Hepburn and World War II*, photo inserts and captions between pages 192–93.

277 *Fritz Sühren:* Larry Loftis, *Code Name: Lise*, 242, 259–60.

277 *tens of thousands of women:* In *KL: A History of the Nazi Concentration Camps* (628), Nikolaus Wachsmann estimates the figure between 30,000 to 40,000, while *The Oxford Companion to World War II* (929) suggests the number could be as large as 92,700.

278 *Corrie's father was inducted:* Yad Vashem: The World Holocaust Remembrance Center. Casper's induction in 2007 can be found in the list of Dutch inductees at https://www.yadvashem.org/yv/pdf-drupal/netherlands .pdf.

278 *street was named after him:* Emily S. Smith, *More Than a Hiding Place*, 107.

278 *Betsie was inducted:* Yad Vashem: The World Holocaust Remembrance Center. Betsie's induction in 2007 can be found in the list of Dutch inductees at https://www.yadvashem.org/yv/pdf-drupal/netherlands.pdf.

278 *"It Is Well with My Soul":* Spafford's original and full manuscript can be seen at spaffordhymn.com.

278 *"It is well . . . with Kik":* Corrie ten Boom, *The Hiding Place*, 218.

279 *Willem ten Boom:* This photo is located in Collection 78, Box 1, Buswell Library Collections.

279 *Do you happen to know":* Corrie ten Boom, *Father ten Boom: God's Man*, 108–9; Peter van Woerden, "For Love of Israel," *The Hiding Place* magazine, Spring 1974, 2–3, 13 (condensed from the full article Peter published in the *Jerusalem Post* magazine, March 8, 1974), located in Box 3, Folder "Publications: The Hiding Place 1973–1982," Buswell Library Collections.

279 *Ten Boom School in Maarssen:* Smith, *More Than a Hiding Place*, 107.

278 Ville du Havre: "Run Down: Midnight Collision Between the Ville Du Havre and the Loch Erne," *Chicago Tribune*, December 2, 1873, 1.

278 *"Saved alone":* Western Union telegram from Anna to Horatio Spafford, December 1, 1873.

280 *For seven years after the war:* Carole C. Carlson, *Corrie ten Boom*, 89; *The Hiding Place*, 218. Note that Corrie's recollection was that Kik had died at the Bergen-Belsen concentration camp, apparently the camp where Kik was originally imprisoned. Given the delay in finding out what happened to Kik, however, Carlson's account that he died in a Russian labor camp seems more plausible.

290 *"Yesterday Marina took me":* Guillermo Font, *Kik ten Boom: The Clockmaker's Grandson*, 43, 271–72.

281 *is called Ten Boomstraat:* Font, *Kik ten Boom*, 26; Smith, 107.

281 *bronze sculpture:* Font, 26.

 family singing group: The Hiding Place, 219. See also Peter van Woerden, "Just So You Understand," *It's Harvest-Time*, January 1958 (inaugural issue), where Peter explains how he and Corrie came together to coproduce the newsletter. Collection 78, Box 3, Buswell Library Collections.

281 *Peter and family at the piano:* This photo is part of Peter's article "Greetings from Geneva," *It's Harvest-Time*, January–February–March 1960, located in Collection 78, Box 3, Buswell Library Collections.

282 *assisted Corrie with her second: Father ten Boom: God's Man*, 15. Note also that Peter visited the Corrie ten Boom Museum in November 1975 and signed the guestbook, which can be found at Beje guestbook, vol. 1 (of 4), Collection 78, Box 2, Folder 2, Buswell Library Collections. Peter's siblings Cocky, Aty, and Noldy visited later, signing the guestbook on October 20, 1976.

282 *Beneath a portrait of Casper:* This photo is located in Collection 78, Box 1, Buswell Library Collections.

282 *the Dutch Resistance Memorial Cross:* Hans Poley, *Return to the Hiding Place*, 207.

282 *earning a PhD:* Ibid.

282 *Eusi, Corrie, and Hans:* This photo of the Beje reunion of Eusi, Corrie, and Hans in 1974 can be found in Poley, *Return to the Hiding Place*, unpaginated photo section, and in Smith, *More Than a Hiding Place*, 81.

283 *taught mathematics at the Dreefschool:* Poley, 200.

283 *"Who should be warned":* Ibid., 201.

284 *"Mary was arrested":* Beje guestbook, vol. 1, Collection 78, Box 2, Buswell Library Collections; Poley, 203 (providing an English translation).

284 *Mirjam de Jong:* Poley, 200.

284 *"Their friendship greatly enriched":* Ibid.

285 *did not survive:* Ibid., 200–201.

285 "een van hen die in de engelenbak": Beje guestbook, vol. 2, found in Collection 78, Box 2, Folder 2, Buswell Library Collections.

285 *almost one thousand infants:* Mark Klempner, *The Heart Has Reasons: Dutch Rescuers of Jewish Children During the Holocaust*, 130–32; Warmbrunn, *The Dutch Under German Occupation*, 170; "The Story of Walter Suskind," http://www.holocaustresearchproject.org/survivor/suskind.html.

286 *who saved the refugees:* Smith, 82, 105.

286 *Eusi was arrested:* Poley, 201.

287 *"to fulfill my promise":* Ibid., 204.

288 *Beje guestbook:* This volume of the Beje guestbook is 1 of 4, and is located in Collection 78, Box 2, Buswell Library Collections.

288 *"30 years after I was hiding here":* Poley, 202–3 (Hans's English translation of Eusi's comments).

288 *Eusi signing the Beje guestbook:* Eusi's comment in Dutch is found in the Beje guestbook, vol. 1, Collection 78, Box 2, Folder 2, Buswell Library Collections.

Appendix

290 *May 25, Mrs. Kleermaker:* Corrie ten Boom, *The Hiding Place*, 76.

290 *May 27, elderly couple:* Ibid., 77.

290 *May 28, couple:* Ibid., 79.

290 *late May, several unidentified:* Ibid., 81.

290 *June 1, mother and baby, other children:* Ibid., 93–94.

290 *May 13, Hans Poley:* Hans Poley, *Return to the Hiding Place*, 15. Note that Corrie has Meijer Mossel ("Eusi") as the next arrival (*The Hiding Place*, 96), but she kept no diary during this time and tried to remember dates and names some twenty-eight years after the events. Hans Poley did keep a daily diary during the war, which revealed that Eusi was, in fact, the *sixth* permanent refugee into the Beje. Poley, *Return to the Hiding Place*, 15–47. Ironically, though Corrie mentions Hans five times in her 1947 autobiography, *A Prisoner and Yet* (15, 18–20), he is not found in her 1971 release, *The Hiding Place*. Hans's date of entry into the Beje on May 13 (as the first permanent refugee) is confirmed by Carol C. Carlson's *Corrie ten Boom: Her Life, Her Faith*, 93, and by Emily S. Smith's *More Than a Hiding Place: The Life-Changing Experiences of Corrie ten Boom*, 104, which was published by the Corrie ten Boom House Foundation in 2010. In the House Foundation's video tour of the Beje, Hans Poley is quoted at length about his stay with the ten Booms (visit virtualtour.corrietenboom.com).

    The logical explanation for Hans's absence in *The Hiding Place* is that the book was written not by Corrie, but by John and Elizabeth Sherrill (see the *they proposed to write* endnote in Chapter 27), who had no direct knowledge of the events and apparently missed Corrie's references to Hans in *A Prisoner and Yet*. For further details on Hans's mysterious absence from *The Hiding Place*, see the first endnote for Chapter 6.

290 *May 14, Hansje Frankfort-Israels:* Poley, 28–29; Smith, 104.

290 *June 8, Mary van Itallie:* Poley, 40; Smith, 104.

290 *mid-June, Henk Wessels:* Poley, 41; Smith, 104.

290 *mid-June, Leendert Kip:* Poley, 41; Smith, 104.

290 *June 28, Meijer Mossel:* Poley, 47–48; Smith, 104.

290 *early July, several unidentified:* Poley, 64.

290 *July 15–18, Jop:* *The Hiding Place*, 99. Corrie doesn't identify the exact date that Jop appeared, only that he arrived after Wessels, Kik, and Eusi, which would place him at the Beje in early July.

290 *July 15–18, Henk Wiedijk:* Poley, 64; Smith, 104.

290 *July 19, Mr. de Vries:* Poley, 75; Smith, 104.

290 *early August, Kik ten Boom with two friends:* Poley, 76.

290 *September 29, Mirjam de Jong:* Poley, 85–86; Smith, 104.

290 *mid-October, several unidentified:* Poley, 64.

290 *late October, Nel:* Poley, 97; Smith, 104.

290 *late October, Ronnie Gazan:* Poley, 97, Smith, 104 (identifying Ronnie's last name as da Costa Silva).

290 *January, Meta ("Martha") and Paula Monsanto:* Poley, 118; Smith, 104.

290 *February 28, Reynout ("Arnold") Siertsema:* Smith, 105.

290 *February 28, Hans van Messel:* Ibid.

Author's Note

291 *"writing a book is an adventure":* Evan Esar, *20,000 Quips & Quotes*, 86.

293 *"When I first met her":* Carole C. Carlson, *Corrie ten Boom: Her Life, Her Faith*, 7.

BIBLIOGRAPHY

Archives, Exhibits, and Official Documents
Buswell Library Archives and Special Collections, Wheaton College, Wheaton, IL
Christians, Incorporated (Certificate of Incorporation, Bylaws, Annual Directors Meeting Minutes, Reports)
Corrie ten Boom House Foundation, Haarlem, Netherlands
Corrie ten Boom Museum guestbook
International Congress on World Evangelization
Jewish Cultural Quarter, Amsterdam
Jewish Family and Children's Services Holocaust Center, San Francisco
Joods Historisch Museum, Amsterdam
Netherlands State Institute for War Documents, Amsterdam
NIOD Institute for War, Holocaust, and Genocide Studies
Trial of the Major War Criminals Before the International Military Tribunal, Official Text English Edition, Nuremberg
United States Holocaust Memorial Museum, Washington, D.C.
Yad Vashem: The World Holocaust Remembrance Center, Jerusalem

Books, Articles, and Presentations
Balfour, Michael. *Withstanding Hitler.* London: Routledge, 1988.
Bankier, David. *The Germans and the Final Solution: Public Opinion Under Nazism.* Oxford: Blackwell, 1992.
Bard, Mitchell. "Concentration Camps: Vught (Herzogenbusch)." *Jewish Virtual Library,* undated.
———. *48 Hours of Kristallnacht: Night of Destruction/Dawn of the Holocaust.* Guilford, CT: Lyons Press, 2008.
Baudot, Marcel, et al., eds. *The Historical Encyclopedia of World War II.* Translated by Jesse Dilson. New York: Greenwich House, 1984.
Benz, Wolfgang. "The Relapse into Barbarism." In *November 1938: From Kristallnacht to Genocide.* Edited by Walter H. Pehle. New York: Berg, 1991.
Bleicher, Hugo. *Colonel Henri's Story: The War Memoirs of Hugo Bleicher, Former German Secret Agent.* London: William Kimber, 1954.
Bluhm, Raymond K., ed. *World War II: A Chronology of War.* New York: Universe, 2011.
Bonhoeffer, Dietrich. *The Cost of Discipleship.* 1937; reprint, New York: Touchstone, 1995.
———. *Letters and Papers from Prison.* Edited by Eberhard Bethge. 1953; reprint, New York: Touchstone, 1997.

Brady, Tim. *Three Ordinary Girls: The Remarkable Story of Three Dutch Teenagers Who Became Spies, Saboteurs, Nazi Assassins—and WWII Heroes*. New York: Citadel Press, 2021.

Brown, Joan Winmill. *Corrie: The Lives She's Touched*. Old Tappan, NJ: Revell, 1979.

Burden, Suzanne. "Meet the Dutch Christians Who Saved Their Jewish Neighbors from the Nazis." *Christianity Today*, November 23, 2015.

Burney, Christopher. *Solitary Confinement*. New York: Macmillan, 1952.

Carlson, Carole C. *Corrie ten Boom: Her Life, Her Faith*. Old Tappan, NJ: Revell, 1983.

Casey, William. *The Secret War Against Hitler*. Washington, D.C.: Regnery, 1988.

Churchill, Winston. *The Second World War*. Vol. 2, *Their Finest Hour*. Boston: Houghton Mifflin, 1949.

———. *The Second World War*. Vol. 3, *The Grand Alliance*. Boston: Houghton Mifflin, 1950.

Clark, George N. *Holland and the War*. Oxford: Clarendon Press, 1941.

Conway, John S. *The Nazi Persecution of the Churches, 1933–1945*. New York: Basic Books, 1968.

Cookridge, E. H. *Inside S.O.E.: The Story of Special Operations in Western Europe, 1940–1945*. Arthur Baker, 1966.

"Corrie Ten Boom—Age Was Inconsequential." *CWN* Series, September 16, 1983.

Corum, James S. "The Luftwaffe's Campaigns in Poland and the West, 1939–1940." *Security and Defence Quarterly* 1, no. 1 (March 2013): 158–89.

Craig, Gordon A. *Germany: 1866–1945*. Oxford: Oxford University Press, 1980.

Crankshaw, Edward. *Gestapo: Instrument of Tyranny*. New York: Viking, 1956.

Crowdy, Terry. *Deceiving Hitler: Double-Cross and Deception*. Oxford: Osprey, 2008.

Dalton, Hugh. *The Fateful Years: Memoirs, 1931–1945*. London: Frederick Muller, 1957.

Dear, I. C. B., and M. R. D. Foot, eds. *The Oxford Companion to World War II*. Oxford: Oxford University Press, 1995.

Deutsch, Harold C. *The Conspiracy Against Hitler in the Twilight War*. Minneapolis: University of Minnesota Press, 1968.

Doerries, Reinhard. *Hitler's Intelligence Chief: Walter Schellenberg*. New York: Enigma, 2009.

———. *Hitler's Last Chief of Foreign Intelligence: Allied Interrogations of Walter Schellenberg*. London: Frank Cass, 2003.

Dörner, Klaus, et al., eds. *The Nuremberg Medical Trial 1946–47: Guide to the*

Microfiche-Edition. Translated by Cath Baker and Nancy Schrauf. Munich: K. G. Saur, 2001.

Dourlein, Pieter. *Inside North Pole: A Secret Agent's Story*. Translated by F. G. Renier and Anne Cliffe. London: William Kimber, 1953.

Dulles, Allen W. *Germany's Underground: The Anti-Nazi Resistance*. 1947; reprint, New York: Da Capo Press, 2000.

Eisenhower, Dwight D. *Crusade in Europe*. Garden City, NY: Garden City Books, 1948.

Eman, Diet, with James Schaap. *Things We Couldn't Say: A Dramatic Account of Christian Resistance in Holland During World War II*. Silverton, OR: Lighthouse Trails, 2008.

Engelmann, Bernt. *In Hitler's Germany: Daily Life in the Third Reich*. Translated by Krishna Winston. New York: Pantheon, 1986.

Evans, Richard J. *The History of the Third Reich*. Vol. 1, *The Coming of the Third Reich*. New York: Penguin, 2003.

———. *The History of the Third Reich*. Vol. 2, *The Third Reich in Power*. New York: Penguin, 2005.

———. *The History of the Third Reich*. Vol. 3, *The Third Reich at War 1939–1945*. New York: Penguin, 2008.

Farago, Ladislas. *The Game of Foxes: The Untold Story of German Espionage in the United States and Great Britain During World War II*. New York: David McKay, 1971.

Fest, Joachim C. *The Face of the Third Reich: Portraits of the Nazi Leadership*. New York: Knopf Doubleday, 1977.

———. *Inside Hitler's Bunker: The Last Days of the Third Reich*. New York: Macmillan, 2004.

FitzGibbon, Constantine. *20 July: A Full and Complete Account of the Fantastic "Officers' Plot" Against Adolf Hitler on July 20, 1944*. New York: Norton, 1956.

Font, Guillermo. *Kik ten Boom: The Clockmaker's Grandson*. Translated by Veronica Zerbini. Cordoba, Argentina: Pacificarnos, 2019.

Foot, M. R. D. *S.O.E.: The Special Operations Executive, 1940–1946*. London: Arrow Books, 1984.

———. *SOE in France: An Account of the Work of the British Special Operations Executive in France, 1940–1944*. London: Whitehall History Publishing, 1966.

Frank, Anne. *The Diary of a Young Girl*. 1947; reprint, New York: Bantam, 1995.

Frankl, Viktor. *Man's Search for Meaning*. Boston: Beacon Press, 1959.

Fritzsche, Peter. *Life and Death in the Third Reich*. Cambridge, MA: Harvard University Press, 2008.

"Gen. Dietrich von Choltitz Dies; 'Savior of Paris' in '44 Was 71." *New York Times*, November 6, 1966.

Gilbert, Martin. *Kristallnacht: Prelude to Destruction.* New York: Harper-Collins, 2006.

Gill, Anton. *An Honourable Defeat: A History of German Resistance to Hitler, 1933–1945.* New York: Henry Holt, 1994.

Gisevius, Hans Bernd. *To the Bitter End: An Insider's Account of the Plot to Kill Hitler, 1933–1944.* 1947; reprint, New York: Da Capo Press, 1998.

Giskes, Hermann. *London Calling North Pole.* 1953; reprint, Echo Point Books & Media, 2015.

Göbel, Esther. "In Memoriam: Betty Goudsmit-Oudkerk (1924–2020)." *Jewish Cultural Quarter,* 2020.

Grunberger, Richard. *Hitler's SS.* New York: Dell, 1973.

Guthrie, Stan. *Victorious: Corrie ten Boom and the Hiding Place.* Brewster, MA: Paraclete Press, 2019.

Gutman, Israel, ed. *Encyclopedia of the Holocaust.* 4 vols. New York: Macmillan, 1990.

Hamerow, Theodore S. *On the Road to the Wolf's Lair: German Resistance to Hitler.* Cambridge, MA: Harvard University Press, 1997.

Handel, Michael. *Strategic and Operational Deception in the Second World War.* London: Frank Cass, 1987.

———. *History of the Second World War.* New York: G. P. Putnam's Sons, 1971.

Hassell, Agostino von, and Sigrid MacRae. *Alliance of Enemies: The Untold Story of the Secret American and German Collaboration to End World War II.* New York: Thomas Dunne, 2006.

Hassell, Ulrich von. *The Von Hassell Diaries, 1938–1944: The Story of the Forces Against Hitler Inside Germany.* Garden City, NY: Doubleday, 1947.

Hazelhoff, Erik. *Soldier of Orange: One Man's Dynamic Story of Holland's Secret War Against the Nazis.* CreateSpace, 2014.

Helm, Sarah. *Ravensbrück: Life and Death in Hitler's Concentration Camp for Women.* New York: Talese/Doubleday, 2014.

"Henriëtte Pimentel: Whoever Saves One Person, Saves a Whole World." *Joodsamsterdam* (translated), May 3, 2016; https://www.joodamsterdam.nl/henriette-pimentel-wie-een-mens-redt-redt-een-hele-wereld/.

The Hiding Place. Official brochure of the Corrie ten Boom Museum.

Hilberg, Raul. *The Destruction of the European Jews.* Chicago: Quadrangle Books, 1961.

Hinsley, F. H. *British Intelligence in the Second World War.* Vol. 1. London: Her Majesty's Stationery Office, 1979.

———. *British Intelligence in the Second World War.* Vol. 3, Part 2. New York: Cambridge University Press, 1988.

———. *British Intelligence in the Second World War.* Vol. 4. New York: Cambridge University Press, 1990.

Hitler, Adolf. *Mein Kampf.* Edited by Rudolf Hess. Translated by James Murphy. 1925; reprint, Haole Library, 2015.

Hoffmann, Peter. *The History of the German Resistance, 1933–1945.* Translated by Richard Barry. Cambridge, MA: MIT Press, 1977.

Höhne, Heinz. *Canaris: Hitler's Master Spy.* Translated by J. Maxwell Brownjohn. 1976; reprint, New York: Cooper Square Press, 1999.

———. *The Order of the Death's Head: The Story of Hitler's SS.* (Originally published in 1966 in *German as Der Orden unter dem Totenkopf.*) Translated by Richard Barry. 1969; reprint, New York: Penguin, 2000.

Holt, Thaddeus. *The Deceivers: Allied Military Deception in the Second World War.* New York: Scribner, 2004.

Höttl, Wilhelm. *The Secret Front: Nazi Political Espionage, 1938–1945.* 1953; reprint, New York: Enigma Books, 2003.

Howard, Michael. *Strategic Deception in the Second World War.* 1990; reprint, New York: Norton, 1995.

Hughes, Roland. "Obituary: John van Hulst, the Teacher Who Saved Jewish Children." *BBC News,* March 30, 2018.

Internationaal Instituut voor Sociale Geschiedenis. "The Potato Blight in the Netherlands and Its Social Consequences (1845–1847)." *International Review of Social History.* Cambridge: Cambridge University Press, 2008.

Jewish Family and Children's Services Holocaust Center. "Oral Histories: Rescue and Resistance," undated.

Johnson, Eric A. *Nazi Terror: The Gestapo, Jews, and Ordinary Germans.* New York: Basic Books, 1999.

Jong, Louis de, and Joseph W. F. Stoppelman. *The Lion Rampant: The Story of Holland's Resistance to the Nazis.* 1943; reprint, New York: Kessinger, 2010.

Kahn, David. *Hitler's Spies: German Military Intelligence in World War II.* New York: Macmillan, 1978.

Kleffens, Eelco Nicolaas van. *Juggernaut over Holland: The Dutch Foreign Minister's Personal Story of the Invasion of the Netherlands.* New York: Columbia University Press, 1941.

Klemperer, Klemens von. *German Resistance Against Hitler: The Search for Allies Abroad, 1938–1945.* New York: Oxford University Press, 1992.

Klempner, Mark. *The Heart Has Reasons: Dutch Rescuers of Jewish Children During the Holocaust.* Amsterdam: Night Stand Books, 2012.

Larson, Erik. *In the Garden of Beasts: Love, Terror, and an American Family in Hitler's Berlin.* New York: Crown, 2011.

LeSourd, Catherine Marshall. "Grand Example." *Cornerstone,* May 1983.

Leverkeuhn, Paul. *German Military Intelligence.* Translated from German by R. H. Stevens and Constantine FritzGibbon. New York: Praeger, 1954.

Liddell Hart, B. H. *The German Generals Talk.* New York: Morrow, 1948.

Loftis, Larry. *Code Name: Lise.* New York: Gallery, 2019.

———. *Into the Lion's Mouth.* New York: Dutton Caliber, 2016.

———. *The Princess Spy*. New York: Atria, 2021.

Longerich, Peter. *Holocaust: The Nazi Persecution and Murder of the Jews*. Oxford: Oxford University Press, 2010.

Lorain, Pierre. *Clandestine Operations: The Arms and Techniques of the Resistance, 1941–1944*. New York: Macmillan, 1983.

Maass, Walter B. *The Netherlands at War: 1940–1945*. London: Abelard-Schuman, 1970.

Mackenzie, William. *The Secret History of SOE: The Special Operations Executive, 1940–1945*. London: St. Ermin's Press, 2000.

Margaritis, Peter. *Countdown to D-Day: The German Perspective*. Oxford: Casemate, 2019.

Matzen, Robert. *Dutch Girl: Audrey Hepburn and World War II*. New York: GoodKnight Books, 2019.

Metaxas, Eric. *Bonhoeffer: Pastor, Martyr, Prophet, Spy*. Nashville, TN: Thomas Nelson, 2011.

———. *7 Women: And the Secret of Their Greatness*. Nashville, TN: Thomas Nelson, 2015.

Michel, Henri. *The Shadow War: Resistance in Europe, 1939–1945*. Translated by Richard Barry. New York: Harper & Row, 1972.

Michman, J. "Vught." *Encyclopedia of the Holocaust*, vol. 4. New York: Macmillan, 1990.

Miller, Francis Trevelyan. *The Complete History of World War II*. Chicago: Readers' Service Bureau, 1947.

Montgomery, Field Marshal Bernard. *Normandy to the Baltic*. Boston: Houghton Mifflin, 1948.

Moore, Pam Roswell. *The Five Silent Years of Corrie ten Boom*. Grand Rapids, MI: Zondervan, 1986.

———. *Life Lessons from the Hiding Place: Discovering the Heart of Corrie ten Boom*. Washington Depot, CT: Chosen Books, 2012.

———. "San Quentin State Prison." *The Hiding Place*, Winter 1977.

Morrison, Jack Gaylord. *Ravensbrück: Everyday Life in a Women's Concentration Camp, 1939–45*. Princeton, NJ: Wiener, 2001.

Naujoks, Harry. *Mein Leben im KZ Sachsenhausen, 1936–1942*. Cologne: Röderberg, 1987.

Nicholas, Lynn H. *The Rape of Europa*. New York: Knopf, 1995.

Norris, Fred. "No Hiding Enthusiasm," *Birmingham and Sandwell Evening Mail*, October 10, 1979.

"Not Lost, but Gone Before: Corrie ten Boom, April 15, 1892–April 15, 1983." *The Hiding Place* Memorial Edition, April 1983.

Paine, Lauran. *German Military Intelligence in World War II: The Abwehr*. New York: Stein & Day, 1984.

Patton, George S., Jr. *War as I Knew It*. 1947; reprint, Boston: Houghton Mifflin, 1995.

Peis, Günter. *The Mirror of Deception: How Britain Turned the Nazi Spy Machine Against Itself.* New York: Pocket Books, 1977.

Pen, Hanneloes. "Betty Goudsmit-Oudkerk (1924–2020) Saved Hundreds of Jewish Children from Deportation." *AD* (translated), June 15, 2020.

Pindera, Jerzy. *Liebe Mutti: One Man's Struggle to Survive in KZ Sachsenhausen, 1939–1945.* Lanham, MD: University Press of America, 2004.

Poley, Hans. *Return to the Hiding Place.* Elgin, IL: LifeJourney Books, 1993.

Presser, Jacob. *Ashes in the Wind: The Destruction of Dutch Jewry.* Translated by Arnold Pomerans. 1965; reprint, London: Souvenir Press, 2010.

Rees, Laurence. *The Nazis: A Warning from History.* London: The New Press, 1998.

Roon, Ger van. *German Resistance to Hitler: Count von Moltke and the Kreisau Circle.* (Translation of *Neuordnung im Widerstand.*) Translated by R. Oldenbourg. London: Van Nostrand Reinhold, 1971.

Roosevelt, Kermit. *The Overseas Targets: War Report of the OSS.* Vol. 2. New York: Walker, 1976.

Rothfels, Hans. *The German Opposition to Hitler.* 1947; reprint, New York: Regnery, 1963.

Rürup, Reinhard, ed. *Topography of Terror: Gestapo, SS and Reichssicherheitshauptamt on the "Prinz-Albrecht-Terrain": A Documentation.* Translated by Werner T. Angress. Berlin: Verlag Willmuth Arenhövel, 2006.

Schellenberg, Walter. *The Memoirs of Hitler's Spymaster.* Edited and translated by Louis Hagan. 1956; reprint, London: Andre Deutsch, 2006.

Schlabrendorff, Fabian von. *The Secret War Against Hitler.* Translated by Hilda Simon. New York: Pitman, 1965.

Segev, Tom. *Soldiers of Evil: The Commandants of the Nazi Concentration Camps.* New York: McGraw-Hill, 1988.

Shirer, William. *The Rise and Fall of the Third Reich.* New York: Simon & Schuster, 1960.

Slim, John. "The Hiding Place." *Birmingham Post,* October 10, 1979.

Smith, Emily S. *More Than a Hiding Place: The Life-Changing Experiences of Corrie ten Boom.* Haarlem, Netherlands: Corrie ten Boom House Foundation, 2010.

Snyder, K. Alan. "Corrie ten Boom: A Protestant Evangelical Response to the Nazi Persecution of Jews." Paper presented to the Annual Conference of the Social Science History Association, Chicago, November 1998.

Snyder, Louis L. *Encyclopedia of the Third Reich.* New York: Marlowe, 1976.

Speer, Albert. *Inside the Third Reich (Memoirs).* New York: Macmillan, 1970.

Spiedel, Hans. *Invasion 1944: The Normandy Campaign—from the German Point of View by Rommel's Chief of Staff, Lieutenant General Hans Spiedel.* New York: Paperback Library, 1968.

Spurgeon, Charles. *Spurgeon's Gold.* 1888; reprint, Morgan, PA: Soli Deo Gloria, 1996.

Stafford, David. *Secret Agent: The True Story of the Covert War Against Hitler.* New York: Overlook Press, 2001.

Stamps, Ellen de Kroon. *My Years with Corrie.* Old Tappan, NJ: Revell, 1978.

Swinford, Nigel. *Corrie ten Boom's Incredible True Story of The Hiding Place.* Musical, Birmingham Hippodrome, October 9–13, 1979.

ten Boom, Casper. *Herinneringen van Een Oude Horlogemaker* ("Memoirs of an Old Watchmaker"). Haarlem, Netherlands: 1937.

ten Boom, Corrie. "Africa on the Crossroad," *It's Harvest-Time*, September–October 1961.

———. *Amazing Love: True Stories of the Power of Forgiveness.* London: CLC International, 1953.

———. "Around the World." *The Hiding Place*, March/April 1978.

———. "Awakening to God's Peace." *The Hiding Place*, January/February 1980.

———. "The Book." *It's Harvest-Time*, December 1970.

———. *Clippings from My Notebook.* London: SPCK, 1983.

———. *Common Sense Not Needed: Bringing the Gospel to the Mentally Handicapped.* Grand Rapids, MI: Revel, 1957.

———. "Corrie and Betsie Traveling the World." *The Hiding Place*, March/April 1978.

———. *Corrie's Christmas Memories.* Old Tappan, NJ: Revell, 1976.

———. *Corrie ten Boom's Prison Letters.* Old Tappan, NJ: Revell, 1975.

———. "Crusading for Christ Throughout Europe." *It's Harvest-Time*, July 1960.

———. *Each New Day.* Old Tappan, NJ: Revell, 1977.

———. "A Family Time." *The Hiding Place*, Fall 1976.

———. *Father ten Boom: God's Man.* Old Tappan, NJ: Revell, 1978.

———. "Fishing for Men in Japan." *It's Harvest-Time*, October–November 1958.

———. "From the Old Chest." *The Hiding Place*, Winter 1976.

———. "God's Timing Is Perfect." *It's Harvest-Time*, January–February 1963.

———. "Go into All the World," *The Hiding Place*, May/June 1979.

———. *He Sets the Captive Free.* Old Tappan, NJ: Revell, 1977.

———. "The Hiding Place." *It's Harvest-Time*, January 1972.

———. "In the Coliseum." *The Hiding Place*, Summer 1975.

———. "Lonely Place." Message before the National Prayer Congress, 1976. Collection 176 Records of the National Prayer Conference, Buswell Library Archives and Special Collections, Wheaton College, Wheaton, IL.

———. "Long Forgotten Memories of the Heidelberg Catechism." *The Hiding Place*, March/April 1978.

———. "The Lord Looseth the Prisoners." *It's Harvest-Time*, March–April 1959.

———. "Mountain-tops and Roof-tops." *It's Harvest-Time*, January–February 1959.

———. "My Books." *It's Harvest-Time*, July 1969.

———. "My First Fifty Years." *The Hiding Place*, Spring 1975.

———. "My Message to the People in Yad Va Shem." *It's Harvest-Time*, May–June 1968.

———. "New Beginnings." *The Hiding Place*, January/February 1978.

———. "New Prison Ministry Underway." *The Hiding Place*, March/April 1978.

———. "News from the Beje." *The Hiding Place*, Summer 1976.

———. "On the Road Again." *The Hiding Place*, Spring 1977.

———. "Open Doors in Germany." *It's Harvest-Time*, January–February–March 1960.

———. "Operation Borneo." *It's Harvest-Time*, August 1958.

———. "Outside His Boundaries." *The Hiding Place*, July/August 1980.

———. "The Paddle of God's Love." *It's Harvest-Time*, September–October 1961.

———. "People We Meet: Hans Rahms." *It's Harvest-Time*, November–December 1964.

———. *A Prisoner and Yet*. 1947; reprint, Fort Washington, PA: CLC, 2018.

———. "A Rare Recording of Corrie ten Boom." Vols. 1 and 2. Listen and Live Audio, 2019.

———. "Report on Russia." *It's Harvest-Time*, January 1969.

———. "Set Apart for God." *The Hiding Place*, Fall 1981.

———. "A Sun-Beam for Jesus." *It's Harvest-Time*, May–June 1958.

———. "Surrendering to God Day by Day." *The Hiding Place*, Summer 1981.

———. "The Three Locks." *The Hiding Place*, Summer 1975.

———. Untitled [Corrie's article on revisiting Ravensbrück prison in 1964]. *It's Harvest-Time*, November–December 1964.

———. Untitled [Corrie's article on the Righteous Among the Nations ceremony in Israel]. *It's Harvest-Time*, May–June 1968.

ten Boom, Corrie, with Bill Brown. "On the Set with Corrie and Bill Brown." *The Hiding Place*, Spring 1974.

———. "On the Set with Corrie and Bill Brown," *The Hiding Place*, Winter 1974–1975.

ten Boom, Corrie, with Jamie Buckingham. *Tramp for the Lord*. Old Tappan, NJ: Revell, 1974.

ten Boom, Corrie, with Carole C. Carlson. *In My Father's House*. 1976; reprint, Eureka, MT: Lighthouse Trails, 2011.

ten Boom, Corrie, with John and Elizabeth Sherrill. *The Hiding Place*. Washington Depot, CT: Chosen Books, 1971.

Thompson, John. *Spirit over Steel: A Chronology of the Second World War*. Carrick, 2014.

Toland, John. *The Last 100 Days*. New York: Random House, 1965.

United States Holocaust Memorial Museum. "Corrie ten Boom." *Holocaust Encyclopedia*, undated.

van Woerden, Peter. "Boom Is Dutch for Tree." *The Hiding Place*, Fall 1975.

———. "For Love of Israel." *The Hiding Place*, Spring 1974.

———. *In the Secret Place*. 1954; reprint, Plainfield, NJ: Logos International, 1974.

———. "Just So You Understand." *It's Harvest-Time*, January 1958.

Vomécourt, Philippe de. *An Army of Amateurs*. Garden City, NY: Doubleday, 1961.

Wachsmann, Nikolaus. *KL: A History of the Nazi Concentration Camps*. New York: Farrar, Straus & Giroux, 2015.

Walker, Robert. "The Hiding Place Revisited." *Christian Life*, January 1975.

Waller, John H. *The Unseen War in Europe: Espionage and Conspiracy in the Second World War*. New York: Random House, 1996.

Warlimont, Walter. *Inside Hitler's Headquarters*. Translated by R. H. Barry. 1962; reprint, Novato, CA: Presidio Press, 1991.

Warmbrunn, Werner. *The Dutch Under German Occupation, 1940–1945*. Stanford, CA: Stanford University Press, 1963.

Webb, Chris. "The Story of Walter Suskind." Holocaust Education & Archive Research Team, 2007.

Wilhelmina, H. R. H., Princess of the Netherlands. *Lonely but Not Alone*. Translated by John Peereboom. London: Hutchinson, 1959.

Wilmot, Chester. *The Struggle for Europe*. 1952; reprint, New York: Wordsworth, 1997.

Winters, Dick. *Beyond Band of Brothers: The War Memoirs of Major Dick Winters*. New York: Berkley Caliber, 2006.

Wistrich, Robert S. *Who's Who in Nazi Germany*. London: Routledge, 1995.

PHOTO CREDITS

252 Courtesy of Hans Poley
263 Courtesy of Corrie ten Boom House Foundation
267 Courtesy of Buswell Library Archives and Special Collections
278 Courtesy of Buswell Library Archives and Special Collections (*top*); courtesy of Corrie ten Boom House Foundation (*bottom*)
279 Courtesy of Buswell Library Archives and Special Collections
280 Courtesy of Corrie ten Boom House Foundation
281 Courtesy of Buswell Library Archives and Special Collections
282 Courtesy of Buswell Library Archives and Special Collections (*top*); courtesy of Hans Poley (*bottom*)
283 Courtesy of Buswell Library Archives and Special Collections (*top*); courtesy of Hans Poley (*middle*); courtesy of Corrie ten Boom House Foundation (*bottom*)
284 Courtesy of Buswell Library Archives and Special Collections (*top*); courtesy of Hans Poley (*bottom*)
285 Courtesy of Corrie ten Boom House Foundation (*top and middle*); courtesy of Buswell Library Archives and Special Collections (*bottom*)
286 Courtesy of Corrie ten Boom House Foundation
287 Courtesy of Corrie ten Boom House Foundation (*top*); courtesy of Hans Poley (*bottom*)
288 Courtesy of Hans Poley (*top*); courtesy of Buswell Library Archives and Special Collections (*bottom*)

INDEX

Page numbers in *italics* refer to illustrations.

Abwehr, 22n, 23, 35–36

Allies
  Battle of the Bulge, 229
  bombing raids, 82, 89, 95, 127–28
  downed pilots, 106, 113–14, 128
  invasion of Sicily, 82
  Operation Manna, 252, 334n252
  Operation Market Garden, 211
  signs of victory, 190, 197–98, 326n198

Altschuler, Otto, 17–21, 100–102

Amersfoort transit camp, 157–58, 176–77, 188–89, 194

Amstelveenseweg prison, 152–53, 158–59

Angels' Den (Beje hiding place)
  capacity, 83, 90
  claustrophobic conditions, 71, 147
  construction, 65–66, 67, 142, 308n64
  emergency drills, 68, 69, 70–71, 81
  escape from, 148, 149, 150, 247, 320n148
  German raid feared as imminent, 81–82, 116
  Gestapo raid, 132, 137, 140–41, 143–44, 147–50, 318n132
  lack of toilet facilities, 137, 143, 148, 149
  location, 64–65, 66
  name, 67
  supplies, 66–67, 129, 137

Annaliese, 91–92

Anschluss, 13, 27

Argument (Allied operation), 127–28

Arnold. *See* Siertsema, Reynout

Association of Christian Prison Workers, 273

Auschwitz, 209n, 222n, 230n, 276, 286, 328n207, 333n240

Bach, Johann Sebastian, *37*

Battle of the Bulge, 229

BBC radio, 25, 29, 30, 31–32, 61–62

Beck, Ludwig, 22n, 126n, 189

Beer Hall Putsch, 263

Beje. *See also* Angels' Den
  alarm system, 67–68, 70, 101
  all-night vigils, 82, 92
  arrival of refugees, 40–41, 43–44, 102, 114
  Corrie's return from Ravensbrück, 246–48
  as Corrie ten Boom Museum, 274n
  daily routine, 61–62
  doorbell code, 137, 138, 319n137
  emergency drills, 64, 68, 69, 70–71, 79, 80–81
  entertainment, 83–84, 89
  German soldiers seeking shelter, 72–73
  Gestapo raid, 1, 132–41, 143–44, 147–50, 318n132
  guestbook, *283*, 284, *284*, *285*, 288, *288*, 310n76, 318n132, 341n282
  Hans hiding at, 55, 57–64, 306n57
  Hans's arrest and, 122
  Hans's birthday, 73–74, 76
  Henny's birthday, 107
  hiding divers, 55, 57–64, 82–83, 84, 306n57
  hiding Jews, 33, 60–61, 64, 74–76
  items looted from, 248
  list of refugees, 289–90
  loneliness and boredom, 83, 86
  Mies's Christmas visit, 108–9, *109*
  number of refugees sheltered in, 309n72
  in Opa's will, 179
  parlor conversation, *115*
  permanent refugees, xi, 60, 289–90, 306n57, 308n64
  as postwar convalescent center, 257, 258, 274, 329n218
  protected by angels, 88, 140, 312n88
  raid warnings, 81–82, 98
  Resistance activities, 104–5, 129
  reunion (1974), 282, *282*, 287, *287*–88
  rooftop, 83, 86–87, *88*, 90, 148, 283, 320n148